# Human Factors for
# Technical Communicators

# WILEY TECHNICAL COMMUNICATION LIBRARY

**RESEARCH**  **WRITING**  **DESIGN**  **EVALUATION**  **MANAGEMENT**

## SERIES ADVISORS:

**JoAnn T. Hackos**   Comtech, Denver, CO
**William Horton**    William Horton Consulting, Boulder, CO
**Janice Redish**     American Institutes for Research, Washington, D.C.

## Other Titles of Interest:

Marlana Coe

# Human Factors
# for
# Technical
# Communicators

**Wiley Computer Publishing**

**John Wiley & Sons, Inc.**

New York • Chichester • Brisbane • Toronto • Singapore

*Library of Congress Cataloging-in-Publication Data*

Coe, Marlana.
    Human factors for technical communicators / Marlana Coe.
        p.    cm.
    Includes index.
    ISBN: 0-471-03530-0 (paper: alk. paper)
    1. Communication of technical information.   2. Human engineering.
I. Title.
T10.5.C54    1996
808'.066--dc20                                                                                    96-50324
                                                                                                              CIP

Printed in the United States of America

10  9  8  7  6  5  4  3  2  1

*For Gail, the most important human factor in my life*

# About the Author

Marlana Coe, owner of Coe Communications in Santa Monica, CA, has a varied background: linguistics, technical communication, computer science, and industrial psychology.

She works with corporate, educational, and governmental clients to design, develop, and test user-centered technical information in both hardcopy and online formats. As an instructor at UCLA Extension, she teaches courses in technical writing, technical editing, human factors, and SGML. She also conducts onsite or offsite seminars on designing, developing, and testing hardcopy and online information, evaluating information and interfaces from a human-factors perspective, and creating information and interfaces for multicultural audiences.

# Contents

# Preface

In the early 1980s, I became interested in the application of ergonomics to information design, development, and use. I sat through endless courses on designing cockpits, compensating for G-forces, and estimating candlefeet of light. This was not what I had in mind. Then I connected with cognitive psychologists who were studying how users access and use information, how reading and action patterns affect users, and the emotional impact of icons and colors. This was it. Where could I find resources that pulled it all together for technical communicators? No where. So, I created some workshops that I delivered to corporations and at regional and international conferences, then a course that I taught (and still teach) at UCLA, then some articles and papers. Then John Wiley & Sons, in the person of editor Terri Hudson, came calling and asked me to put it all together in book format.

And so I did, and here it is. However, it is important to be clear on what this book is and is not.

This book is a kick in the pants to get you started thinking about a human-factors approach to designing and developing written technical communication. It presents a cognitive-psychology point of view. It is a book about users—how they sense, perceive, learn, remember, read, and act. It explores ways you can use user psychology to create strong technical communication.

This book is not a "how-to." This book is one level higher and deals with the cognitive psychological theory of designing and developing technical communication that is truly user-centered.

## Audience

This book is for anyone who designs, writes, edits, or tests technical information. It is also for managers and other decision makers whose ultimate responsibility is quality technical communication.

## Structure of the Book

I structured this book around examples, extended examples, and problem-solving scenarios. The human-factors approach to technical communication is a four-part process of designing and developing user-oriented information:

1. Understand the psychological and physical sensory and perceptual process users employ to access information.

   Chapters 2 through 7 explore sensation, perception, learning, memory, problem solving, accessing information, and action structures.

2. Create dynamic, robust user partnerships to design and develop information.

   Chapter 8 examines how to build and use these partnerships to design and develop information.

3. Build a strong, user-centered subtext to carry the text of information.

   Chapters 9 through 11 discuss designing and creating the medium, navigation, and presentation that compose information's subtext.

4. Design and develop user-oriented text.

   Chapter 12 looks at creating the content that is the information's text.

The following is a roadmap to the topics in this book. You may use this book sequentially or in a random-access fashion. However, there are threads of themes and examples that run throughout the book. Used sequentially, this book provides a solid technical-communication human-factors learning experience for either the newcomer to the technical profession or the seasoned professional. Used in a random-access fashion, the book serves as a human factors reference.

| Chapter | Topic | What to expect |
| --- | --- | --- |
| 2 | Sensation and perception | Physicality and psychology of sensation and perception as the basis for everything we do and think, emphasizing the symbiotic nature of the two types of processes and how they interact on a continuum |
| 3 | Learning | Learning styles, knowledge, and motivation |
| 4 | Memory | Stages, theories, and processes of memory |
| 5 | Problem solving | Types of logic and the approaches and obstacles to problem solving |
| 6 | Accessing information | Text and subtext of information, physicality and psychology of reading, and emotional and cultural associations of subtext |
| 7 | Action structures | Basic and enhanced action structures and opportunistic and reactionary actions |
| 8 | Building user partnerships | Building strong user partnerships as a basis for a systematic human-factors approach to technical communication |
| 9 | Choosing a medium | Media type and subtype |
| 10 | Building the navigational infrastructure | Hardcopy and online navigational infrastructures |
| 11 | Presenting information | Layout and fonts |
| 12 | Designing and developing content | Helping users use the content of your information to identify and respond to problems in their environment |
| A | Writing for other cultures | Types of translation, ten areas of concern when writing for other cultures, cultural associations of icons and color |
| B | Human factors resources | Names and addresses of other resources on human factors for technical communicators |

# Trademarks

Adam is a trademark of Coleco.

ClarisWorks is a registered trademark of Claris Corporation.

CorelDraw! is a registered trademark of Corel Corporation.

eWorld is a trademark of Apple Computer, Inc.

Helvetica is a registered trademark of Allied Corporation.

HyperCard is a registered trademark of Apple Computer, Inc.

Info Mapping is a registered trademark of Info Mapping, Inc.

MacDraw is a registered trademark of Claris Corporation.

MacIntosh is a registered trademark of Apple Computer, Inc.

Microsoft is a registered trademark of Microsoft Corporation.

Quicken is a registered trademark of Intuit.

SuperPaint is a copyright of Silicon Beach Software, Inc.

Times is a registered trademark of Allied Corporation.

UNIX is a registered trademark in the U.S. and other countries
licensed exclusively through X/Open Company, LTD.

Windows is a registered trademark of Microsoft Corporation.

Word is a registered trademark of Microsoft Corporation.

WordPerfect is a registered trademark of Novell, Inc.

# Acknowledgments

There are many guiding spirits to thank for the evolution of this book. I must thank:

- My mother, grandmother, aunt, and sister for a solid foundation that enables everything I do

- My partner, Gail, for believing in me and not letting me out of the house 'till I completed this book

- Lil, Leigh, Michael, Marti, Pat, and Roberta for moral support and just the right amount of solicitous nagging

- Barbara and Howard for ensuring that I had the emotional wherewithal to complete this book

- Chia and Tsunami for playing with me when I could not type another word

- Terri Hudson and John Wiley & Sons for suggesting this book

# CHAPTER ONE

# Introduction

*When Mary Wollstonecraft Shelley's hero, Frankenstein, endowed his synthetic robot with a human heart, the monster which before had been a useful mechanical servant suddenly became an uncontrollable force.*

A. A. Berle Jr.

What is the discipline of human factors? While the field is fascinatingly complex, the answer is relatively simple: Human factors is designing and developing products for people. Right, you are saying, that much you knew. Now comes the hard part—how do you, as a technical communicator, do it? This book lays out a theory-based human-factors methodology for designing, developing, and testing technical information.

The field of human factors falls into two broad categories: engineering and cognitive psychology. On the engineering side are ergonomics and anthropometry. Ergonomics is the study of human capabilities and limitations in the design of machines and objects, work processes, and work environments. Anthropometry is the study of human body measurements. Ergonomics and anthropometry are the oldest types of human factors. During the second World War, the military brought in engineers to determine why bombs were missing their targets, planes were crashing, friendly ships were being sunk, and whales were being attacked with depth charges. The engineers decided these problems were caused by mismatches between machines and their operators—in short, human error. And so, ergonomics was born. In fact, outside the United States, the general field of human factors goes by the name ergonomics.

Recently, however, cognitive psychology has become a more visible player in the human-factors game. Cognitive psychology is the study of human behavior in light of the internal, mental processes that drive it. The psychologists of the Army-Air Force Psychology Unit knew they could gain more insight into why bombs were missing their targets if they studied the perception, memory, problem-solving philosophies, and learning styles percolating in the psyches of the bombardiers. So was born the cognitive psychology branch of ergonomics or human factors.

Optimally, designing for people takes into account not only the ergonomics of design, but also the cognitive implications of design. At its best, human factors involves understanding the physicality of how people interact with and use objects as well as the psychology of how their mental processes interact with each other to understand and use objects.

Designing successful technical communications requires a human-factors relationship between technical communicators and users. Technical communicators design information for users, and there is a covenant of trust between these two human elements that serves as the foundation for human factors in technical communication.

This covenant is simple in its goal, but complex in it maintenance. Basically the agreement states that there is an implied trust that users place in you, the technical communicator, when they read and use your information. Users trust that you respect and understand their goals; that you have chosen the right method and means of communication; and that the content that you are communicating is accurate.

As Figure 1.1 shows, the human factors metaphor for technical communication is the proverbial onion. The users' world is at the center. At the point farthest from the users' world is the information text, which is its content. In order to get to the text, users have to peel back the layers of the subtext: medium, navigation, and presentation. Users trust that you have chosen the appropriate medium; that you have designed clear, intuitive, and "holeless" navigation; and that you have created a supportive, intuitive presentation that allows the content to shine through.

It is important to keep in mind that users never enter the world of the technical communicator or of the information, but that the technical communicator and the information always enter the world of the users. The adage "When in Rome, do as the Romans do" is particularly pertinent to the profession of technical communication. Users inhabit their world; you and your information do not. They bring your information into their world to read, use, and apply.

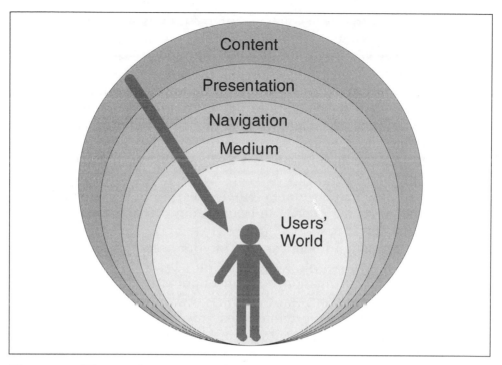

**Figure 1.1** Human factors metaphor for technical communication.

The users' world comprises a myriad of themes, interpretations, experiences, expectations, habits, abilities, goals, motivations, reading strategies, learning styles, and problem-solving philosophies. When your information enters this world, users expect it to respect and understand all the components that compose that world. They expect you to recognize that your information is an invited guest in their world, that they control their world, and that they are trusting you and your information not to violate any mores of their world.

You may also deal with users who have lost their trust of technical communication. Past experiences may have destroyed their trust and colored their approach to and use of your information. You must re-establish the covenant of trust with these users.

Users are not heartless robotic Frankenstein monsters. They are not cookie-cutter beings whose white-cell count, brain-wave patterns, and arterial paths you might look up in a handbook. They are human beings, who carry with them a complete range of cultural, social, and educational needs, wants, expectations, and goals. They are truly uncontrollable forces with whom you have entered into an unspoken agreement, and the onus of retaining that agreement is on you, the technical communicator.

The key to maintaining this agreement is to keep users at the heart of everything you do in designing and developing information. Buzz words for this concept are "user-centered design," "user-oriented systems," and "user-driven information." You can use any, all, or none of these terms to describe a human-factors approach to technical communication. I use them all, plus I make up some. The demand of human factors and technical communication is that you as a technical communicator thoroughly understand your users and their needs and expectations, and that you construct information that reflects your understanding of your users and meets their needs and expectations. That is the covenant of trust in a nutshell.

Thorough understanding of your users means knowing the physical and psychological processes they use in accessing, processing, and applying your information. You must understand that users bring your information into their world to solve problems—you are a solutions broker. Constructing information that meets users' needs and expectations means that you are in full control of the information. You know what to present to users and how to present it. You are not an editorial "pass-through" who takes information and regurgitates it in a user-friendly style; you are an information craftsperson.

To take a human-factors approach to technical communication is to understand that users are the final arbiters; they must drive every design and development decision. Remember, if they do not use your information, it simply does not exist.

My favorite definition of human factors is an answer that Sir Alfred Hitchcock gave in response to the question, "How long should a film be?" Hitchcock replied, "The length of a film should be directly related to the endurance of the human bladder." Now there is a man who understood his users and built his product with their needs and expectations at the heart of everything he did.

# CHAPTER TWO

# Sensation and Perception

*All our knowledge has its origins in our perceptions.*

Leonardo da Vinci

Sensation and perception are two ends of a continuum we use to take in sensory data, then interpret, store, retrieve, and apply it at will. This continuum is the foundation for everything we think and do. At the sensation end of the continuum is a set of physical processes by which we collect data from the world. At the perception end is a set of cognitive processes we employ to organize, interpret, store, retrieve, and apply the data that sensation provides.

Perception is the result of processing sensory input. Without sensation, perception would have no raw data to process, and without perception, humans would be sensory data collectors without the ability to cognitively process that sensory data. Without cognitive processing, the data is useless. As Figure 2.1 illustrates, sensation is the physicality, while perception is the psychology[1] of what we do.

We need four things to collect sensory data:

1. Stimulus in the world
2. Sensory organ, which has sensory receptors that the stimulus excites and that encode the stimulus into a neuronal impulse
3. Nerve pathway to carry the neuronal impulse to the brain
4. Area of the brain to receive and process the neuronal impulse

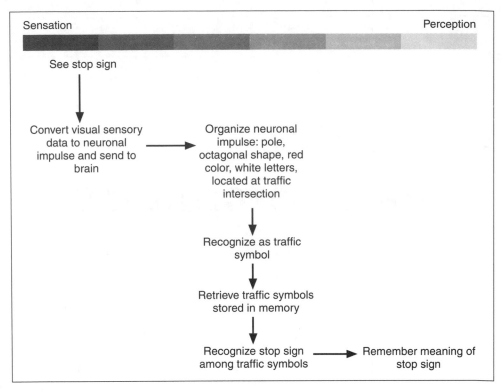

**Figure 2.1**  Sensation-perception continuum.

The brain receives all sensory input as encoded neuronal impulses, regardless of the type of sensory input. Just how the brain translates the different types of neuronal impulses—an auditory from a visual, for example—is a mystery, but the individual sensory organ that sends the impulse and the part of the brain receiving the impulse seem to play large roles in how the brain distinguishes the types of sensory input.

As Figure 2.2 illustrates, the areas of the brain that receive different impulses are mutually exclusive. The occipital lobes, which process visual impulses, do not receive auditory impulses, for example. This man's ear cannot hear the rose. It can neither see nor smell it. Likewise, our eyes cannot take in the smells of Dodger Stadium, and our nose cannot read *The Wall Street Journal* (no matter how much of a nose for news we might have).

As you are reading these words, the stimulus is the electromagnetic energy of black squiggles on white paper; the sensory organ experiencing

**Figure 2.2**  Unique sensory domains.

the stimulus is your eye, whose sensory receptors encode the stimulus into a neuronal impulse; the nerve pathway that carries the impulse is the optic nerve, which takes visual input to the brain; and the area of the brain receiving input from the optic nerve is the occipital lobes. This is the physical process of getting the sight of the words on paper to your brain.

Once your occipital lobes receive the encoded neuronal impulse, cognitive processes such as memory, reading, and learning begin trying to decipher the sensory data.

Long ago, you learned and remembered how to read in general, and the English language in particular. If you have mastered an English vocabulary that contains the words on these pages, if you can retrieve the semantic meaning of that vocabulary, if you can remember the rules of grammar in order to make sense of the words, and if you have schemata that you can use to compare what these words are saying to your understanding of the world, then you can understand the sentences in this book. This is the psychological process of organizing, interpreting, and understanding the sensory data.

To further illustrate the interaction of sensation and perception, consider the scenario that Figure 2.3 illustrates.

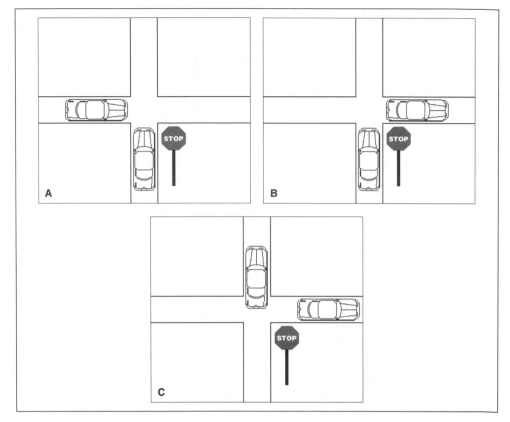

**Figure 2.3** Sensation and perception.

Roberta is driving to work and comes to a stop sign.

Her eyes take in the stimulus of the stop sign: red, octagonal, with the word "STOP" in white letters. Her visual sensory receptors encode the stimulus into a neuronal impulse. Her optic nerve carries the neuronal impulse to her occipital lobes.

Once her occipital lobes receive the encoded neuronal impulse, her perceptual processes begin to organize, interpret, and understand the meaning of the stop sign.

At some earlier point in her life, Roberta learned what a stop sign is. She stored that information in memory as a stop-sign schema, and every time she encounters a stop sign, she retrieves the schema.

Her stop-sign schema tells her that she must stop until it is safe to proceed, so she puts her foot on the brake and stops her car. She looks both ways; her eyes take in the sensory data of a car coming through the intersection; her perceptual processes tell her that she cannot cross the intersection while the car is coming through it, so she and her car wait at the stop sign.

Her eyes take in the sensory data that the car has cleared the intersection and that there are no other vehicles coming through the intersection. Her perceptual processes interpret this as meaning she can drive through the intersection, so Roberta takes her foot off the brake, presses down on the accelerator, and maneuvers her car through the intersection.

Amazingly, when Roberta came to that stop sign, all her sensory and perceptual processing took less time than it took me to write the preceding scenario (or you to read it). The processes of sensation and perception take place at blindingly fast, micro-second speeds, and not all the processes are conscious ones. A great deal of our sensory and perceptual processing is automatic and unconscious. The brain is continually receiving input that it processes but does not bring to our conscious awareness. The methods we use to process information unconsciously are called preattentive processes, while the methods we use to process information consciously are called attentive processes.

## Preattentive and Attentive Processes

Preattentive processes are autopilot or automatic processes that do not involve higher, cognitive functions; they are primarily a result of sensory input. Preattentive processes are data-driven, bottom-up processes that operate quickly, randomly, and without conscious knowledge.

For example, as you are holding this book, you automatically recognize where the book ends and your hands begin. This is not something you had to learn. You derive the recognition of where the book ends and your hands begin from noncognitive processing of the visual and tactile data your senses are taking in. You are not using cognitive processes such as memory, understanding, and learning.

On the other hand, attentive processes do involve cognitive processes such as learning, memory, and understanding. Attentive processes are concept-driven, top-down processes that operate slowly, serially, and only with conscious effort on your part.

For example, as you are reading these words, you are relying on the English vocabulary that you have stored in memory to interpret these black squiggles; on semantic meanings you have stored in memory to organize the text into a meaningful whole; and on the knowledge base that you have stored in memory so you can critically evaluate what you are reading.

Preattentive and attentive processes are not mutually exclusive. When readers use your information, they use combinations of these processes to interpret the input of your information. Users know where their noses end and your help screen begins, for example. But simultaneous to this preattentive recognition are the attentive processes of understanding organization, structure, navigation, and semantics. Preattentive and attentive processes combine to help users make sense of, store, retrieve, and apply your information.

## Sensory Data Filters

Sensory data bombards us constantly. There is no way we can take it all in or process it. We are aware of only a fraction of the sensations in our world. Protecting us from the vast array of sensations in the world are three phenomena:

1. Thresholds
2. Cocktail-party effect
3. Sensory adaptation

### Thresholds

We have two types of thresholds: absolute and just noticeable difference (JND).

Absolute threshold is the smallest amount of stimulus that we can detect fifty percent of the time. It depends not only on the sensory data we take in from the world, but on our psychological state as well. Experience, expectation, and motivation all play a part. Absolute thresholds are not static; the same stimulus can produce different responses at different times.

When you are alert and highly motivated to detect a particular stimulus, your absolute threshold is higher than when you are bored, tired, and not interested in detecting the stimulus. If you are an astronomy buff and eagerly have been awaiting an infrequent meteor shower, you are more apt to detect it, even if it is faint, than if you are sitting on your balcony brooding over the loss of your prize orchid. In fact, the whole sky could probably light up, and you would turn your back in mourning for your rare cymbidium.

Your information interacts with the users' absolute threshold. Users do not always approach the information in an optimal psychological state. They pick up your pages or read your screens when they are worried because the plumber could not fix the leaky washing machine, when they are upset because their boss just rescinded their vacation, and when they are irritated because the photocopier just chewed up the master of their overdue quarterly status report.

As you design and create information, you have to take into account users' absolute thresholds and understand that those thresholds can change from minute to minute. You have to design and create information that users can access easily regardless of their psychological state. Rare are the users who always absorb your information when they are at the height of interest, energy, and motivation. This is another dimension you have to consider when you perform your audience analysis. Even when users are bored, irritated, or upset, they must be able to access your information easily, and the burden of ensuring this accessibility is on you, the technical communicator.

JND is the smallest amount of sensation we can detect between any two stimuli fifty percent of the time. JND is proportional. If you are returning from the grocery store on your bicycle with a 20-pound bag of potatoes perched precariously on the handle bars, you are acutely aware of that weight. If, however, you are returning from the grocery store in your car with that 20-pound bag stowed safely in the trunk, you do not even notice the weight. In both cases, the stimulus is an extra 20 pounds, but proportionally, that 20 pounds is a greater percent of your bicycle's total weight than it is of your car's.

Not only does the technical information interact with users' absolute thresholds, it also interacts with their JNDs. Is understanding the structure and layout of your information like pedaling 20 pounds of potatoes or like driving a car whose trunk contains 20 pounds of potatoes? Is the navigation and searchability of your information a large proportion of users' energy and effort, or so easy it almost appears effortless?

You have to exploit your users' thresholds by understanding them and using them to your advantage. How hard do you think your users are going to struggle to access your information? And how often do you think they are going to tire themselves out trying? If users spend less time and effort accessing the information, they can spend more time and effort assimilating it.

The following are some ways you can take advantage of users' absolute and JND thresholds:

- Use an optimal medium.

  There are a plethora of media available to technical communicators: hard copy, online, video, multimedia, interactive, and Computer-Based Training (CBT). Match the medium to your information. There is no "best" medium. The information and the needs of your users should determine which medium you use.

- Use graphics, icons, color, and emphasis.

  Users need these visual cues to use information successfully. The lower users' interest, energy, and motivation, the more they depend on the cues.

  Use the cues judiciously, however. Using too many graphics, icons, colors, or emphases defeats the strategy of taking advantage of users' absolute thresholds. They become indifferent to boldface type, for example, if you use it with too heavy a hand.

- Chunk information.

  Chunking information makes it stand out, affords more white space, and makes it easier to remember. Incorporate lists, charts, and other "grouping" mechanisms where appropriate.

- Use navigation cues that are clear, recognizable, consistent, and meaningful.

  In hardcopy information, navigation cues are page numbers, running headers and running footers, table of contents entries, index entries, references, and cross-references. In online information, navigation cues are hyperlinks (textual and graphical), table of contents entries, index entries, and interface controls (objects such as buttons and check boxes that users manipulate).

## Cocktail-Party Effect

Like thresholds, the cocktail-party effect helps shield us from the continuous flood of sensory data. The cocktail-party effect is our ability to zero in on what is important to us while filtering out the data that is not important, much in the same way one might concentrate on a particular conversation in the midst of a noisy, chit-chat filled room. Say you are in a budget meeting, and it is well into the second hour. Your boss is giving a multimedia presentation with pie charts exploding left and right. Your coworker very softly asks you if you want to escape for lunch. You immediately are able to drown out the presentation (and the attendant oohs and ahhs as each new pie explodes in dazzling color) and zero in on the whispered question. At this point in time, your boss' ramblings are superseded by the thought of lunch with your colleague.

As users strive to access and assimilate your information, have you made it easy for them to filter out the bombardment of sensory data and allowed them to focus on the importance of your information? Have you designed your information so they can easily and quickly find and focus on what is important? Some ways of enabling users to filter through the cocktail-party effect are:

- Use the litmus test of "if-users-don't-need-it-throw-it-out" to determine what information to provide.

  Often technical communicators clutter their work with useless information because "the developer said to put it in," they feel they need to cover their derrieres, they are not in control of the information and are unable to evaluate it critically, or they are not in touch with their users and truly do not know what users do and do not need. There is only one criterion for including information: users need it to complete their task.

- Give users the main points in the body of the information, and relegate supporting details to appendixes.

  Most users are interested only in the main points. Even those who are interested in the detail need the main points as a structure on which to hang the detail. Move the detail to an appendix; those who are interested will look there. Those who are not interested are not distracted by a slew of interloping facts and figures.

- Use graphics to support or replace text.

  Putting information in a graphical format makes it stand out from prose. Using color, different fonts and line weights, and exploded diagrams adds more distinction. Graphics should support text or replace text; you should never use graphics just for the sake of adding pretty pictures.

Do not overlook the most widely used graphic: white space. In hardcopy information, you want to achieve 25 to 40 percent white space. In online information, you want to achieve 40 to 60 percent white space (on the smallest screen your users use).

- Use tables to present information that lends itself to the column-row arrangement.

If you find yourself thinking in a matrix paradigm while writing your information, chances are that information is a candidate for tabular presentation. Tables are graphics; as such, they help information stand out and create more white space. They also facilitate users' information retrieval.

- Use clear, well-defined hierarchies and heterarchies to communicate relationships in your information.

Heads are the most recognizable clue to hierarchies and heterarchies. Heads should be distinct and set apart from the body of the text by font, point size, and emphasis. And, of course, heads should be consistently presented.

Within the hierarchies and heterarchies, develop your information's content to reflect the structure. In a hierarchy, be sure that you work from general to specific. In a heterarchy, be sure that the information you present is of equal value and that you have a good reason for sequencing the topics. Since all topics in a heterarchy are of equal value, some sequencing strategies are:

- Alphabetical
- Amount of information
- Frequency of occurrence
- Order of occurrence
- Users' familiarity with the information

- Separate the types of information.

Separate concept, process, procedure, and reference information and clearly label each type. You can label information explicitly with a label such as Information Mapping advocates or implicitly with a clearly defined structure so that your users know the type of information you are communicating.

Do not mix a little concept, a little process, a little procedure, and a little reference information. This is a Molotov cocktail that will blow to smithereens your users' ability to focus on the immediately important information.

## Sensory Adaptation

If, in the previous budget presentation, your boss had saved the musically enhanced, dazzlingly colored, exploding pies for only the most important information, you and the others in the audience would have taken notice every time a slice of pie whizzed across the screen. But, since your boss made the mistake of bringing a full-frontal technical assault to every piece of information in the presentation, you and the others in the audience had to stifle yawns at even the most spectacular effects. After a while, you ceased to even notice the sights and sounds of the presentation. This is sensory adaptation at work. Sensory adaptation occurs when our senses get used to a stimulus and do not respond to it.

Perhaps it is midnight, and your alarm clock's ticking is marking the passing of each second. You have gotten so used to it that it does not bother you. In fact, you probably do not even notice it. You have become "sensory adapted" to your alarm clock's ticking. You have not, however, become sensory adapted to your alarm clock's alarm, which is why it is so effective in jolting you upright out of a pleasant dream.

Likewise, had your boss confined the software's full capabilities to a few pertinent pieces of information, the effects would have functioned like your clock's alarm instead of like your clock's second hand. Just because you have the technical capability (coulda) of 1,412 different fonts and 1.6 million colors does not mean you should (shoulda) employ them. You must critically evaluate what you want (woulda) to emphasize and be careful to design and create information to which users do not become sensory adapted. Do not fall into the coulda-shoulda-woulda mistake of using all the fonts, colors, and graphics at your technical disposal. Instead of making your information stand out for users, going overboard with sensory stimuli only encourages sensory adaptation to all those wonderful fonts, colors, and graphics.

Thresholds, cocktail-party effect, and sensory adaptation are mechanics of sensation. Stimuli in the world excite sensory receptors in our various sensory organs; our sensory receptors encode the stimuli into neuronal messages and send the encoded messages along to appropriate parts of the brain. These parts of the brain receive the encoded neuronal messages, and the process of perception begins.

## Perceptual Filters

Just as there are mechanics of sensation that affect our acquisition of sensory data, so are there mechanics of perception that affect our perceptual processing of that data. We use six perceptual mechanisms to filter perceptions and help us interpret them:

1. Perceptual set
2. Figure-ground relationships
3. Laws of grouping
4. Goodness of figures
5. Shape-recognition strategies
6. Perceptual illusions

### Perceptual Set

A perceptual set is a predisposition to interpret data in a given manner. In other words, we perceive what we expect to perceive. If a group of astronomers exploring the possibilities of extraterrestrial life gave you photographs of lights in a dark sky, would you be inclined to interpret them as signs of extraterrestrial life? And if another group of astronomers charting new stars gave you those same photographs, would you be more inclined to interpret them as new stars?

Our perceptual set is a reflection of our experiences; environment; expectations; assumptions; learning; and physical, mental, and psychological conditions. A perceptual set is temporary, though it may be recurring. Very often, perceptual sets impede our ability to perceive reality, and once we have perceived an irreal reality, it is difficult to correct that perception.

Figure 2.4 is a classic example of a perceptual set. If someone told you that Figure 2.4 is a figure of a young woman, you would have no trouble seeing the young woman. If someone else told you it is a figure of an old woman, how difficult is it to shift your perceptual set and see the old woman? Can you shift your perceptual set so that you can alternate between seeing the young woman and the old woman?

**Figure 2.4** Perceptual set.

As users bring your information into their world, it runs smack dab into their perceptual sets. Sometimes, this is a boon to users' learning and sometimes it is a hindrance. Part of your audience analysis should be an exploration of your users' perceptual sets. Discover which are apt to help users assimilate your information and which are apt to hinder them from assimilating it. Exploit those perceptual sets that help users learn your information, and change those that hinder them.

## Figure-Ground Relationships

In order to interpret the visual stimuli our eyes take in, we must see objects as being separate from other stimuli and as having a distinct, meaningful form. Every object has at least two parts: the object itself that we recognize as a distinct whole, called the figure, and the object's surroundings, called the ground. As you are reading this, you are making a distinction between the words on the page and the paper of the page. The words are the figure, and the paper is the ground.

Sometimes, figure and ground reverse themselves and you see figure as ground and ground as figure. Figure 2.5 is a classic example of figure-ground relationships. Can you see the vase in Figure 2.5? Can you see two faces in profile?[2]

**Figure 2.5** Figure-ground relationships.

As you design and develop your information, remember to design distinct, meaningful whole parts that fit well with their surroundings. Ensure that the surroundings are the appropriate medium, organization, and presentation.

## Laws of Grouping

Once we have differentiated figure and ground, we interpret the figure as a meaningful object. To help us interpret the figure, we use laws of grouping. These laws are a Gestalt approach to perceptual organization that focus on seeing well-organized, meaningful wholes instead of disparate, isolated parts. Six laws of grouping help us interpret figures as meaningful objects:

1. Proximity
2. Similarity
3. Continuity
4. Symmetry
5. Closure
6. Common fate

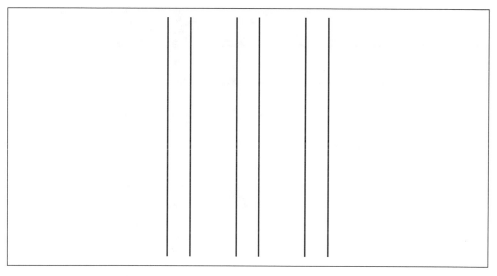

**Figure 2.6** Proximity.

## Proximity

If objects are near each other, we tend to group them. Do you see six lines or three pair of lines in Figure 2.6?

Proximity applies not only to lines, of course. Users group objects such as text, tables, and graphics that are close to each other. They also group online controls such as hypergraphics and icons with adjacent text.

As you design and develop information, exploit users' tendency to group objects in close proximity and remember this tendency when you place objects either on paper or screen.

## Similarity

If figures are similar, we tend to group them. In the first group of Figure 2.7, do you see rows or columns? What about the second group?

There are two phenomena at work here. Not only do we tend to group similar objects, but we also strive for the simplest interpretation of a set of objects. It is by far easier to interpret Figure 2.7 as rows and columns of triangles and circles than to interpret it as a row or column of triangle-circle-triangle.

The more complex the groupings, the more you must enable your users to detect similarity. In text, graphics, tables, and charts, find the best way to exploit your users' propensity toward similarity.

**Figure 2.7**  Similarity.

## Continuity

We tend to perceive smooth, continuous patterns rather than discontinuous ones. Do you see a sine wave along a line or a line with alternating semicircles in Figure 2.8?

Users crave continuity, and if you do not provide it, they attempt to improve it on their own. Part of the covenant of trust is that you design and develop the medium, presentation, organization, and content of your information in such a way as to take advantage of continuity.

If you breach the covenant on the point of continuity, users get lost in the information. This weakens any hope you had of communicating with those users. The continuity must be intuitive and transparent to users; they should not be aware of the craft of writing behind your information any more than we should be aware of the craft of acting behind a

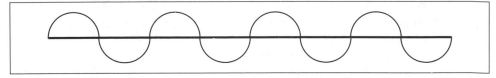

**Figure 2.8**  Continuity.

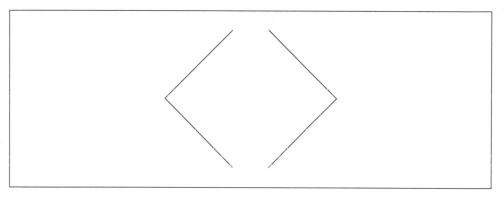

**Figure 2.9** Symmetry.

Katharine Hepburn classic. Users should always see the flowing sine wave and never even be aware of the possibility of disjointed, alternating semicircles.

### Symmetry

If symmetrical figures bound an area, we perceive a whole, coherent, symmetrical figure. Do you see a diamond in Figure 2.9?

Users are like the proverbial visitor who always straightens pictures on walls and doilies on tables. They prefer that their world be symmetrical, and when they turn to your information, they expect you to honor that preference. If you do not, they find ways of imposing the symmetry they want (or they simply do not use your information).

Design and develop your information symmetrically so that users can expend effort assimilating the information instead of trying to make it symmetrical. Symmetry is not a concept that applies only to the physicality of page or screen layout. It applies also—and perhaps more important—to the design and development of concepts, organizations, and modules of information.

### Closure

If a figure has gaps, we tend to complete it, filling in the gaps to create a whole object. Do you see the great state of Texas in Figure 2.10?

Users want whole information. They trust that you are presenting whole objects to them. If you do not provide it, they do—sometimes erroneously. Give them complete modules of information; do not make them fill in the gaps.

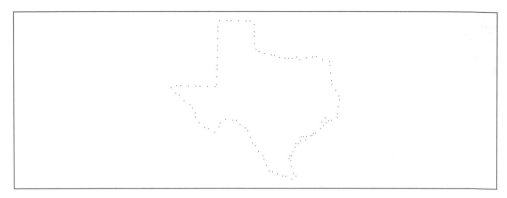

**Figure 2.10** Closure.

## Common Fate

We see objects moving in the same direction (toward a common fate) as a unit. Do you see a squadron of planes or seven individual planes in Figure 2.11?

Did you count the planes to see if there really are seven of them? Since they compose one unit, you see them as a single entity, not as seven discrete subentities.

Likewise, users should see your sentences, table entries, and lists as single logical entities. It is easier for users to store single logical entities in memory and retrieve them from memory than it is to work with individual subentities.

Your information modules should take advantage of users' desire for objects of common fate. Let the content be transparently obvious in a

**Figure 2.11** Common fate.

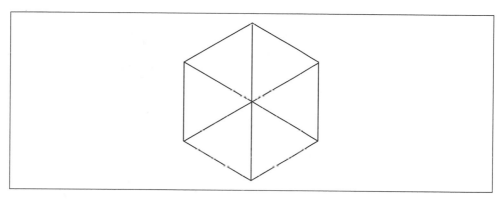

Figure 2.12  Goodness of figures.

module of information rather than the nuts and bolts that make it a module. Let users always see a paragraph as a logically developed concept rather than a grouping of individual sentences.

## Goodness of Figures

In addition to laws of grouping, we use a concept called the goodness of figures or the law of Prägnantz to help us interpret visual input. According to this concept, we opt for the simplest interpretation of an object.

In Figure 2.12 do you see a two-dimensional figure (a polygon with six sides), which is the simpler interpretation?  And with a little more effort, do you see a three-dimensional figure (a cube), the more difficult interpretation?

Users opt for the simplest interpretation of all information, regardless of its sensory origin. When you design and develop your information, evaluate your designs and constructions to ensure you have enabled users to make the simplest interpretation. The simplest interpretation should always be intuitive and transparent; the less time and effort users have to spend examining the information, the more time and effort they can spend assimilating it.

## Shape-Recognition Strategies

After we make figure-ground distinctions to separate visual stimuli from their surroundings, we use laws of grouping to make an organized whole of the figure. Then we use three shape-recognition strategies to determine whether we recognize the figure:

**Figure 2.13**  Prototype matching for shape-recognition.

1. Prototype matching

   We store in memory generalized shape patterns that we compare to objects to see if we can find a match. Since the patterns are generalized, we can recognize unlimited variations on an object's shape. What shape do you see in Figure 2.13? And what letter do you see in Figure 2.14?

2. Template matching

   Unlike prototype matching, we store in memory detailed shape patterns that we compare to objects to see if we can find a match. It must be an exact match, so in order to recognize all of the hearts and Ps in Figures 2.13 and 2.14, you have to have a template for each variation. As you can see, template matching requires enormous memory storage as well as tremendous effort in storing and retrieving the correct template.

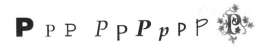

**Figure 2.14**  Prototype matching for letter recognition.

3. Distinctive features

We distinguish letters by their distinct feature patterns. Ts have only two lines, whereas Ds have one line and one arc. Some letters, such as Ms and Os, do not share features, while other letters, such as Ps and Rs, do. Using this strategy, we match patterns by analyzing the distinct parts of the letter as opposed to using prototype matching or template matching, in which we match patterns by comparing and contrasting the whole object, not its individual parts.

Exploit the prototypes your users have stored in memory. Use graphics, metaphors, and extended examples that users can match right away. Using banking metaphors, for example, hardly helps users of automotive information. Using unknown technical jargon in software information is equally disorienting to users. As a technical communicator, you are teacher and translator, and the best teachers and translators know that the more familiar the constructs, the stronger the learning and understanding.

A familiar context also plays a large part in shape-recognition. We see what we expect to see. We use our knowledge of context to help us interpret the objects we see. What is out of context in Figure 2.15?

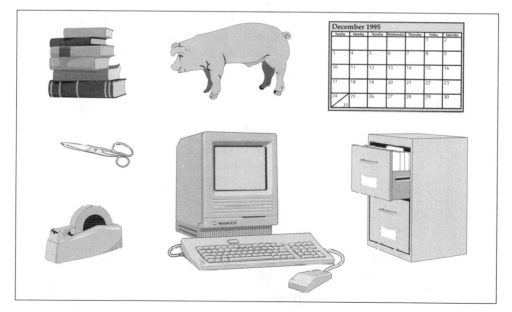

**Figure 2.15** Context in shape-recognition.

We expect to see a computer, filing cabinet, tape dispenser, scissors, books, and calendar in an office. We do not expect to see a pig. We can easily recognize the standard office objects and do not think them remarkable in their surroundings; we look twice to make sure that what we see is a pig and do find it remarkable that it should be grouped with objects from an office.

Likewise, context influences how we perceive letters and words, which we recognize by shape. We recognize and remember individual letters and whole words better if they are in a meaningful context. This is called the word-superiority effect. The letter t in the word "peanut" is easier to recognize than it is in the nonword "kletiu," and the word "telephone" is easier to recognize than are the same letters arranged in the nonword "netlehoep."

We also recognize letters as parts of meaningful words more easily than we recognize single letters. This is called the word-letter phenomenon.[3] The letter "m" in the word "game" is easier to recognize than the single letter "m."

Context is the all-important glue that holds your information together, and users import the context of your information right along with the information itself. The glue should be strong, yet intuitive and transparent. Medium, navigation, presentation, and content should work together to make the information easily accessible. In other words, do not put a pig in the middle of your information design or development—unless, of course, you are writing a pamphlet about tofu substitutes for slaughtered swine, in which case you might want to show a picture of a long-lived, contented pig.

## Perceptual Illusions

Perceptual illusions impact how we perceive objects. An illusion is something that appears true but is false, and a perceptual illusion is a perception that appears true but is false. This section examines six visual perceptual illusions:

1. Pöggendorff effect
2. Ponzo illusion
3. Relative size
4. Müller-Lyer illusion
5. Subjective contours
6. Necker cube

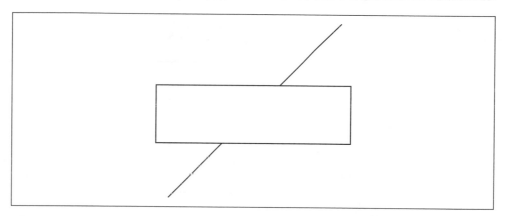

**Figure 2.16** Pöggendorf effect.

While these illusions deal expressly with graphical information, the cognitive lessons we learn from these perceptual illusions apply to textual information as well.

### Pöggendorff Effect

Why does the diagonal line appear to be offset in Figure 2.16? The rectangle offsets the diagonal line and disrupts our visual flow along the line.

The Pöggendorf effect lends itself to text application easily. Think of the diagonal line as a concept you are developing in text. Think of the rectangle as a tangent or a superfluous piece of information. What happens to the original concept? If your users maintain a grasp on the thread of the original concept, that grasp is weaker, more diluted because the "rectangle text" got in the way.

### Ponzo Illusion

Why does Line A look longer than Line B in Figure 2.17? Because of the inward slanting lines bracketing Lines A and B, we perceive Line A as farther away, yet it appears to be the same length as Line B. Since distant objects can look the same size as near objects only if they are larger, we perceive that Line A is longer than Line B. Thus, the Ponzo illusion is a result of environment manipulation. The environment or context of your information is important to users. Users trust that you have set up an honest environment, so do not manipulate it so that it appears to be something it is not.

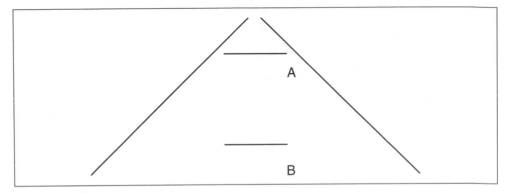

**Figure 2.17** Ponzo illusion.

## Relative Size

Why does Circle A appear to be larger than Circle B in Figure 2.18? This is the "big fish in a little pond" syndrome. We perceive Circle A as being larger than Circle B, because relatively smaller circles surround Circle A, while relatively larger circles surround Circle B. Circle A appears to be a big fish in a little pond, whereas Circle B appears to be a little fish in a big pond.

Does your text suffer from either "big fish in a little pond" or "little fish in a big pond" syndrome? Either is deceptive to users, and as such, betrays their trust. Once again, users trust that you have chosen the appropriate medium, navigation, and presentation for the information. Keep in mind that if you design and develop your information in such a way that you either overplay or underplay it, you are betraying that trust.

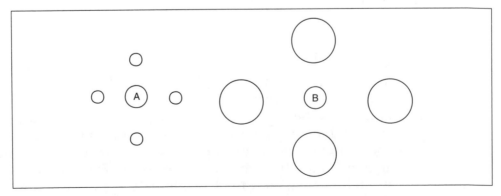

**Figure 2.18** Relative size.

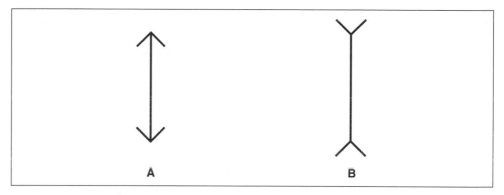

**Figure 2.19** Müller-Lyer illusion.

### Müller-Lyer Illusion

Why does Line B appear to be longer than Line A in Figure 2.19? Line B's arrowhead tails orient us away from the line, giving the illusion that the line is longer than it is, while Line A's arrowhead tails orient us back toward the line, giving the illusion that the line is shorter than it is.

The arrowhead tails of Line A fold back upon the line; there is no transition away from the line. Line B, however, uses the arrowhead tails as transitions away from the line, thereby elongating the perception of the line. Textual transitions work the same way. Without smooth transitions, the abruptness of a piece of information stunts that information. This concept of transition means more than textual bridges; it means always pointing the way for the user. Never leave your users wondering "What next?" Provide pointers out of your wilderness of information and maintain your users' trust.

Minimalist documentation and structured writing such as Information Mapping advocate doing away with textual bridges. Do not confuse these text-chaining transitions with navigation cues. While most users truly do not need text-chaining transitions, they are lost without pointers to what they should do next.

As you design the structure and navigation of information, design in intuitive, transparent navigational transitions.

### Subjective Contours

Why do we see white shapes in the middle of the figures in Figure 2.20?

We try to make meaningful wholes out of all the parts we perceive, and it is easier to see whole, meaningful black-lined and white-lined

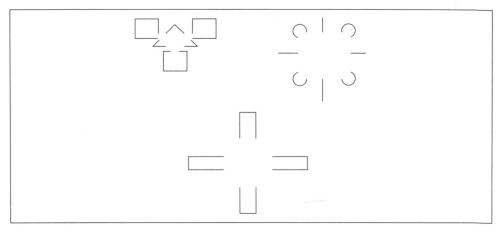

**Figure 2.20** Subjective contours.

shapes in these figures than it is to see meaningless, disorganized parts. The goodness of figures concept is at work here.

It is not only in graphics that users try to make meaningful wholes out of disorganized parts. Users desperately want all of your information to be meaningful, and if it is not, they attempt to bring some meaning to it themselves. The meaning they bring to it may or may not be the meaning you intended. Be sure your meaning is always whole and that there is no need for users to complete your information.

### Necker Cube

Do you see the cube in Figure 2.21?

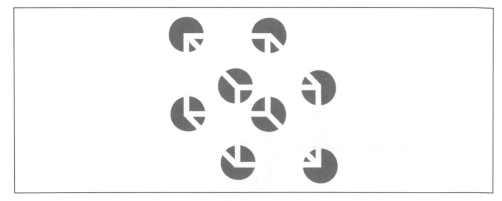

**Figure 2.21** Necker cube.

The Necker cube is another example of our determination to make meaningful wholes from disorganized parts. Instead of meaningless parts that are circles with lines etched in them, we prefer to perceive a meaningful whole that is a cube. Can you change your perception of the figure-ground relationship so that the cube sometimes floats behind the circles and sometimes in front?

Never allow users the ambiguity of changing perceptions. Your information should not float with unclear meanings and disorganized construction. Users do not look to technical information for mind puzzles and games of illusion. When you allow ambiguity into your information, you breach the covenant of trust with users.

## Summary

Sensation and perception are two ends of a continuum of processes we use to take in sensory data and bring meaning to that data. This continuum is the foundation for everything we think and do. Sensation is the physicality, and perception is the psychology of dealing with data in the world.

Three mechanisms protect us from the continuous bombardment of sensory data: thresholds, cocktail-party effect, and sensory adaptation. Six mechanisms affect how we perceive sensory data: perceptual set, figure-ground relationships, laws of grouping, goodness of figures, shape-recognition strategies, and perceptual illusions.

### Further Reading

Ackerman, D. *A Natural History of the Senses.* New York: Random House, 1990.

Barlow, H.B. and J.D. Mollon, eds. *The Senses.* Cambridge: Cambridge University Press, 1982.

Beck, J. (Ed.). *Organization and Representation in Perception.* Hillsdale, NJ: Erlbaum, 1982.

Boff, K.R., L. Kaufman, and J.P. Thomas, eds. *Handbook of Perception and Human Performance.* New York: John Wiley & Sons, 1986.

Elsendoorn, B.A.G. and H. Bouma, eds. *Working Models of Human Perception.* London: Academic Press, 1989.

Gelman, David, et. al. "Is the Mind an Illusion?" in *Newsweek,* April 20, 1992, pp. 71–72.

Gibson, J.J. *The Senses Considered as Perceptual Systems.* Boston: Houghton Mifflin, 1962.

Gregory, R. L., ed. *The Oxford Companion to the Mind*. Oxford: Oxford University Press, 1987.

Harnad, S., ed. *Categorical Perception: The Groundwork of Cognition*. Hillsdale, NJ: Erlbaum, 1984.

Hershenson, M. *The Moon Illusion*. Hillsdale, NJ: Erlbaum, 1989.

Howe, E.S. and C.J. Brandau. "The Temporal Course of Visual Pattern Encoding: Effects of Pattern Goodness." *Quarterly Journal of Experimental Psychology*, 35A, pp. 607–633.

Jastrow, R. *The Enchanted Loom: Mind in the Universe*. New York: Simon and Schuster, 1981.

Katsuki, Y. et al., eds. *Brain Mechanisms of Sensation*. New York: John Wiley & Sons, 1981.

Koffka, K. *Principles of Gestalt Psychology*. New York: Harcourt Brace, 1935.

Köhler, W. *Gestalt Psychology: An Introduction to New Concepts in Modern Psychology*. New York: Liveright, 1947.

Matlin, M.W. and H.J. Foley. *Sensation and Perception*. Boston: Allyn and Bacon, 1992.

Minsky, M. *The Society of Mind*. New York: Simon and Schuster, 1986.

Pomerantz, J.R. and M. Kubovy. *Perceptual Organization*. Hillsdale, NJ: Erlbaum, 1981.

Rock, I. *The Logic of Perception*. Cambridge: MIT Press, 1987.

Shaw, R.E. and J. Bransford, eds. *Perceiving, Acting, and Knowing*. Hillsdale, NJ: Erlbaum, 1977.

## Notes

1   There are three types of sensation: exteroceptive, interoceptive, and proprioceptive. Exteroceptive sensations collect data about our external environment and include the five Aristotelian sensations of sight, hearing, taste, smell, and touch as well as sensations of temperature, pain, and pressure. Exteroceptive sense organs are on the exterior of the body and include the eyes, ears, tongue, nose, and the temperature, pain, pressure, and touch receptors of the skin. Interoceptive sensations collect data about our internal environment and include such sensations as pain, hunger, thirst, nausea, fatigue, and suffocation. The interoceptive sense organs are mainly in the abdominal and thoracic organs. Proprioceptive sensations collect data about body position and movement. The proprioceptive sense organs are in the muscles, tendons, joints, and organs of balance in the ear.

2   M.C. Escher's work is a particularly good example of figure becoming ground and ground becoming figure.

3   M. Matlin and H. Foley (1992, pp. 147–148).

# CHAPTER THREE

# Learning

*There's one thing more painful than learning from experience, and that is not learning from experience.*

Anonymous

Technical communication has the responsibility of helping users learn. Whereas quite a few people may favor a bit of mystery, romance, or poetry for entertainment and escape, who picks up an environmental impact report to forget about the day's traumas? Users want to learn from what you write, whether it is how to write a software utility, fix a carburetor, or invest in mutual funds. So what is learning? Learning is a relatively permanent change in behavior as a result of experience.

Given this definition of learning, does Otto learn in the following scenario, and if so, what does he learn?

Otto has not played volleyball since his high school days, which were around the time Elvis was mustered out of the service. His neighbors convince him to play in a beach pick-up game one Sunday afternoon. He plays his heart out and falls into bed that night in happy exhaustion.

His alarm clock sounds off bright and early Monday morning, and Otto can barely move. Every muscle in his body is screaming at him, and he can barely stagger to the bathroom.

All week long, he treats himself extra gently, taking long, hot soaks, and getting plenty of rest. The next Sunday, when he finally can move without pain, his friends try to recruit him for another game.

He shakes his head and says with a grin, "I'll keep score."

Has Otto learned anything? Although this one example is not enough to determine the relative permanence of Otto's behavior change, we can say that he has at least learned this: out of shape 50-plus year olds cannot cavort on the beach like high schoolers without paying a price.

As you design and develop your information, you need to understand how users learn, what they learn, and why they learn. The "how" is learning theory and learning styles; the "what" is knowledge; and the "why" is motivation.

## Learning Theory

Learning theory is a codified set of hypotheses that theorize about how people learn. Very broadly, learning theory falls into two categories: behaviorist (also called connectionist) and cognitive (also called Gestaltist).[1]

Behaviorist learning theory suggests that it is better to focus not on mental acts that we cannot observe, but rather on objective, quantifiable behavior; the connection between actions; and the role of reward in behavior. Although pure behaviorist learning theory is now out of fashion, components of behaviorism must always be an important part of learning theory, since the real measure of learning is behavior.[2]

Cognitive learning theory suggests that it is better to focus on mental acts that we cannot observe such as conceiving, believing, and expecting than on strictly objective, quantifiable behavior.[3]

Behaviorist and cognitive learning theories may seem like the North and South Poles, but in reality, we learn in both ways. We stitch a seamless blend of behaviorism and cognition from these components:[4]

- Experience
- Schemata
- Habits
- Reinforcement
- Interference
- User curves

### Experience

Learning is a result of experience. We are constantly experiencing the world. We experience hurricanes, happiness, and hepatitis. Although each of these experiences is vastly different from the other, they are all experiences and they all lead to learning.

The sensation-perception continuum forms the basis of experience. Experience uses sensation and perception either to form a new schema or to evaluate perception in light of an existing schema. A schema is a mental framework or model that we use to understand and interact with the world.

Perhaps you have never been in a hurricane. You take in the sensory data that all wind has been sucked from the air and the air is stiller than you have ever felt it, and you notice that the air has taken on an eerie yellow tinge. You perceive this data and build a schema from this perception.

Then, suddenly, frighteningly strong winds begin to rip at houses, cars, and trees, and more rain than you thought clouds could possibly hold pours in cataracts from the sky. You perceive this data as quickly as your senses can take it in, and you modify your schema to include this new data.

After hours that seem like days, the wind and rain subside. You perceive this sensory input and once again modify your schema. Now you have experienced a hurricane; you have built a schema and labeled it hurricane; you have learned what a hurricane is. The next time the air is uncannily still and has a yellowish cast, you will pull your hurricane schema out of memory and know what to expect. Because you have now formulated expectations, the next time you see all the external signs of a hurricane, you will anticipate that the culmination of these external signs will be a hurricane.

Figure 3.1 illustrates the components of experience.

As you can see, experiences hinge on schemata we have created and stored in memory. We interact with the world based on these schemata.

## Schemata

When faced with an experience, we either create a new schema or modify an existing one. This modification might involve adding new data, subtracting existing data, or completely overhauling the schema.

You have your hurricane schema safely tucked away in memory. You sense the air becoming still and yellow, you perceive this data and haul out your hurricane schema to evaluate your perception. It looks like a hurricane, it sounds like a hurricane, it feels like a hurricane ... it must be a hurricane.

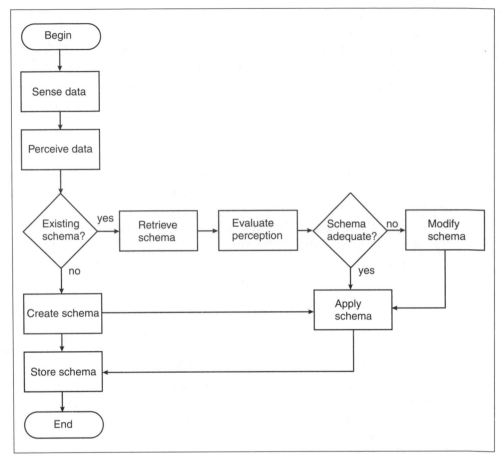

**Figure 3.1**  Experience flowchart.

But this time, the winds are weaker and less rain falls, so you have to modify your hurricane schema. You now have an enriched model of what a hurricane is; you have added the possibility that a hurricane does not always behave in the same way. Eventually, if you experience enough hurricanes, you will have a sophisticated hurricane schema that takes into account all the variables your experiences have presented to you.

Our schemata help us create connections between stimuli and learning. They are the bridge between the external world and the internal worlds that are in our heads. Often, these connections become so strong that we do not consciously have to trot out our schemata. For example, take another look at Roberta and the stop sign from Chapter 2:

Long before the gleam of a driver's license appeared in Roberta's teenaged eye, she knew that vehicles stop, or are supposed to stop, at stop signs. The first time she ever saw a stop sign, her eyes took in the sensory data of its size, shape, color, and markings; she perceived this as a whole symbol communicating something. She observed that vehicles stop at this symbol, so she created a schema labeled stop sign, and this schema said that vehicles stop when they come to a stop sign.

Through the years she modified this schema to include the difference between two-way and four-way stop signs, the fact that fire engines with their lights whirling and sirens screaming do not stop, and the stopping-distance variables that weather dictates.

When Roberta started driving, she was very aware of stop signs and perhaps even nervous every time she came to one. In time, however, her reaction to stop signs became automatic. She probably rarely thinks about them, despite the fact that she encounters them dozens of times each day.

She still has her stop-sign schema, but she does not modify it unless she senses and perceives new data about stop signs. If she travels to a country where people drive on the other side of the road, for example, Roberta might bring it out and evaluate the new sensation and perception of driving and stopping on a different side of the road. Otherwise, she is unconscious of her stop-sign schema, although she uses it daily.

Users populate their world with conscious and unconscious schemata. To be successful, your information must either leverage users' schemata or enable them to quickly and easily create new schemata. The easiest way to leverage users' schemata is to use examples that center on schemata they already have in memory. Be careful, though, because experience and the schemata it engenders are products of individual users' times, culture, education, and social milieu. A member of Generation X might not understand a reference to the fox-trot, while a veteran of the second World War might think heavy metal is what a tank is made of. Likewise, a reference to Main Street, USA would carry little meaning in Beijing.

To help users create schemata, draw on universal experiences that transcend time, culture, education, and social milieu. If users cannot relate your information to something in their world, your information does not exist in their world. Use metaphors, examples, and problem-solving scenarios that they recognize and to which they can relate.

If your users must create schemata, help them understand why. Posit the new schemata as enhancements to their interaction with your information. Help them lay a foundation and build their schemata layer by layer. Always show them the benefit of new schemata; they should never be in the position of trading in old schemata that produced results for new schemata that are ineffective. Simplicity is key in helping users build schemata, and the cliché about a picture's being worth a thousand words is never more appropriate than when you are guiding users to create schemata. If you fail in either leveraging existing schemata or helping users create new schemata, your information fails.

To leverage users' existing schemata:

- Use universal metaphors and examples.

  If you are writing for a broad audience or an international audience, you must use metaphors and examples to which everyone can relate. Use metaphors and examples that are from daily life, are not culture-specific, and are simple.

     For example, in this book, I use the stop-sign example several times, because I am confident that everyone who reads this book can relate to a stop sign and its meaning.

- Use specific metaphors and examples you know your users' schemata match.

  Use specific metaphors and examples only if you are writing for a narrow audience. If you are writing a policy and procedures manual for a credit union, for example, you can be confident that your users can relate to credit-union metaphors and examples. Of course, users new to credit-union environments probably will not immediately understand the references, but they are likely to learn, and your information should help them learn.

To help users quickly and easily create new schemata:

- Build on existing schemata.

  Compare and contrast the schema you want your users to build with schemata they already have. This gives them a peg on which to hang the new schema and enables them to relate to it and remember it more easily.

- Start with the general and add the specific.

  Use a pyramid approach to schema building. Start with a broad, general base and work your way up to the narrow specifics.

- Build complexity layer by layer.

  Anything new is at first complex, so approach schema building as a complex task on the part of your users. Give them one layer of information at a time until you have given them the entire schema.

- Control the pace of the schema creation.

  Schema building should not be like opening a fire hydrant and getting blown away by a gush of water. It should be a healthy trickle whose velocity you control with your knowledge of the information and your understanding of users' needs.

Schemata are our bridge from what is in our heads to what is in the world. When users bring your information into their world, they apply their schemata to it. The more you can leverage users' existing schemata, the easier learning from your information is for them. If you cannot leverage existing schemata, you must enable users to create quickly and easily new schemata based on your information. Use the audience and task analysis phase of information development to find out what your users' existing schemata are.

Everyone balks at change. Users rarely want to change simple things like the color of an icon much less the ingrained schemata they use to understand information. Make change as painless and transparent as possible. Never make whimsical changes, and never ask your users to change unless you thoroughly endorse the change yourself. If you are dishonest, they detect it.

## Habits

Roberta's connection between stop sign and stopping is, for the most part, permanent. Unless she suffers a medical catastrophe, she is likely to remember this connection long beyond her driving years. Like Pavlov's dogs who drooled when they heard a dinner bell regardless of whether there was any dinner, Roberta stops when she sees a red, octagonal symbol with the word STOP in big, white letters. She probably would stop if she saw a red, octagonal symbol with the word GO in big, white letters, too, because she is conditioned to the connection between the symbol and the action. This is why each traffic sign has a unique shape and color.

Connections between symbols and their corresponding actions are called habits, and we organize our lives around thousands of habits. A habit is a learned connection between a stimulus (stop sign) and a response (stopping). The strength of that connection is called the habit strength. Each habit has its own habit strength.

Each habit also has its own habit family, which is a set of related habits. Within each habit family is a habit-family hierarchy, a pecking order for habits. The most effective habits are highest in the habit family hierarchy and are the ones we tend to use first in a new situation. For example:

> Betty has a habit family of computer hot keys, keys she relies on to perform computer tasks quickly. She learned this habit family from her experiences with various hardware and software, and she relies on these habits when she encounters new situations.
>
> Betty comes from a UNIX background, where CONTROL-C gets her out of almost any predicament. She is perfectly happy working in a UNIX shell, secure in the knowledge that CONTROL-C is her cavalry. She learned this connection early in her UNIX career, and it has rescued her time and again.
>
> What happens when she starts working in a Virtual Machine (VM) environment and finds herself in a situation from which she wants to extricate herself? She hits CONTROL-C...and wonders why it does not work. She relied on a habit, on a learned connection that had always rescued her. She moves down her habit-family hierarchy, trying CONTROL-Z, then CONTROL-A. Nothing works. She has to reevaluate her hot key habit family, realizing that maybe she needs a UNIX hot key branch and a VM hot key branch of the habit family.

As well as understanding your users' schemata, you must understand their habits, habit strengths, and habit families. You can exploit the habits they already possess, and if you know the habits that are likely to interfere with your information, you can carefully steer your users on the road to new habits.

You have to design this "new habit" training into your information. Leverage old habits by comparing and contrasting the new (desired) habit with the old (undesired) habit. Some examples of leveraging old habits and creating new ones are:

- Make remembering new key combinations easy by creating free-standing reference cards.

- Ease users into change in command structures by mapping the old command habit to the new command with gentle online reminders.

- Pull new terminology out of the body of your information to stand alone at the front as a mini-glossary map that correlates old (undesired) terms to new (desired) terms.

- Use your index to help users map new terminology and concepts with familiar terminology and concepts.

Sustain your users' trust by recognizing and admitting that their existing habits have served them well and by promoting new habits as a means of enhancing, not merely replacing, what they do and how they do it. Always posit new habits as necessary to enhance your users' learning experience.

## Reinforcement

If CONTROL-C did not save Betty from unwanted UNIX situations, she would not have developed it as a habit. Each time she pressed CONTROL-C, an unpleasant situation disappeared and was replaced by a pleasant situation. This result reinforced her learning that CONTROL-C is an escape route.

As another example of reinforced learning, consider Brian, who is learning the landscaping business:

Brian worked side-by-side with his boss learning the colors, textures, cycles, and needs of year-round landscaping. Every time he successfully created a flowing bank of colorful, generous begonias, instead of tightly packed little clumps with hard rootballs that withered and died, his boss would slap him on the back and buy him lunch at McGinty's.

This was unusually pleasant behavior from his boss, so Brian developed the habit of spreading begonias' roots and giving them room to grow. His boss' behavior reinforced Brian's learning to landscape begonia beds.

An integral part of learning, reinforcement is the process of using events or behaviors, called reinforcers, to produce learning. There are both positive and negative reinforcers.

Although some psychologists would argue that there are distinct, if subtle, differences between positive reinforcers and reward, most agree that lay people can use the terms interchangeably. We cannot, however, use the terms negative reinforcer and punishment interchangeably. A negative reinforcer removes an unpleasant condition, such as turning off the electrical current when you have your finger in a socket. Punishment, on the other hand, is the introduction of an unpleasant condition, such as your mother's washing out your mouth with soap when you discovered and practiced words she would have prefered you had neither discovered nor practiced.

CONTROL-C is a negative reinforcer, because it ends an unpleasant condition, such as a seemingly interminable UNIX grep. Stopping at a stop sign is a positive reinforcer, because it creates a pleasant condition, such as preventing a Mack truck's flattening you and your car.

Reinforcement helps us learn, but to be effective, reinforcement must be systematic. Three schedules of reinforcement help us systematize reinforcement:

1. Continuous reinforcement is reinforcing a behavior each time it occurs. For example, each time you try to sell Aunt Jane a magazine subscription for your child's summer-camp fund, she buys one.

    Continuous reinforcement is the quickest route to learning. It does not take long for either you or your child to learn that you can count on Aunt Jane for at least one magazine subscription. Continuous reinforcement also sets up the strongest expectations, so that when the reinforcement stops, the learning stops quickly. Should Aunt Jane not buy magazine subscriptions twice in a row, you probably would learn not to count on her the next time Camp Lakeside needs a new roof for the mess hall. Learners do not continue to learn once continuous reinforcement has stopped.

2. Intermittent reinforcement is sometimes reinforcing a behavior, sometimes not; there is no pattern or consistency. For example, you ask your boss for one day of compensation time for each three days of uncompensated time you have worked. Your boss sometimes gives you the day and sometimes does not, so you learn that sometimes you get a comp day. You also learn to be hopeful that you will get a day off.

    With intermittent reinforcement, initial learning is slower than with continuous reinforcement, but learning and hope do not cease with intermittent reinforcement as they do with the cessation of continuous reinforcement. Learners continue to learn even when there is no reinforcement.

3. Vicarious reinforcement is learning to perform those actions we see others rewarded for and to eschew those actions we see others punished for. For example, if you see a coworker put money in a soda machine and get two sodas for the price of one, you will put some money in that machine. If, however, you see a coworker lose money in a soda machine, you will not put any money in that machine.

   If the soda machine you had been avoiding suddenly begins giving free soda, you change your learning and your actions to accommodate this new observation. With vicarious reinforcement, learners continue to learn to perform those actions they see others rewarded for and to eschew those actions they see others punished for. The pattern of learning changes only when the observation changes.

You must choose a schedule of reinforcement for your users. Obviously the medium of information plays a part in which schedule you choose. Vicarious reinforcement works well in videos, CBT environments, and interactive multimedia. It is hard, however, to build vicarious reinforcement into hardcopy information.

The level of user for whom you are writing also plays a part in which schedule you choose. Power-level users, or users fairly high up on the technical information user curve, are annoyed and irritated with continuous reinforcement. These users really want reinforcement only when they are attempting self-initiated tasks or trying to do something in an unconventional way. Entry-level users find a warm, fuzzy security blanket in continuous reinforcement, but the danger is twofold: what happens when the continuous reinforcement stops and what happens as these users mature and move up the technical information user curve to more sophisticated levels?

Schedules of reinforcement should be user-defined in the way and frequency with which users access their reinforcement. You can make online reinforcement (such as a sound or flashing icon) user-controlled, so that your users can turn off the reinforcement. You can make hardcopy reinforcement (such as the results of an action and reviews of what users have learned) optional by either clearly labeling them in the body of your information or moving them to an appendix. Power-level users skip over the reinforcement, and entry-level users rely on it less and less as they become more confident. User-defined schedules of reinforcement allow users to determine just how much reinforcement they need as well as choose when they need it.

The type of information you are communicating also impacts the schedule of reinforcement you choose. As information moves up the scale of complexity, the more need users have for reinforcement. Often basic, easily assimilated information requires no reinforcement, while other conceptually or technically difficult information obviously demands some schedule of reinforcement.

## Interference

Very often, habit families interfere with new learning. They become baggage that gets in the way of successfully performing new tasks. The reverse is also true; new learning can retroactively interfere with something already learned.

For example, Loni is having trouble learning English as a second language, because her native French keeps interfering. Ashley is having trouble learning Microsoft Word, because her WordPerfect habits keep getting in the way.

But interference is not always a negative phenomenon. Interference can also aid learning. If Ashley has learned MacDraw, she can apply the same approach, understanding, and actions to learning SuperPaint.

You have to determine how to turn your users' interference to the best advantage. Exploit previously learned information to help users learn your information. Compare and contrast the differences between your information and previously learned information when the interference is likely to impact your users' learning in a negative way.

## User Curves

User curves are a way to plot and track the stages of users' learning. They help you determine what type of information users need at each stage of learning, break the information down into components and subcomponents, and understand what assumptions are safe to make. User curves also help you understand how to move your users along the curves if they want to make that journey.[5]

For example, Gail is writing a procedure explaining how to create form letters in Microsoft Word.

A high-level explanation of the task is that users need to create a data document and a text document then merge the two. If Gail breaks this down into the modular components of the knowledge, skill, and understanding necessary to accomplish this task, she finds that users need to:

- Know what equipment and information they need
  - A personal computer that runs Windows
  - Microsoft Word for Windows
  - Paper
  - A printer
  - Names and addresses
  - Text of the form letter
- Understand how to function in their environment
  - Use their computer and printer
  - Ensure that the two machines are communicating with each other
- Be able to perform specific tasks
  - Use Microsoft Word and Windows
  - Create a data document
  - Create a text document
  - Use the merge menu option

If Gail's users do not have this knowledge, understanding, and skill at their disposal, they cannot create form letters. She can break each of these components into subcomponents. For example, how many subcomponents are there in knowing how to use Word and Windows? And what are the subcomponents of those subcomponents? What is Gail safe in assuming? That users can type? Use online help? Understand how to select a menu option? Know how to connect their printer to their computer? Can read English?

There are three user curves that impact how users learn technical information:

1. Technical information user curve
2. Piaget's cognitive developmental curve
3. Erikson's psychosocial curve

## Technical Information User Curve

The technical information user curve plots the stages of learning users go through in learning technical information from entry-level users to power-level users. It includes an outsider-level user who wants to remain outside the formal stages of the user curve.

There are five distinct stages on the technical information user curve[6]:

1. Entry

   The entry-level user can perform an action as directed and observe the response; this user does not perceive beyond the immediate experience.

2. Beginner

   The beginner-level user focuses on the most basic aspects and requires many positive explanations and examples; this user begins to build simple symbolic models, but cannot extrapolate those models and apply them elsewhere.

3. Intermediate

   The intermediate-level user can learn more than the basics; this user begins to examine logic, but cannot yet theorize based on the logic.

4. Power

   The power-level user has a systemic understanding and ability to derive new applications; this user is able to perform abstract reasoning.

5. Outsider

   The outsider-level user is an infrequent user who performs narrowly defined tasks, so does not need the broader perspective and schematic knowledge traversing the curve brings. This user wants to learn to do specific tasks and nothing else.

Figure 3.2 shows the technical information user curve.

Users can approach learning at any stage and, with practice, move up through the various stages. They also can choose not to participate in the curve and remain at the outsider stage.

When you were about eight years old, you probably started learning your multiplication tables. In the beginning, they made no sense; you could not for the life of you understand why $6 \times 9 = 54$ was important. You listened to your teacher and mimicked what you heard. You were at the entry stage of learning multiplication.

With a little practice, however, you moved beyond just echoing back what your teacher said. You began to ask questions and try to find answers. You began to take a few tentative steps in mastering multiplica-

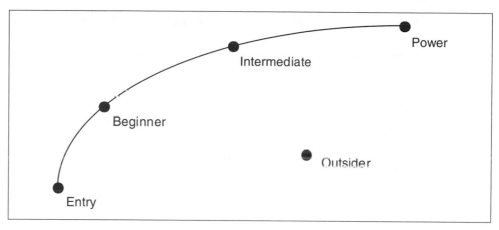

**Figure 3.2** Technical information user curve.

tion by creating your own mental models of the multiplication tables, but you did not use those models anywhere but in the classroom during arithmetic. You were at the beginner stage of learning multiplication.

You practiced...and got better. You began to show off at home a little, trying to explain the intricacies of third-grade math to your little sister or brother, shaking your head in eight-year old disgust when the little one just was not interested in how many fours make twenty. You were at the intermediate stage of learning multiplication.

Then multiplication fever hit you. You whipped out your flash cards at the least provocation and feverishly recited all of the multiplication tables, even the hard 12s. You were invincible. You saw applications for multiplication everywhere and began to explain to your parents how they could multiply gallons of gas times miles per gallon to get total miles per tank. You understood multiplication inside and out. You had arrived at the power stage of learning multiplication.

Of course, you could have stayed at any one stage and not progressed to the next, or, having attained a certain stage, could have slid back to the previous stage. Your motivation, practice, and application of the information allowed you to traverse the multiplication learning curve. It is possible that as you read this, you are trying to dredge up the answer to 12x11 (132); it is possible that the power-level user of eight is only the intermediate-level or beginner-level user of 30-something.

And it is equally possible that you never have 12x11=132 on the tip of your tongue. For this particular information, you may choose always to be an outsider-level user, someone who has to calculate this information each time and is content to do so. If 12 × 11=132 is important in your life, you learn it; if not, you whip out your solar-powered, pocket-sized, combination fax machine/calculator/foot massager and let it figure out the answer on those rare occasions when you need it.

### Piaget's Cognitive Developmental Curve

Jean Piaget's cognitive developmental curve plots the stages of development people go through in cognitive learning. It begins with viewing the world in purely concrete, objective terms and ends with being able to abstract and theorize about the world. Piaget's work revolves around the concepts of thesis, antithesis, and synthesis. The hurricane example can explain these terms:

> The first time you experience a hurricane, you create a hurricane schema; this is the thesis. The next time you encounter a hurricane, and it is not like the first one you encountered; this is the antithesis. You modify your hurricane schema to accommodate the new data you have perceived; this is the synthesis. The synthesis now serves as a thesis for the next antithesis, which leads to the next synthesis. This approach is a never-ending spiral of creating and modifying schema.[7]

Thesis/antithesis/synthesis is the means to traverse Piaget's cognitive developmental learning curve. We cannot move from stage to stage until we have created the thesis, encountered the antithesis, and formed the synthesis. Piaget identifies four stages along his cognitive developmental curve:

1. Sensorimotor

   The child experiences the world through actions performed on actual objects. The child cannot create mental representations or schema of the world. Actions are at first reflexive, progressively moving to controlled. The child first views objects as having no permanence; when an object is out of the child's sight, the object no longer exists.

   The child progresses to a stage of looking for an object no longer in view, but is unable to progress to the stage of creating a mental path of discovery and following that path to find hidden objects. The accomplishment of this last stage marks the end of the sensorimotor stage.

2. Preoperational

The child can represent objects with words and images but cannot reason logically. Six limitations apply to this stage:

1. Concreteness

   The child can interact only with concrete objects that are physically present.

2. Irreversibility

   The child cannot mentally rearrange objects or conceive of them in a different pattern.

3. Egocentrism

   The child believes that everyone experiences the world as he or she experiences it.

4. Centering

   The child focuses on only one aspect of a situation, excluding all other aspects.

5. States versus transformations

   The child focuses on the condition of an object rather than on the actions that created a given condition.

6. Transductive reasoning

   The child reasons by moving from Notion A to Notion B and back to Notion A; the notions have nothing in common other than that the child is focusing on them.

3. Concrete operational

The child can think logically about concrete events and can classify, combine, and compare. The six limitations of the preoperational stage begin to dissolve. The hallmark of this stage is the concept of conservation, which is the recognition that a substance's quantity is not affected by the actions we perform on that substance.

There are three types of conservation:

1. Number

   Five jelly beans are five jelly beans, whether we put them in a pile or line them up one after another.

2. Substance

   A pound of clay is a pound of clay whether we form it into a ball or a long rope.

3. Quantity

   Eight ounces of water is eight ounces of water whether we pour it into a tall, thin container or into a short, fat container.

4. Formal operational

   The child can reason abstractly and understands formal structures, problem formulation, and logical consequences. The child forms hypotheses and probabilities and looks at all aspects of a situation, including symbolic situations. Scientific modes of reasoning begin to emerge. This is the adult stage of thought.[8]

Figure 3.3 show's Piaget's developmental learning curve.

Although Piaget's theories deal with children's cognitive learning development, they are valid for all learning situations. We can extrapolate Piaget's theories and apply them to user learning. We can overlay the two curves and see their likenesses and note the similarities between the descriptions of the learning stages.

Figure 3.4 shows the correlation between the technical information learning curve and Piaget's developmental learning curve.

Think back to the first time you used a computer. You were content just to figure out how to turn it on and off, see the relationship between

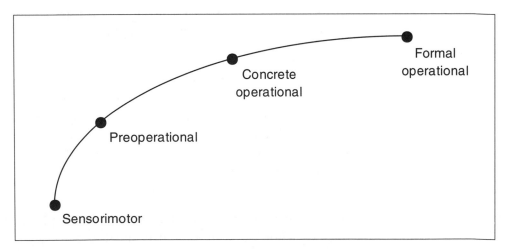

**Figure 3.3** Piaget's cognitive developmental curve.

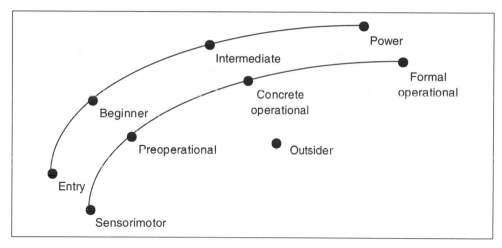

**Figure 3.4** Technical information user curve and Piaget's cognitive developmental curve.

moving the mouse and the movements of the cursor, and being able to drag and drop objects. When objects such as files left the screen, you were terrified they were gone forever. This is a sensorimotor stage of learning.

With practice, you began to understand the computer a little. You developed mental models of files and directories, their structures, and how they are related. You realized that just because an object is not visible does not mean you have lost it forever. This is a preoperational stage of learning.

With even more practice, you could think logically about how a computer works and understand more about it, perhaps even applying its structure and workings to your own daily life. You developed mental models of classifications, combinations, and comparisons you applied when using the computer. This is a concrete operational stage of learning.

Finally, you developed a systemic understanding of the computer, could create macros to automate routine tasks, and formulate and solve problems you encountered. This is a formal operational stage of learning.

Take a few minutes and think of other learning processes and apply Piaget's curve. Learning to read music? Learning to fix a voltage regulator? Learning to invest in index mutual funds?

Although Piaget never identified an outsider level, is it possible that there is an outsider level of cognitive learning? It probably is possible, although it would not be part of the "normal" learning process and would indicate a learning dysfunction. Dyslexia might force a learner to the outsider level as might other learning challenges such as neural damage, difficulties with second languages, and attention deficit disorder. This does not equate to the outsider-level user on the user curve, because opting to remain an outsider-level user is not an indication of user dysfunction. For example, you might have 17 software programs on your personal computer. You may be a power-level user for six of them, an intermediate-level user for eight of them, a beginner-level user for one of them, and an outsider-level user for two of them.

### Erikson's Psychosocial Curve

Erik Erikson's psychosocial curve plots the stages of development in social learning. It begins with learning to trust through experiencing satisfaction or failure and ends with effectivity and mastery of social situations. Whereas Piaget plotted a child's cognitive processing development, Erikson examines a person's social development, at each stage of which he identifies what he calls psychosocial tasks. Although Erikson identifies eight stages of psychosocial development, we are interested in the first four, because they correspond to the technical information user curve and Piaget's cognitive developmental curve:[9]

1. Trust

   If a child's needs are met, the child develops a sense of trust and feels that the world is reliable and predictable.

2. Self-confidence

   The child develops independence and self-confidence.

3. Initiative

   The child develops initiative and self-control.

4. Competence

   The child develops effectivity and mastery.

Figure 3.5 shows Erikson's psychosocial learning curve.

Although Erikson's stages explicitly apply to children's psychosocial development, they apply as well to users' development, and we can overlay Erikson's stages on both the technical information user curve and Piaget's cognitive developmental learning curve.

Figure 3.6 shows the correlation among the technical information, Piaget's developmental, and Erikson's psychosocial curves.

Think about the first time you made a cake. You relied on the recipe to tell you what you needed and to guide you through all the steps. After

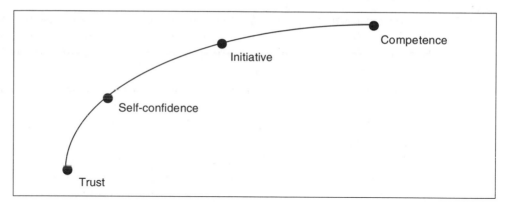

**Figure 3.5** Erikson's psychosocial curve.

successfully baking a few cakes, you felt safe with the recipe; you thought it reliable and predictable. You trusted it. This is the trust stage of psychosocial development; it is also a very sensitive and critical stage. If your cake had turned out to be slightly more tasty than mildewed cardboard, you would not have learned to trust the recipe. Instead, you would have learned to mistrust it, and probably would not have used it again. If this were the case, you would not traverse the psychosocial curve for this particular recipe.

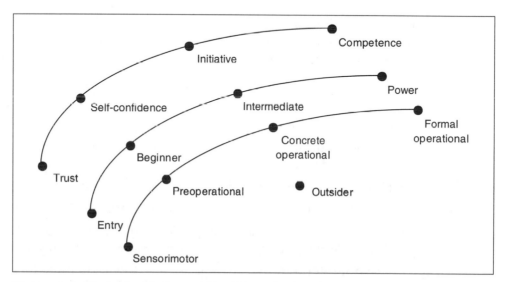

**Figure 3.6** Technical information, Piaget's developmental, and Erikson's psychosocial curves.

With practice, you began to leave the safe harbor of the recipe, using it as a guide, not as a life preserver. You gained some independence and began to feel self-confident about your culinary abilities. This is the self-confidence stage of psychosocial development.

With more practice, you began experimenting. You substituted some applesauce for a portion of the sugar, but you did not go wild. You remained within the confines of a cake, but you felt you could take more initiative. This is the initiative stage of psychosocial development.

With even more practice, you were turning out two and three-tiered works of art. You rarely consulted the recipe; you felt empowered. You had mastered your craft. This is the competence stage of psychosocial development.

Like Piaget, Erikson did not identify an outsider stage, but is it possible? Once again, it is possible, but probably not part of "normal" psychosocial development. Certain psychological or social abnormalities could prevent someone's traversing the curve, or perhaps early psychological traumas could prevent someone's successfully developing the trust that is the foundation for moving up the curve. Once again, too, this does not equate to the outsider level of the user curve. It is not abnormal, for example, for you not to want to be a power-level user of all 17 software programs you have on your personal computer.

These three user curves give you a new dimension in plotting user profiles. As you perform your audience analysis before beginning any project, plot where your users fall on each of these curves. Going back to Gail's task of creating a procedure for mass-producing form letters in Microsoft Word, Gail does her audience analysis and finds that her users:

- Are mostly clerical staff in large, corporate environments
- Understand how to use a computer and Microsoft Word to perform the daily requirements of the job
- Are not comfortable venturing out of clearly understood and tightly prescribed procedures
- Have strong habits based on most frequently performed jobs
- Do not want to become power-level computer or Microsoft Word users
- Have no interest in how things work, but a high interest in getting the job done quickly and efficiently and right the first time
- Are not interested in learning beyond the immediate task
- Have acute concerns about losing data and recovering from errors

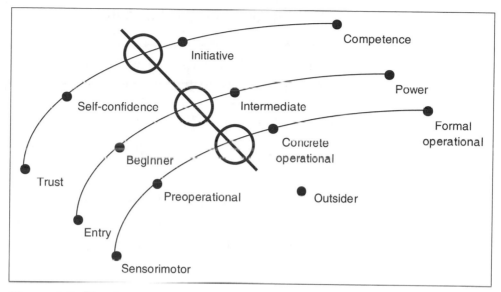

**Figure 3.7** Plotting users on user curves.

Based on this analysis, Gail plots her average target user on the three curves as shown in Figure 3.7.

Users trust that you not only know at which stage of each of these curves they are, but that you know what they need both to function at a given stage and to move on to the next stage. Combine the three curves and there are five user profiles:

1. Entry-sensorimotor-trust

   These users need:

   - Clear, concrete, uncluttered information and structure

   - Controlled focus

   - Explanations of the results of actions

2. Beginner-preoperational-self confidence

   These users need:

   - Help in creating appropriate, simple schemata

   - Encouragement to ask questions

   - Many simple examples

3. Intermediate-concrete operational-initiative

These users need:

- Insight into the logic structure of the information
- Open-ended examples that they may extrapolate from their own environment
- Safety net as they explore

4. Power-formal operational-competence

These users need:

- Systemic understanding of the information
- Opportunities to apply analytical and problem-solving skills
- Frameworks that launch original thought about and application of the information

5. Outsider

These users need:

- Recognition that not every user wants to traverse the user curve
- Modular components of information that enable them to come to information over and over
- Reliable maps that guide them to just the information they want

Users fall all across the curves. You have users at each of the levels as well as between all of the levels. Your greatest challenge is in making one piece of information satisfy all of these users' needs (or in recognizing that you do not want one piece of information to satisfy all of these needs). Some ways of meeting this challenge are:

- Design and develop stand-alone, random-access pieces of information with plenty of graphics and terminology definitions.
- Separate the four major types of information: concept, process, procedure, and reference.
- Move supporting detail out of the body of information and into auxiliary information such as appendixes.
- Enable users to define their schedules of reinforcement.
- Teach by metaphor, extended example, and problem-solving scenario.
- Design and develop to universal schemata to which all users can relate.

## Learning Styles

Learning styles indicate how we learn best. Some people learn best primarily through doing, some through imagining, some through reasoning, some through theorizing and others through some or all of these. Our left brain-right brain orientation influences our optimal learning style. Basically, there are four learning styles:

1. Doing
2. Imagining
3. Reasoning
4. Theorizing

Table 3.1 summarizes the major characteristics of these four learning styles.

**Table 3.1** Four Learning Styles

| *Doing* | *Imagining* | *Reasoning* | *Theorizing* |
|---|---|---|---|
| Relies on experiments and plans | Relies on imagination | Relies on deductive reasoning | Relies on theoretical models and inductive reasoning |
| Enjoys new experiences | Views experiences from multiple perspectives | Prefers hypothetical experiences | Tries to integrate disparate experiences |
| Takes risks | Brainstorms before acting | Acts in narrow, prescribed manner | Thinks of risks at an abstract level |
| Adapts to circumstances | Internalizes circumstances | Does not adapt well to changes in circumstances | Raises circumstances to theoretical level |
| Uses trial and error for problem solving | Relies on insight for problem solving | Uses hypotheses for problem solving | Relies on syllogistic reasoning for problem solving |
| Is at ease with people | Is people-oriented | Is not at ease with people | Is at ease with people on a theoretical level |
| Is impatient | Likes to counsel people | Has narrow technical interests | More concerned with sound logic than facts |
| Excels in marketing or sales | Excels in human resources and counseling | Excels in engineering | Excels in research and development |

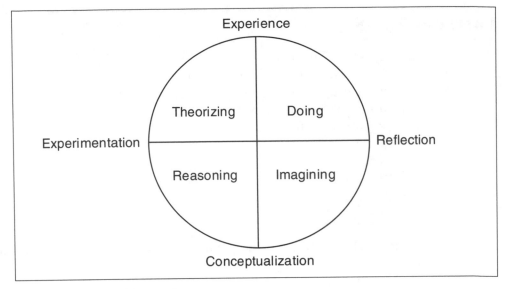

**Figure 3.8** Learning styles.

You can think of these four learning styles as the quadrants of a circle bisected by two continuums: experience–conceptualization and experimentation–reflection, as shown in Figure 3.8.

Orientation summarizes the characteristics of left-brain orientation and right-brain orientation.(See Table 3.2.)

Combining the four learning styles with left-brain right-brain orientation, we get the following four learning profiles:

**Table 3.2** Left-Brain Right-Brain Orientation

| Left Brain | Right Brain |
|---|---|
| rational | intuitive |
| reasoning | creative |
| modular | holistic |
| analytical | feeling-oriented |
| sequential | random |
| hierarchical | heterarchical |
| nonspatial | spatial |

1. People who have a Doing learning style seek meaning in experience, want to understand how learning relates to their experiences, and want to know the reason for learning something.

   These people ask Why?

2. People who have an Imagining learning style seek meaning in reflecting on experience, want to integrate experience with stored knowledge, and want to know fully what the new learning is.

   These people ask What?

3. People who have a Reasoning learning style seek meaning in abstracting experience, look for individual applications of learning, and want to know how new learning works.

   These people ask How?

4. People who have a Theorizing learning style seek meaning through using experience to extend stored knowledge with new learning, want to analyze the new learning for relevance, and want to see relationships and connections between the new learning and stored knowledge.

   These people ask If?

These, then, are the questions you have to answer in your information. As part of your audience analysis, plot your users in the appropriate quadrant. Most information must satisfy more than one learning style. If you satisfy why, what, how, and if, you give users with each learning style the vehicle to learn in the most comfortable way. Some ways to answer the questions in your information are:

- Why?

    - Explain background, history, and application of new learning
    - Describe benefits of new learning
    - Relate new learning to stored knowledge

- What?

    - Explain concepts, process, and procedure of new learning
    - Show how users can integrate new learning with stored knowledge
    - Point to other sources of reference material for the new learning

- How?

  - Explain the workings of the new learning
  - Give individual applications of the new learning
  - Set up sound, logical hypotheses with narrowly defined parameters

- If?

  - Explain the relevance of the new learning
  - Show relationships and connections among the components of the new learning and between the new learning and stored knowledge
  - Set up what–if scenarios

## Knowledge

We have defined learning as a relatively permanent change in behavior due to experience. We learn what hurricanes are, what a stop sign means, how to speak French, and how to create magnificent works of computer art. These things that we learn are knowledge.

There are basically two types of knowledge: knowledge of and knowledge how. Knowledge of encompasses facts, figures, and feelings; knowledge how is knowing how to do something. We know that Paris is the capital of France, we know that *livre* is the French word for book, and we know that an airplane will take us to Paris if we have enough *francs*. This is knowledge of, also called declarative knowledge.

Knowing what steps to perform to make the airline reservation, pack our clothes, and get to the airport is knowledge how, also called procedural knowledge.

Knowledge resides in two places: in the world and in our heads. We spend the better part of our lives trying to get knowledge back and forth between these two places. It is your job as a technical communicator to ensure this knowledge transfer, and communication is the key.

To be successful, communication requires four things:

1. Knowledge

   Knowledge is the what. What is being learned? This is the information you are teaching.

2. Giver

The giver is the first of the two whos. Who is giving the knowledge? Your product, that is, your information is the giver.

3. Receiver

The receiver is the second of the two whos. Who is receiving the knowledge? Your users are the receiver.

4. Feedback

Feedback is evidence that the receiver has received the knowledge. How does the giver know the receiver got the information? There are several ways your users can give you feedback:

- Usability tests
- Customer support calls
- Focus groups
- User groups
- User response cards
- Site visits
- Phone surveys
- Questionnaires

User feedback is not something users think about providing; most often, you have to go after it. Going after user feedback is a worthwhile endeavor and helps you build a trusting relationship with your users. Be sure you show that you are putting their feedback to good use, though, or you will irreparably damage your relationship. If, during a focus group, you commit to changing a particular set of help screens, for example, your users are going to look for that change in the next release.

A word of caution, though: learning how to evaluate feedback is often more difficult than obtaining it. Some things to consider when evaluating users' feedback are whether it is:

- Representative or isolated
- Statistically significant
- Practical to implement
- Biased

The best way to maintain a steady stream of user feedback is through strong user partnerships, and Chapter 8, "User Partnerships," discusses this subject in detail.

Figure 3.9 shows the communication model for knowledge transfer. "Says" and "hears" are in quotation marks, because they are representations of giving and receiving knowledge. We do most of our communicating and learning nonverbally. The giver does not have to be a person. The giver might be written material (such as this book), nature (such as a hurricane), or an object (such as a stop sign). The giver might also be ourselves as we strive for knowledge of self.

We often overlook the feedback component of the communication model. Without feedback, communication has not taken place, and without communication, no learning can occur. A corporate annual report can graphically illustrate that the corporation's return on profit has decreased alarmingly in the last year. You can read that report and store that knowledge away, but have you learned anything?

If you attend the annual shareholders' meeting and demand accountability, advise your former and now despised love interest to sink a lifetime's savings in the corporation's stock, or make a conscious decision to ride the roller coaster of this corporation's fortunes and leave your money in its ill-managed hands, you have demonstrated feedback, and you have learned.

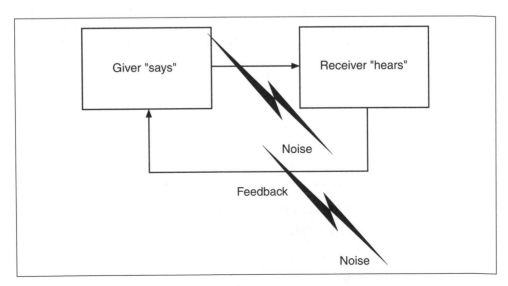

**Figure 3.9** Communication model.

If a child touches a hot stove, gets burned, and develops a healthy wariness of stoves, this is swift and obvious feedback. Feedback is not always swift or obvious, however. How long has it taken you to learn some of life's more abstract lessons regarding love, trust, and honor?

Anything that interferes with the giving and receiving of knowledge and feedback is noise. Noise hinders communication and hampers learning. An example of noise might be old baggage that says CONTROL-C eliminates any computer predicament, a perceptual set that does not allow for perceiving things in a new or unique way, or a lack of a particular schema that prohibits being able to process information and learn from it.

Very often, knowledge transfer from the world to our heads leads to automatism. What do you do when you see a large, octagonal, red sign with the word STOP in big, white letters? You stop—automatically. Ideally, you want your users to reach the point of automatism. The best written information writes itself out of existence by firmly and subtly moving users to the point of automatic response, where they no longer need the information.

## Motivation

Why do we learn to stop when we see a stop sign, get the clothes off the line and round up the cats when we feel a hurricane coming, or dump stock from a corporation that is heading for the financial graveyard? We learn because we are motivated; motivation is the why behind learning. Motivation is a need, desire, or incentive that energizes behavior and directs it toward a goal.[10]

Abraham Maslow identifies three supersets of needs, which form a pyramid or hierarchy of needs.

1. Basic needs

    Basic needs are both physiological and safety needs. Physiological needs are needs such as hunger, thirst, and sex. Safety needs are needs for structure, law, and limits; the need to feel free from chaos, anxiety, and fear; and the desire to experience the world as reliable, predictable, and stable.

2. Psychological needs

    Psychological needs include the need to feel love, a sense of belonging, and a sense of self esteem. Belonging and love needs are needs for giving and receiving affection, being part of a group or family, and not being lonely or alienated. Esteem needs are both the need to think highly of oneself, which is a result of achievement, mastery, and competence, and the need to enjoy a good reputation, prestige, and status, all of which are derived from others' perception of us.

3. Self-actualization

Self-actualization is the need to be what we must be to find happiness, to fulfill our individual potential, and to be all that we are capable of being.

Figure 3.10 shows Maslow's needs hierarchy.

There are two important points to remember about this hierarchy of needs:

1. Types of needs are not pure; needs are mixtures of different types.

What is the mixture of needs motivating us to stop at a stop sign? We have a need to:

- Keep our driving record clean so our insurance premiums remain low

- Keep ourselves physically safe so we do not experience pain

- Not hurt others so we do not have to bear the guilt of having hurt someone

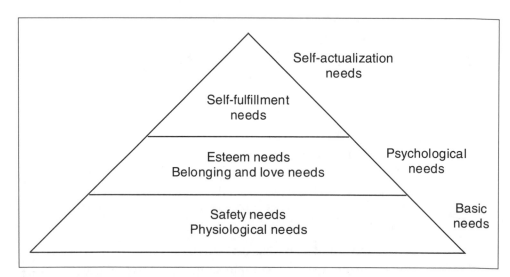

**Figure 3.10** Maslow's needs hierarchy.

- Stay out of jail so we can be near our friends and family and have the freedom to do what we want when we want

- Not pay for car repairs so we can keep our money and save for a comfortable retirement or spend it doing something we want to do such as go to Hawaii

- Keep our driver's license so we have the freedom to go wherever we want, so we are like the majority of those we know who have driver's licenses

- Maintain our self-image of being good drivers so that we have high self-esteem

Motivation comes from complex mixtures of needs from up and down the needs hierarchy. Even a basic need like sex can be part physical, part belonging, and part self-esteem.

2. Needs lower in the hierarchy are not wholly satisfied before needs higher in the hierarchy make themselves felt.

The structure of the needs hierarchy would imply that we completely satisfy basic needs before we feel psychological needs. This is not true; often lower needs are only partially satisfied before we begin the work of satisfying higher needs.

Dorothea Dix is probably right when she says people do not want to kiss when they are hungry. However, if we are not so hungry that our entire focus is on procuring something to eat, we can experience belonging and love as well as self-fulfillment needs, even if we are late for lunch and our stomachs are growling.

We flow from one level of the needs hierarchy to another, continuously satisfying multiple mixtures of needs simultaneously. If you go to lunch with your boss, is it because you are hungry? Want to get a jump on the new project? Hope to pick up some gossip? Are bucking for a promotion? Want her job? Hope to make her think you are a good employee? Genuinely like her? Want her to think you genuinely like her? Most probably, you go to lunch with her for a variety of reasons, the motivation behind which runs the gamut of the needs hierarchy.

Users trust that you understand and meet their needs at each stage of the needs hierarchy. What, then, do users need at each of the three stages?

- Basic needs

  - Media in which they are comfortable learning the information

  - Logical structures for the presentation of the information

- Evidence that what you are teaching is accurate, reliable, and predictable
- Psychological needs
    - A feeling of being part of a broader user community
    - A sense of mastery and competence
    - A sense that they are not being talked down to or patronized
- Self-actualization needs
    - Encouragement to apply the information in new and unique ways and frameworks that allow them to achieve this application
    - Freedom to take the information and use it as a foundation for applications beyond the immediate situation
    - Suggestions for further exploration of the information

Once again, the great challenge is making one piece of information meet all of these needs. Some ways of meeting this challenge are:

- Providing clear road maps to the types and levels of information; not every user needs to read the basics, for example, just as not every user needs to read the "For Advanced Users" section
- Constructing bridges of application between the information and users' worlds
- Giving examples that illustrate how to solve users' problems
- Including what–if scenarios
- Presenting evidence of your respect for your users
- Pointing out Further Reading information for those users who want to pursue their learning beyond your information

## Summary

Technical communication is a vehicle of learning. The how, what, and why of learning are learning theory and style, knowledge, and motivation. Experience, schemata, habits, and reinforcement compose learning style. There are three user curves that create a user profile: technical information, Piaget's cognitive developmental, and Erikson's psychosocial. There are two types of knowledge: knowledge of and knowledge how. Communication is the key to knowledge transfer. There are three supersets of motivational needs: basic, psychological, and self-actualization.

## Further Reading

Bjorklund, D.F. *Children's Thinking.* Pacific Grove, CA: Brooks/Cole, 1989.

Bower, G.H. and E.R. Hilgard. *Theories of Learning* 5th edition. Englewood Cliffs, NJ: Prentice-Hall, 1981.

Brockmann, R.J. *Writing Better Computer User Documentation: From Paper to Hypertext.* New York: John Wiley & Sons, 1990.

Brown, G. *Human Teaching for Human Learning.* New York: Viking, 1971.

Flavell, D. *Cognitive Development* 2nd edition. Englewood Cliffs, NJ: Prentice-Hall, 1985.

Gagne, R. "The Acquisition of Knowledge," *Psychological Review* 69.

_____"Military Training and Principles of Learning," *American Psychologist* 17.

Ginsburg, H.P. and S. Opper. *Piaget's Theory of Intellectual Development,* 3rd edition. Englewood Cliffo, NJ: Prentice Hall, 1988.

Glickman, S.E. and B.B. Schiff. "A Biological Theory of Reinforcement" in *Psychological Review* 74.

Guthrie, E.R. *The Psychology of Learning.* Gloucester, MA: Smith, 1960.

Hull, C.L. *Principles of Behavior.* New York: Appleton-Century-Crofts, 1943.

Maslow, A. H. *Motivation and Personality,* 3rd edition. New York: Harper & Row, 1987.

Mazur, J.E., ed. *Learning and Behavior.* Englewood Cliffs, NJ: Prentice-Hall, 1986.

Piaget, J. *Six Psychological Studies.* New York: Random House, 1967.

Schneider, M.L. "Models for the Design of Static Software User Assistance," *Directions in Human/Computer Interaction,* A. Badre and B. Shneiderman, eds. Norwood, NJ: Ablex, 1982.

Seligman, M.E.P. "On the Generality of the Laws of Learning," *Psychological Review* 77, pp. 406–418.

Seward, J.P. "An Experimental Study of Guthrie's Theory of Reinforcement" in *Journal of Experimental Psychology* 30, pp. 247–256.

Siegler, R.S. *Children's Thinking.* Englewood Cliffs, NJ: Prentice-Hall, 1986.

Skinner, B.F. *The Behavior of Organisms: An Experimental Analysis.* New York: Appleton-Century-Crofts, 1938.

_____"Reinforcement Today," *American Psychologist* 13, pp. 94–99.

Spiro, R.J. "Remembering Information from Text: The 'State of Schema' Approach" in *Schooling and the Acquisition of Knowledge.* R.J. Spiro, R.C. Anderson, and W.F. Montague, eds. Hillsdale, NJ: Erlbaum, 1976.

Sternberg, R.J., ed. *Mechanisms of Cognitive Development.* New York: Freeman, 1984.

Sullivan, E.V. "The Acquisition of Conservation of Substance through File-Mediated Models" in *Recent Research on the Acquisition of Conservation of Substance*. D.W. Brison and E.V. Sullivan, eds. Toronto: Ontario Institute for Studies in Education, 1967.

TIP (theory into practice) database at http://gwis2.circ.gwu.edu:80/~kearsley/

## Notes

1   The TIP (theory to practice) database lists 48 distinct learning styles.

2   E. L. Thorndike, B. F. Skinner, E. R. Guthrie, I. P. Pavlov, C. L. Hull, G. Ryle, and J. B. Watson are the most prominent proponents of behaviorist learning theory.

3   M. Wertheimer, W. Kohler, K. Koffka, K. Lewin, and J. Piaget are the most prominent proponents of cognitive learning theory.

4   E. C. Tolman created what he called a "purposive behaviorism," which is a first attempt at blending behaviorist and cognitive learning theory. Purposive behaviorism is concerned with both the external behavior an organism exhibits and with the cognitive processes that create that behavior, including motivation, which pure behaviorists do not recognize as a contributing factor to behavior. R. C. Bolles created a neoTolmanian theory that attempted to predict behavior in terms of three variables: signal, response, and reinforcers.

5   R. Gagne proposes hierarchical organizations for educational and training material in "The Acquisition of Knowledge" in *Psychological Review* 69: pp. 355–365 and in "Military Training and Principles of Learning" in *American Psychologist* 17: pp. 83–91.

6   M. L. Schneider calls the first four stages parrot, novice, intermediate, and expert in "Models for the Design of Static Software User Assistance," in *Directions in Human/Computer Interaction*, Albert Badre and Ben Shneiderman, eds. Norwood, NJ: Ablex Publishing, Co., 1982: pp. 137–148. R. Brockmann calls the outsider the casual learner in *Writing Better Computer User Documentation*, R. John Brockmann. New York: John Wiley & Sons, 1986: p. 59.

7   Piaget identified assimilation and accommodation as the mechanisms for traversing this thesis/antithesis/synthesis spiral. Assimilation is the application of a schema to the world, and accommodation is the modification of a schema based on new data from the world.

8   J. Bruner offers three stages of cognitive development: enactive, in which a child sees the world in terms of actions (correlates to Piaget's sensorimotor stage); iconic, in which a child sees the world in terms of images (correlates to Piaget's preoperational stage); and symbolic, in which a child sees the world in terms of language and symbols (correlates to Piaget's operational thinking stage) in *Studies in Cognitive Growth*, J.S. Bruner and H. Kennedy. New York: John Wiley & Sons, 1966.

9   Stages 5–8 of Erikson's psychosocial learning curve are identity, intimacy, generativity, and integrity.

10   There is a minor school of thought that theorizes that motivation is generalized and without a specific goal or direction.

# CHAPTER FOUR

# Memory

*Memory is the cabinet of imagination, the treasury of reason, the registry of conscience, and the council chamber of thought.*

Saint Basil

If sensation and perception are the necessary precursors to learning, memory is the natural consequence. Whether knowledge is facts, schemata, events, sensations, or feelings, you put it in a place called memory using a mechanism called memory, and the knowledge, schemata, events, sensations, and feelings themselves are also called memories. Memory is at once a storage place, a means of moving data into and out of that storage place, and the data itself.

Memory is a physical change in the neuronal structure of the brain; this change indicates the persistence of learning and is called an engram. We infer the presence of engrams from changes in behavior. If you were blithely to go about planting marigolds when signs of a hurricane were all around you, we could infer that you have not learned what a hurricane is.

Without memory, there would be no need for technical communicators. Your users would not be able to interpret, store, or recall those black squiggles you put on paper or screen. They would not remember how to turn on their computer, pick up a document, or read.

Memory is the great organizer. It accepts everything we feed it, stores it away, and usually presents it to us when we ask for it. When we need to know what 11x12 is, what to do at a stop sign, or what an eerie yellow stillness portends, memory serves up 132, stop, and hurricane.

As a technical communicator, you must understand the stages, theories, and mechanics of your users' memory in order to create information that takes advantage of the memory processes.

## Stages of Memory

Memory has three stages:

1. Sensory registers
2. Short-term memory
3. Long-term memory

These three stages work together to enable us to think, speak, read, remember—in short, do any cognitive processing. As Figure 4.1 shows, the sensory registers are the portals for sensations; short-term memory is the processing unit; and long-term memory is the storage facility.

When users import your information, they take it in via their sensory organs—usually their eyes or ears. Then the information registers with the visual or acoustic sensory register, and undergoes filtering before moving into short-term memory. Once in short-term memory, users rehearse the information if they want to store it in long-term memory; otherwise, they forget it. Rehearsing the information encodes it into long-term memory, where it lives forever. When users want to use a piece of information, they retrieve it from long-term memory into short-term memory, where they use it to do something, decide something, say something, understand something—anything that requires cognitive processing.

Sensory registers are sensation-driven, and are the physicality of memory. Short-term memory is perception-driven, and so is the psychology of memory. Long-term memory combines both physicality (neuronal changes to the brain) and psychology (cognitive storage mechanisms).

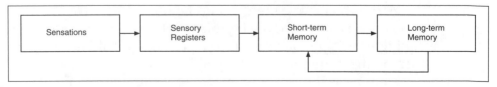

**Figure 4.1** Stages of memory.

## Sensory Registers

Sensory registers are the first stage of memory. They are sensations' gateway to our memory. Images, sounds, and touches enter memory through their respective registers. Thresholds, cocktail-party effect, and sensory adaptation filter the sensations, then move them on to short-term memory for processing—either encoding into long-term memory or forgetting.

There are as many sensory registers as there are senses.[1] Sensory registers are the most short-lived of the three stages of memory. Visual memory traces remain in the visual sensory register for less than a second, while other sensation traces can remain in their respective sensory registers for up to four seconds.[2]

Sensory registers have two functions: to take in sensation and to provide a bridge to short-term memory. These two functions reflect the dual-level processing that takes place in the sensory registers. Sensations imprint themselves on the sensory registers like sharp, focused, detailed photographs. For the very short amount of time a sensation is in a sensory register, we are exquisitely aware of every detail; we store sensations in sensory registers exactly as we receive them from our senses. However, each succeeding sensation overwrites the preceding one, so in order to ensure that each sensation finds its way into short-term memory, the sensory register creates visual afterimages and acoustic afterechoes that serve as bridges to short-term memory.

For example, have you ever "seen" an object that is no longer in front of you? This is a visual afterimage. Often, we see more in the visual afterimage than we were able to see in the real object. Have you asked someone to repeat a remark even as you hear an echo of the remark in your mind? This is an acoustic afterecho. Afterimages and afterechoes extend sensations so sensory data can move into short-term memory.

As sensations move across this bridge into short-term memory, filtering takes place. Thresholds, cocktail-party effect, and sensory adaptation winnow out the meaningless data and pass on the meaningful data to short-term memory.

Since short-term registers are the sensation-driven physicality of memory, your responsibility to your users is to facilitate their registering your information with their sensory registers. Users move from sensing black squiggles (sensory registers) to perceiving information (short-term memory) along the sensation-perception continuum at speeds that would put the most powerful processor chips to shame. The navigation, presentation, and organization of your information facilitates users' movement along that continuum.

The way users sense your information in their sensory registers controls the schemata of your information that they build in short-term memory. Clear, consistent, intuitive navigation, presentation, and organization facilitate users' ability to sense your information. For example, users build meaningful schemata in short-term memory of the hierarchical relationship of heads and subheads in your information. Visual differences such as point size, font, emphasis, border, and spacing are all sensations users meld into a meaningful perception, which serves as the foundation for their hierarchical-heads schemata.

## Short-Term Memory

Short-term memory is the second stage of memory. Filtered sensory data arrives from the sensory register, undergoes processing, and moves on to long-term memory. We perform additional filtering in short-term memory by purging data such as telephone numbers, grocery lists, and meeting schedules that we no longer need.

Short-term memory is a limited-capacity working memory. It is where we do all of our memory processing such as rehearsing, encoding, and retrieving data. It enables us to use language and think. As John Brown says, "Descartes asserted, 'I think, therefore I am.' It is equally true to say 'I think, therefore I have short-term memory.' Indeed any mental activity extended in time, including the production and comprehension of language, must involve... [short-term memory]."[3]

Contrary to the way we handle data in the sensory registers, we do not store data in short-term memory exactly as we receive it from the sensory registers. We store representations or schemata of the data. This implies that perception takes place between the sensory input to the sensory registers and the storing of schemata in short-term memory. Data remains in short-term memory anywhere from 30 seconds to a few hours.[4]

Short-term memory holds meaningful chunks of information. Miller called the number of chunks we can store in short-term memory the magical number seven plus or minus two.[5] We can accurately hold five to nine meaningful chunks of data in short-term memory. If we do not process (rehearsing and encoding) this data into long-term memory, it is lost (forgetting).

For example, you can hold the florist's seven-digit telephone number in short-term memory long enough to dial it. If you do not call the florist often enough (rehearsing) to encode the number into long-term memory, it is lost, and you have to look it up each time you want to order an arrangement of cymbidiums.

Short-term memory is a finite storage area; as new data comes in, it replaces existing data. If your neighbor starts talking to you about a new World Series record for RBIs while you are trying to hold the florist's number in short-term memory, you wind up dialing a hybrid of the florist's number and RBI statistics. If, however, you concentrate on the florist's number and refuse to let the RBIs into short-term memory, your cymbidiums will be on their way.

Because the florist's number is not meaningful to you, it completely fills your short-term memory. But a chunk does not have to be just one digit or one letter. You can store meaningful chunks of digits such as your Social Security number, telephone number, and ATM PIN in short-term memory. You can also store meaningful chunks of letters as words, words as sentences, and sentences as paragraphs in short-term memory.

For example, the letters "radtoniyci" are not meaningful; unless you can use a mnemonic device to make them a meaningful chunk, you cannot store them all successfully in short-term memory. The same letters arranged as the word "dictionary", though, form one meaningful chunk. You can store the word dictionary in short-term memory along with other meaningful chunks.

You can combine smaller chunks to make larger chunks. "I am looking up the word in the dictionary." is a meaningful chunk. You can combine this sentence with other meaningful chunks, but if you combine it with a non sequitur, you lose the meaningful edge and reduce the number of chunks you can store in short-term memory. Whereas "I am looking up the word in the dictionary. Then I will correct my report." is a meaningful chunk, "I am looking up the word in the dictionary." "Carry only cat squirts weed them spinach driveway." is not.

With enough rehearsing, however, you can encode even "I am looking up the word in the dictionary. Carry only cat squirts weed them spinach driveway." into long-term memory. You can then astound your friends at a cocktail party six years from now with your uncanny ability to recall that meaningless bit of drivel.

So far, we have considered short-term memory as one centralized memory store. This is the slot theory, which says that we have five to nine slots in short-term memory, and that each slot can hold a meaningful chunk of data. L. R. Squire alludes to another theory of short-term memory, which states that just as there are multiple sensory registers, so too are there multiple short-term memories. He says that "one can consider working memory as a collection of temporary capacities intrinsic to information-processing subsystems."[6]

This opens up the possibility that there are short-term memories for verbal, textual, and graphical data as well as data taken in through other senses. Each of these short-term memories functions like the centralized short-term memory in the slot theory. This multiple short-term memory theory makes more and more sense as we watch users reading documentation, understanding language and graphics, performing tasks, thinking, evaluating, jotting down notes, and remembering to do fundamental things like turning pages—all of which require processing in short-term memory.

Your short-term memory responsibility to your users is to facilitate their schemata-building by presenting your information in meaningful chunks that do not violate the capacity of short-term memory. G. Miller's magic number is the origin of the technical communication tenet that five to nine is the best range for items in a list and that seven is the optimal number. The fact that short-term memory has a limited-capacity to store information is the origin for the technical communication tenet of meaningful chunking.

## Long-Term Memory

Long-term memory is the third and final stage of memory. Once data arrives in long-term memory from short-term memory, it lives there forever, even if we cannot always retrieve it. When we discuss sensory registers and short-term memory, we are concerned with capacity and temporal duration. These limitations do not apply to long-term memory, because data that arrives in long-term memory remains there forever, and there is no limit to the amount of data that we can store in long-term memory. When we discuss long-term memory, we are concerned with the type and organization of data we store, not how much data we can store or for how long.

We store information in long-term memory based on its information type. Just as with knowledge, there are two types of memory: memory what and memory how. Memory what is declarative memory such as memory for events, facts, and images. Remembering that Austin is the capital of Texas, Uncle Otto was a clown at your fifth birthday party, and coffee that has been on the burner too long is bitter are examples of declarative memory.

Memory how is procedural memory such as memory for motor skills, cognitive skills, and reflexes. Remembering how to read, how to recognize a familiar face in a crowd, and how to avoid fire are examples of procedural memory.

The ancient part of the brain (the brain stem) processes procedural memory, while the more highly evolved part of our brain (the limbic system) processes declarative memory. This gives credence to the view that declarative memory is a relatively recent evolutionary phenomenon.

It is important to separate the types of information you are presenting to users. Separate information that calls on users' declarative memory from information that calls on their procedural memory. Clearly label (either explicitly with a label or implicitly with structure) your information in order to facilitate its encoding.

### Declarative Memory

We use a partnership of short term and long term memory to process declarative memory, which has five divisions:

1. Episodic

   Episodic memory is memory for events, such as a special Christmas, your first dance, and the first time you tried—and failed—to create a perfect baked Alaska.

   A special type of episodic memory, called flashbulb memory, is a clear, detailed, poignant memory of an event that was surprising, emotional, and often stressful. A common example of a flashbulb memory is the memory of learning that President Kennedy had been shot.[7]

2. Associative

   Associative memory is memory for the tags we associate with data when we store it in long-term memory. When we store data in long-term memory, we store schemata of data; we label these schemata with tags that help us retrieve the data.

   Figure 4.2 illustrates one path of many you might take to recall that your Spanish teacher's husband's secretary married the bartender at Babs' Tavern. As Figure 4.2 shows, associative memory is not linear. It is like a hyperlinked online help system where there are multiple paths to the same piece of information and where you can link in circles and switchbacks literally forever.

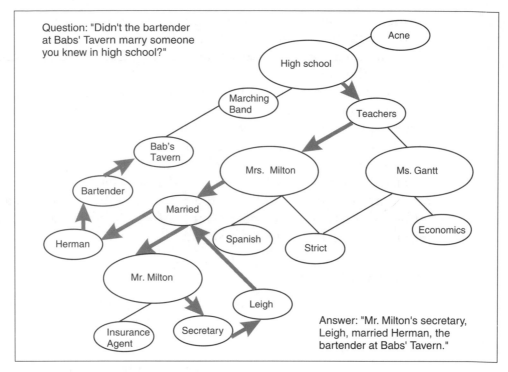

**Figure 4.2** Associative memory.

3. Semantic

Semantic memory is memory for the meaning of facts, concepts, and vocabulary such as poinsettias are poisonous to cats, honor often requires difficult decisions, and tar is a "dark, oily substance consisting mainly of hydrocarbons, produced by the destructive distillation of organic substances such as wood, coal, or peat."[8]

We use a combination of declarative and procedural memory to use most if not all information. For example, to give the definition of the word "tar," you would look it up in the dictionary and get the meaning of the word, which involves semantic memory; however, the process of looking up the word is a procedure and involves procedural memory.

4. Lexical

Lexical memory is remembering the graphological and phonological features of words. The meaning of words is stored in semantic memory.

For example, you store the definition of the word "tar" in semantic memory, but you store its shape, letter order, and pronunciation in lexical memory.

5. Image

Image memory is remembering pictures, not only pictures we see, but mental images we construct from pictures, events, and picture-evoking words. Imagination comes from image memory. Although you may never have been to Hawaii, you can still picture yourself reading a good whodunit under a yellow-and-orange striped beach umbrella on a Kauai beach.

Image memory is one of the most robust of our memory divisions.[9] Data we store either in an image format or accompanied by an image is easier to recall than data we store in nonimage format. The more vivid and interactive the image, the stronger its association with the data and the easier the data is to recall.

For example, if someone were to tell you to remember the words "cat" and "ball," you could store two separate images, one of a cat and one of a ball. But if you store a robust, interactive image of a black and white tuxedo cat playing in a blue-tiled bathtub with a small green and red ball, then you have a long-lasting image that you can recall more quickly and easily.

The longer the list of items you need to remember and the more disparate the items, the more important storing them as robust, interactive images becomes. For example, try to remember the following list of words without creating a robust, interactive image: candle, shovel, lipstick, tea bag, paperclip, command, perch, zeal, beacon, hint.

In order to memorize this list, you unconsciously create images, make associations, and devise other mnemonic devices to help you remember.

Now create a robust, interactive image using all of these words. A scenario like the following is not only fun to create, but you also have a far greater chance of remembering the words.[10]

Burning with *zeal* like a saint's votive *candle*, I decided to take *command* of the insufficiently guarded *beacon* that sat on its high, rocky *perch* like a cheap *lipstick* balancing on the end of a snow *shovel*. Just the *hint* of a thirst was beginning to tickle my throat, so I took a *paperclip* and attached a chamomile *tea bag* to my ragged collar so I could sip tea after I successfully had completed my mission.

Your users do not need to understand and enable the five divisions of declarative memory, but you do so that you can:

- Exploit episodic and flashbulb memories to create metaphors, extended examples, and problem-solving scenarios that your users readily can relate to. Leveraging episodic and flashbulb memories your users already have helps them create schemata from your information.

- Design and develop your information based on consistent tags you want users to associate with data as they store it in long-term memory. Exploiting tags users already have or helping them create new tags makes storage and retrieval of information easier, quicker, and more reliable.

- Take advantage of the separation of semantic and lexical memory that enables users to concentrate separately on the look of a word and on the meaning of a word. Include a mini-glossary at the beginning of information modules or a common glossary at the end of a collection of information modules. Never use terminology you have not defined.

- Use the strength and predominance of image memory in your information to help users store robust, interactive images that are easy and quick to retrieve. Use graphics to enhance or replace text; use graphic metaphors; and use graphic language in your extended examples and problem-solving scenarios. Use interactive multimedia that replicates your users' world as much as possible. Take to heart the adage that a picture is worth a thousand words.

## Procedural Memory

We use only long-term memory to process procedural memory, which has seven divisions:

1. Motor skill learning

   Motor skill learning is memory for performing motor skills such as swallowing, blinking, and wriggling our fingers.

2. Cognitive learning

   Cognitive learning is learning that involves higher cognitive functions such as understanding, interpretation, and expectation. The physical skills of tap dancing involve motor skills, but the interpretative art of it involves cognition.

3. Perceptual learning

Perceptual learning is learning in which we perceive the sensory data differently with exposure and practice. The first time you are playing the goalie position and a puck hurtles at you at 70 miles per hour, you may throw your stick in the air and run for cover, but with enough exposure to speeding pucks and enough practice in diverting them, you can lead your team to a Stanley Cup.

4. Classical conditioning

Classical conditioning is memory for a response that is a result of a paired stimulus and reinforcer and that continues even when the reinforcer is not present.

The most famous example of classical conditioning is Pavlov's ding-dong-drool in which the ringing of a bell (stimulus) precedes food (reinforcer) and eventually creates salivation (response) even when the food is not present.

5. Priming

Priming is memory for cues that activate memory. If someone were to mention the word "yellow" to you over and over, then ask you to name a fruit and a disgusting character trait, you would be most likely to say lemon and cowardice, for example.

"Yellow" activates the memory of both "lemon" and "cowardice." Since the word "yellow" activated the semantic memory of the words "lemon" and "cowardice," priming may seem to be a type of declarative memory. There are, however, three reasons why priming is a type of procedural memory. Memory that priming activates:

A. Is short-lived whereas declarative memory is long-lived.
B. Is available only through the sense that activated it, whereas declarative memory is available to all senses.
C. Does not include the declarative memory bracketing information such as when and where the memory occurred.[11]

6. Habituation

Habituation is memory for decreases in attention to repeated sensations. The first night you try out your new alarm clock, the ticking may keep you awake all night, but by the third night, you have sensory adapted to it, and do not even recognize it as a sensation.

7. Sensitization

Sensitization is memory for sensitivities to specific events or situations. If your neighbor's house had burned down when you were a child, you would be sensitized to fire.

Figure 4.3 shows the divisions of long-term memory.

You can assume certain divisions of procedural learning, while exploiting others. As you design and develop your information, you can:

- Take for granted users' motor skill learning.

  One of the assumptions you can make about your users (unless you know you are writing for users challenged in this area) is that they have a full complement of functioning motor skills.

- Tap into users' cognitive and perceptual learning.

  As you design and develop information, you must enable cognitive learning with clear, concise, consistent, intuitive choice of media, navigation, presentation, and content. You must design and develop

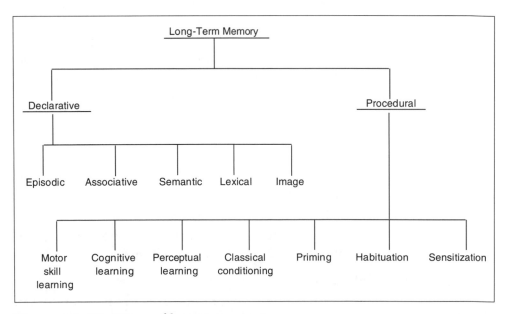

**Figure 4.3** Divisions of long-term memory.

information that lets users build schemata layer by layer. The first time users come in contact with an idea, they may feel like running the other way, but by the fifth or sixth time, you have enabled their perceptual learning and helped them build a schemata that functions successfully.

- Create your own models of classical conditioning.

You can adapt the theories of classical conditioning to move your users to the point of automaticity with your information. For example, say you are writing an installation guide for a data server. This installation process has six distinct, sequential procedures. For each procedure, users must complete a worksheet of site-specific values. For the first two worksheets, you can explain what the worksheets are and why users need to complete them before beginning a procedure. By the third worksheet, this introductory information is no longer necessary.

An alternative is to place this information in an "About This Manual" section at the beginning of the manual; however, can you be sure that all the users read this section?

Adapting theories of classical conditioning for nonsequential, random-access information is more difficult. Classical conditioning depends on the sequence of stimulus-reinforcer-response. There are some universally accepted classical conditioning models in technical communication, however, such as index entries, glossary entries, and table of contents entries. Users trust that you use these entries as do all of the other technical communicators in the world. They do not expect an index at the beginning of a piece of information, nor do they expect glossary entries to contain anything but definitions of terms.

- Use priming to set up your users' expectations and responses.

Always use priming in a positive way. If, for example, you set up users' expectations that a procedure is difficult, they are apt to find it difficult. This is negative priming. If, on the other hand, you prime them to expect ease and success with the procedure, they are apt to find the procedure easy and be successful at it.

- Guard against habituation.

Overuse of any element leads to habituation. Too much bold, color, italics, beeping, movement, tables—in short any element of technical communication—leads to habituation, and that element loses its power. For example, judiciously using italics to communicate emphasis enables users' learning, while overuse of italics renders italics meaningless and enables users to miss important information.

- Consider the sensitization users carry with them.

Respect users' sensitizations and exploit those that enhance your information while deflecting those that degrade your information. For example, if your users have had horrible experiences with online help systems, design your online help system so as to avoid the pitfalls users encountered in the past. And if they have had wonderful results from a particular style of reference card, model your reference card on that past success.

## Theories of Memory

To reiterate, memory is a physical language that the brain writes on itself with neurons. It is a physical, neuronal change in the brain called an engram or memory trace. There are two prevailing theories about how the brain writes these engrams:

- Localized
- Holographic

### Localized Memory

The localized memory theory says that memory is synaptic changes in the brain. A synapse is the junction between two neurons or nerves. There is a microscopic gap between the neurons that deal with memory; this gap is called the synaptic gap and is the facilitator of memory.[12]

Sensory neurons receive input in the form of electric impulses. These impulses travel the length of the sending neuron to the synaptic gap. At the synaptic gap, the sending neuron releases neurotransmitters, which are chemical messengers that carry communication between neurons. In less than one ten-thousandth of a second, these neurotransmitters cross the synaptic gap to the receiving neuron, where they bind to receptor sites as snugly as a hand fits into a custom-made glove.

Once bound to the receiving neuron, the neurotransmitters release ions (electrically charged atoms) that morphologically change the receiv-

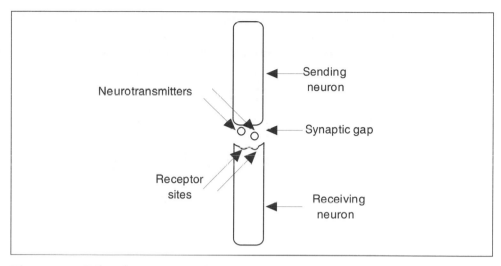

**Figure 4.4**  What happens at the synaptic gap.

ing neuron, causing it to send an impulse. The cycle starts again with the receiving neuron's becoming the sending neuron. This cycle creates neuronal pathways or circuits that change the morphology of the neurons involved. These circuits are engrams. It is important to note, however, that engrams are not so much physical locations as theoretical necessities. Figure 4.4 illustrates the localized theory of memory.

The human brain contains approximately ten billion neurons and ten trillion synaptic gaps; each neuron may make as many as ten thousand connections with other neurons. Unlike other human cells, neurons do not die. You have a full set of neurons within three months of conception, and you retain this set of neurons until you die.[13] There are approximately 50 different types of neurotransmitters, although only a small subset of neurotransmitters carry memory-related communication.[14]

## Holographic Memory

Unlike the localized memory theory, which says that memory is stored in specific neuronal circuits, the holographic memory theory states that memory is distributed throughout the entire brain much like a holographic image is distributed over an entire photographic plate.[15] One memory is a change that involves trillions of synapses, and each synapse is involved in billions of different memories.[16] K. Lashley, who coined the term "engram," called this theory of memory distribution "equipotentiality."

It was not until the relatively recent invention of the hologram that scientists had an analogy for the equipotentiality theory. According to this theory, there are some striking similarities between a hologram and a memory:

- Holograms and memories are extremely durable.
- Each hologram and each memory can store millions of images while retaining the integrity of each image.
- Every piece of a hologram and every piece of a memory contains the information for the whole, but with a loss of clarity and detail.
- Initial context helps retrieve both a hologram and a memory.
- Association is an intrinsic characteristic of both memories and holograms.
- Both holograms and memories hold a remarkable amount of data.[17]

There is some evidence to support both memory theories. E. Kandel's and J. Schwartz's work with sea snails points to the storage of memory at specific synaptic gaps[18], while K. Lashley's work with rats[19] points to the distribution of memory throughout the brain. This may indicate that specific types of memory are stored at specific sites, while the processing of memory is distributed throughout the brain.

# Mechanics of Memory

Whether memory is localized or holographic, how do users get information into and out of memory? What helps and hinders them in remembering? To answer these questions, we must consider the memory process, memory cues, and forgetting.

### The Memory Process

As Figure 4.5 shows, there are five steps in the memory process.

### Receiving Sensory Data

The sensory registers receive data from our senses and extend sensory traces long enough to help the data move into short-term memory, where we encode it. The sensory registers momentarily record virtually all sensory data in extraordinary detail. Thanks to thresholds, the cocktail-

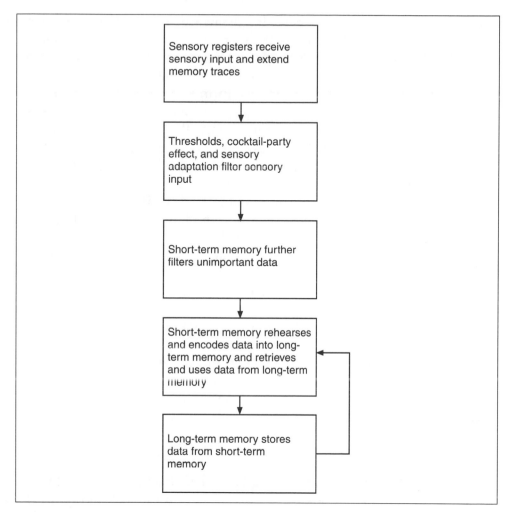

**Figure 4.5** The memory process.

party effect, and sensory adaptation, all sensations do not move from the sensory registers to short-term memory. We experience millions of sensations daily, but we process a relatively small subset of sensations into short-term memory and an even smaller subset into long-term memory. One function of memory is to filter data that is not important or useful to us.

It is difficult to fathom just how many sensations register in the sensory registers. Look around you right now. How many colors, textures, sizes, patterns, and interplays of light do you see? You see so many that you usually are not consciously aware of them. Listen. How many different sounds do you hear? You hear so many that you filter out the ones that are not important to you. In a garden or when supper is cooking, how many smells are you aware of? How many are you filtering out? How many tastes can you identify in Indian curried vegetables? How many tactile sensations do you experience when you rub your cat's belly?

Of the many sights, sounds, smells, tastes, and touches that we take in, we encode relatively few. We encode those pieces of information that we need to survive and function. The meaning of survive and function depends on circumstances. In prehistoric times, survive and function had literal meanings. Our ancestors lived or died depending on what they remembered of their predators, food supplies, and shelters. In modern times, forgetting the rules of the road could have life or death consequences. In the corporate arena, forgetting facts and figures during a presentation could mean the life or death of a career. We encode the data that we need, and those needs change depending on our circumstances.

When users bring your information into their world, their immediate circumstances dictate what is important and what is not. What they choose to encode on one occasion may not be what they choose to encode on another. Keep your navigation, presentation, and content clean and uncluttered. Present only what users need; eliminate anything that does not directly enhance the information you are communicating. Remember the coulda-shoulda-woulda syndrome and do not fall prey to it.

## Encoding Data

In short-term memory, we further filter unimportant data such as last night's menu, losing lottery ticket numbers, and your third grade teacher's birthday. Then we translate meaningful sensory data from the sensory registers into neuronal impulses that the brain can understand. There are three ways of encoding verbal information:

1. Visual encoding

   Visual encoding is encoding the image of words. For example, take "hlpqghncvt." These letters have no meaning (semantic encoding) and you cannot pronounce them (acoustic encoding). The only way you could encode them is by their physical appearance (visual encoding), and you most likely will forget them before you have read the next sentence. Visual encoding is the least durable kind of encoding.

2. Acoustic encoding

Acoustic encoding is encoding the sound of words. As you are reading this sentence, you are "saying" the words to yourself and encoding their sound. Very often, we store words according to sound in short-term memory before storing them semantically (by meaning) in long-term memory. Acoustic encoding is the second-most durable kind of encoding.

3. Semantic encoding

Semantic encoding is encoding the meaning of words. When encoding new data semantically, we often associate it with something we already know. This association helps us move the data into long-term memory. Semantic encoding is the most durable kind of encoding.

To encode data, we must hold it in short-term memory. We do this by rehearsing it, that is, by concentrating on it and saying it over and over to ourselves. The more we rehearse information, the better able we are to retain it. Rehearsing information encodes it into long-term memory. If we do not rehearse information, it has a short-term memory life expectancy of approximately 3–12 seconds.[20] With enough rehearsal, however, we can move it into long-term memory, where we retain it indefinitely.[21]

How many times have you gone to the grocery store secure in the assumption that you could remember a simple list of:

Orange juice

Cat food

Celery

Light bulbs

Lasagna noodles

only to find when you get home that you bought orange juice, cat food, and lasagna noodles, but completely forgot the celery and light bulbs?

Remembering the first and last items in a list is known as the serial position effect. We remember the first items, because we have rehearsed them more, and they have moved into long-term memory. This is the law of primacy. We remember the last items, because they are still in short term memory. This is the law of recency. After some time has passed, though, we remember only the first items, because we have processed them into long-term memory. We forgot the middle items completely, and the last items enjoyed a brief but temporary life in short-term memory.

Some things do not require rehearsal. As you are leaving to go to the store (to forget to buy celery and light bulbs), you remember that you are in your kitchen, that it is afternoon, and that this is the second trip to the grocery store today. You do not have to rehearse this information. This is called automatic processing. The encoding of space (where you are), time (when you are), and frequency (how often you are) are inborn in our information-processing mechanisms.

Users are looking for meaning. Do not make them hunt for it. Meaning in your information should be obvious. Rely on semantic encoding above acoustic and visual encoding. Exploit the serial position effect and the laws of primacy and recency by putting your most meaningful list items in the first and last list positions.

### Storing Data

We encode data into long-term memory, which is our lifetime memory storage facility. Once data is in long-term memory, it lives there forever. Although we may not be able to get it out of storage, it is there.

We store data as representations, not as re-creations. We create and modify schemata using the representations we store. We do not remember something exactly the way we saw it or heard it; we store a unique, personal version of it. Have you ever argued with someone over a conversation the two of you had? Have you ever insisted that someone said something that person vehemently denies having said? Both of you stored away individual versions of the conversation, neither of which has the accuracy of a tape recording.

We store and cross-store data in long-term memory. When we store information, we tag it for easy retrieval (associative memory). We store many pieces of information under one tag, and we store the same information under different tags. Long-term memory is an intricate web, a network of linked data, and there are many paths to each piece of data.

Figure 4.6 shows how you might store the memory of the red bicycle Aunt Jane gave you for your tenth birthday. Not only does the memory of the red bicycle have a tag to help you retrieve the memory, it appears under several different tags, giving you more opportunities to retrieve it.

Leverage long-term memory storage and associative memory in the way you design and develop your information's navigation, presentation, and content. Enable users to employ existing tags to store informa-

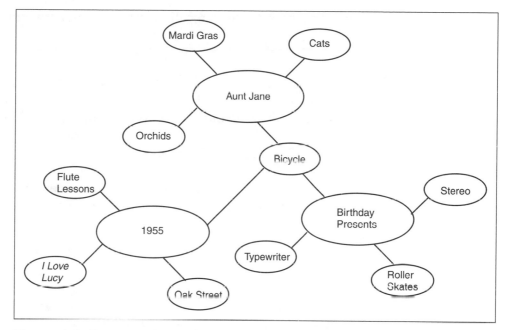

**Figure 4.6** Cross-storing information under multiple tags.

tion and help them create new associative tags. Give users several ways to the same piece of information. Use references and cross-references. Take the web of memory from your users' minds and externalize it in your information. Strive for the ultimate in transparency: emulation of your users' own memory processes.

### Retrieving Data

Just as we store representations of information and not re-creations, we retrieve representations. From the faithful re-creations that our senses input to the sensory registers, we encode representations, thereby altering the data, and we retrieve representations, once again altering the data. Is it any wonder that three witnesses to the same crime give four different accounts of that crime? There are three types of retrieval:

1. Recalling

   Recalling is bringing something into conscious awareness. You have stored 11 × 12 = 132; when you need it, you retrieve it from long-term storage into short-term storage. You use it, then store it back into long-term memory.

We instantly are able to recall information in active memory. It is memory on demand.

2. Recognizing

Recognizing is being aware that you have experienced something before. Who were the members of your high school graduating class? You probably cannot recall their names, but if someone recites a list of names, you can recognize those names as belonging to people who graduated with you.

We are able to recognize information in passive memory but not call it up on demand. As you might suppose, we store far more information in passive memory than we do in active memory.

3. Relearning

Relearning is learning something again and takes less time than initial learning. It may have taken you a week to learn how to ride the red bicycle Aunt Jane gave you, but even after not having ridden a bicycle in 30 years, it would take you less time to relearn how to ride it now. The axiom is true; you never forget how to ride a bicycle...or anything else you have learned. You may have to refresh the memory with relearning, but the initial learning still exists. Relearning is memory that lies dormant until the act of learning again awakens it. You cannot call it up on demand, and you cannot access it with memory prods. Only learning the same knowledge again activates it, and that activation is obvious from the shortened relearning period.

Recalling, recognizing, and relearning all support the notion that memory never leaves long-term memory. As a technical communicator, you must acknowledge that much of your information should pass into users' passive memory. They select only the most immediately meaningful information for active memory. Some of your information, too, is a candidate for relearning, especially those tasks users perform infrequently or those concepts that do not directly impact their day-to-day functioning.

The more meaningful information is, the easier it is to retrieve. The red bicycle Aunt Jane gave you is probably a more meaningful memory to you than it is to your aunt. You have no trouble recalling every detail of that gleaming Schwinn, while your aunt may have only a vague recognition that it was red, (if you prod her memory enough).

With enough prodding, your aunt should be able to retrieve the memory of the bicycle, because she knows it is stored in her long-term memory. We search our memories only for data we know we have stored there. For example, if you were to ask your aunt about the red bicycle she gave Cleopatra to ride along the banks of the Nile, she would not even try to retrieve the information. She knows that she does not have it in long-term memory.

How many times has someone asked you the name of a certain flower and the answer was right on the tip of your tongue? You know the answer starts with a "k;" perhaps you even know the first syllable is "kal." You remember having them in pots on the patio of your first apartment; you can see their vibrant colors; you recall the special ceramic pot the yellow one was in. You remember everything except the name of the "kal" flower. As soon as someone else says "kalanchoe" though, you recognize it immediately. This maddening mezzanine between recall and recognition is the tip-of-the-tongue phenomenon.[22, 23]

Just as with learning, interference can inhibit the accuracy of the data we retrieve from long-term memory. Newly stored information can interfere with our ability to retrieve longer-stored information, and longer-stored information can interfere with our ability to retrieve newly stored information. For example, you can remember your old phone number, but for the life of you, you cannot remember your new one.

Interference can also be beneficial to memory. We can use older memories to help encode and store new memories, and we can use new memories to strengthen older ones. For example, you can remember your new address, because it is your old address divided in half.

## Memory Cues

When you pictured the patio of your first apartment in an attempt to come up with "kalanchoe," you were using a memory cue to help you retrieve information from long-term memory. There are four types of memory cues:

1. Context

   Recall of information is better if we are in the same context in which we encoded the information. This is the type of memory cue you used when you pictured your first patio in an attempt to remember "kalanchoe." Context is one of the tags we store data under, so when we are in the same context, it is easier to find the appropriate tag for the information we want. This type of memory cue is called context-dependent.

Users trust you to set up the context that enables their memory. Two ways to set up context for your information are:

A. Referring to a central metaphor, extended example, graphic, or problem-solving scenario

B. Using consistent navigation, presentation, and organization

2. State

Recall of information is better if we are in the same state in which we encoded the information. In fact, some data is not available to us unless we are in the same mood. If you told an uncharacteristically racy story while you were having a few too many at the local pub on St. Patrick's Day, you might not remember the story at all the next day when you are sober. The next time you imbibe a bit too much, though, you can remember every unsavory detail of the story. This type of memory cue is called state-dependent.

While it probably is not a good idea to encourage your users to rush down to the local pub before using your information, it is a good idea to induce a state of optimum recall. Three ways of inducing this optimum state are:

A. Picking up a continuing thread

B. Setting up introductory and prerequisite information in a boilerplate fashion

C. Using references and cross-references to knit your information together both forward and backward

3. Sensory Tickler

Sensations often unlock memories. The most famous example is M. Proust's madeleine in his *A arecherche du temps perdu*. The taste and smell of the madeleine unlocks a forgotten memory of his aunt's bedroom. A sight, sound, scent, taste, or touch can act as a memory tickler and bring back memories of which we are usually unaware.

There are four ways to activate users' sensory ticklers:

A. Use sensory-vivid language

B. Invoke universally accessible sensory metaphors

C. Use sensory-oriented graphics

D. Encourage users to relate your information to a past sensory-centric experience

**Figure 4.7** Mnemonic device.

4. Mnemonic Device

When you began learning to read music so you could play the piccolo in your school's marching band, your band director might have given you the mnemonic device in Figure 4.7.

Mnemonic devices draw together disparate pieces of information around a central, organized anchor that is memorable. In the treble clef mnemonic device, the organized, memorable anchor is "Every good boy does fine," and it draws the disparate notes together. Do you still say the months of the year on your knuckles to remember which ones have less than 31 days?

Mnemonic devices work well for declarative information that does not require higher cognitive processing. They do not work well for information users need to understand, interpret, or evaluate. Whenever possible, create central mnemonic devices for your users to help them remember facts, events, and meanings and refer often to those devices. Users remember mnemonic devices better if they have a graphic flavor, so either use a graphic as the mnemonic device or use graphic language to build the mnemonic device.

## Forgetting

Forgetting is the inability to retrieve information. Despite memory cues, we forget data we have stored in long-term memory. There are seven theories of forgetting:

1. Lost engrams

   Psychologically, we never lose engrams from long-term memory. We may, however, physiologically lose them. We may experience neuronal damage or decay that destroys all or part of an engram. The lost engram theory of forgetting applies only to the localized theory of memory. The holographic theory of memory indicates that even if there is the tiniest part of the holographic memory available, we can reconstruct the memory.

   Similar to lost engrams are faded engrams. Over time, some engrams may fade, making retrieval harder. This is important to remember if you write for an aging audience.

2. Modified schemata

   Since we modify schemata both as we store and retrieve them, it is possible that we transform the data so much that we forget its original form and retrieve only its changed form.

   Once again, the key to successful information design and development is to help users build robust, meaningful, easily retrievable schemata.

3. Repression

   Freud theorized that we unconsciously forget painful memories. Repression is a means of self-preservation.

   Repression rarely is a factor in technical communication, because normally users do not invest emotion in technical information. However, it is possible that something you write could activate repression in a user; this would be an idiosyncratic response, though, and not one you would strive to manipulate in your information.

4. Interference

   Newly stored data interferes with longer-stored data and vice-versa.

   Make use of previously stored data. Take advantage of what works and distance your information from what doesn't.

5. Weakened associations

   When we store data, we tag it. Multiple pieces of data are associated with one tag, and the same piece of data is associated with multiple tags. These tags may sometimes break down, blur in uniqueness, or get lost in the sheer number of tags we create to store information.

Exploit users' existing tags and help them create new associative tags. Use hierarchies, categories, and graphics to help them sort out their tags and maintain order among them.

6. Faulty encoding

We may not thoroughly process information in short-term memory to ensure retrieval from long-term memory. We may encode part of the information, but not all, or we may encode tags in such a way that we cannot retrieve the information. Something could have interrupted the encoding process so that we do not know the tag under which we stored the information.

Help users avoid faulty encoding by presenting your important data at key points in your information. If the first occurrence of the information suffers from faulty encoding, you can repair the damage at the subsequent occurrence.

7. Motivated forgetting

Motivated forgetting is intentional forgetting. Sometimes, we just do not want to remember something that is painful or embarrassing.

Users are motivated to forget information they find hard to understand or apply, information to which they cannot relate, or information that leads them to failure. As you design and develop your information, write for understanding and application, relevance, and success on the part of your users.

Forgetting is not necessarily a bad thing. It is a way of clearing the clutter, of filtering important information, and of insulating ourselves from memories that are too unpleasant to recall.

Other than users with eidetic memory,[24] users forget at least some of what they have read. Users come away from your information with a schema; when they apply that schema, they may discover holes. To fill those holes, they might re-access your information, not to relearn so much as to selectively remember. They can never remember it all, so forgetting is endemic to their interaction with your information. Be sure you design and develop your information so that users can selectively retrieve the information they need to complete, enhance, and modify their schemata as necessary.

## Summary

Memory is at once a storage place, a means of moving data into and out of that storage place, and the data that is in storage. Memory is a physical change (an engram) in the neuronal structure of the brain. We infer memory from changes in behavior (learning).

There are three stages of memory: sensory registers, short-term memory, and long-term memory. Sensory registers are the gateways to memory, short-term memory is the processing unit of memory, and long-term memory is the lifetime storage facility of memory.

There are two types of memory: declarative (what) and procedural (how). Declarative memory has five divisions, and procedural memory has seven divisions. There are two theories of memory: localized and holographic. The localized theory of memory states that memory is morphological synaptic changes in the brain. The holographic theory of memory states that memory is distributed throughout the entire brain much like a holographic image is distributed over a photographic plate.

There are five stages in the memory process: receiving sensory data, filtering sensory data, rehearsing and encoding data, storing data, and retrieving data. There are four types of memory cues: context, state, sensory tickler, and mnemonic devices.

Forgetting is the inability to retrieve information. There are seven theories of forgetting: lost engrams, modified schemata, repression, interference, weakened associations, faulty encoding, and motivated forgetting.

### Further Reading

Anderson, J.R. *Language, Memory, and Thought*. Hillsdale, NJ: Erlbaum, 1976.

_____. *Cognitive Psychology and Its Implications*. San Francisco: Freeman, 1980.

Baddeley, A. *Your Memory: A User's Guide*. London: Prion, 1993.

_____. *Human Memory*. Needham Heights, Massachusetts: Allyn and Bacon, 1990.

_____. *The Psychology of Memory*. New York: Harper & Row, 1976.

Begley, Sharon et. al. "Mapping the Brain," *Newsweek*, April 20, 1992.

Bentov, I. *Stalking the Wild Pendulum*. London: Wildwood House, 1978.

Bower, G. "Mental Imagery and Associative Learning," *Cognition in Learning and Memory*. L.W. Gregg, ed. New York: John Wiley & Sons, 1978.

Brown, J. "Short-term Memory," *The Oxford Companion to the Mind*. Oxford: Oxford University Press, 1987, pp. 713–714.

Brown, M. *Memory Matters*. New York: Crane-Russet, 1978.

Brown, R. "Flashbulb Memories," *Cognition*, 5, pp. 73–99.

Emmons, Steve. "The Mystery of Memory," *The Los Angeles Times*, January 11, 1994, p. B1.

Fischler, M. and O. Firschein. *The Eye, the Brain, and the Computer*. New York: Addison-Wesley, 1987.

Gregg, V. *Human Memory*. London: Methuen, 1975.

Hill, W.F. *Learning: A Survey of Psychological Interpretations*, 5th edition. New York: Harper & Row, 1990.

Katona, G. *Organizing and Memorizing*. New York: Columbia University Press, 1940.

Miller, G.A. "The Magical Number Seven, Plus or Minus Two: Some Limits on Our Capacity for Processing Information," *Psychological Review* 63, pp. 81–97.

Myers, D.G. *Psychology*. New York: Worth Publishers, Inc, 1989.

Russel, P. *The Brain Book*. New York: The Penguin Group, 1979.

Squire, L.R. *Memory and Brain*. Oxford: Oxford University Press, 1987.

## Notes

1   W. F. Hill (1990). *Learning: A Survey of Psychological Interpretations* (5th ed.). New York: Harper & Row, Publishers. (p. 203).

2   D. Myers (1989, p. 258).

3   J. Brown (1987, p. 71).

4   M. Fischler and O. Firschein (1987, p. 37).

5   G. A. Miller (1956, pp. 81–97). As early as 1859, Sir William Hamilton conducted experiments in which he threw down handfuls of marbles and found that seven was the most anyone could remember with certainty.

6   L. R. Squire (1987, p. 137).

7   R. Brown coined the term "flashbulb memory" in "Flashbulb Memories," *Cognition* 5: pp. 73–99.

8   The American Heritage Dictionary (1984).

9   P. Russel (1979, p. 115) reports 99.6 percent accuracy for image memory.

10  G. Bower (1972, p. 67) reports that recall is 95 percent accurate when test subjects use robust, interactive images.

11  L. R. Squire (1987, p. 161).

12 A synaptic gap is approximately one five-thousandth of a millimeter wide. The Spanish Nobel Laureate Santiago Ramón y Cajal called these tiny gaps "protoplasmic kisses."

13 P. Russel (1979, p. 33). There have been studies that attempt to prove that neurons die; however, these studies have been inconclusive.

14 Norepinephrine, acetylcholine, adrenocorticotrophic hormone, vasopressin, oxytocin and the endorphin family have been found to influence memory. See L. R. Squire (1987 pp. 44–53).

15 The holographic memory theory is also known as the distributed memory theory.

16 Karl Pribram of Stanford Medical School first postulated the holographic memory theory.

17 P. Russel (1979, pp. 154–157).

18 Eric Kandel and James Schwartz conditioned sea snails to withdraw their gills at the movement of water. They observed the neuronal pathways before and after conditioning and were able to pinpoint synaptic changes.

19 Karl Lashley trained rats to run a maze then cut out parts of the rats' brains and retested their memory of the maze. Regardless of how much or which part of the brain Lashley cut out, the rats were still able to remember the maze.

20 D. Myers (1989, p. 259).

21 H. Ebbinghaus demonstrated the importance of rehearsal to information retention by creating nonsense syllables and rehearsing them. He found that the more he had rehearsed his nonsensical syllables on Day 1, the more he could remember on Day 2. Ebbinghaus also found that learning meaningful information takes approximately one-tenth the effort that learning meaningless information takes.

22 R. Brown and D. McNeill coined the term "tip-of-the-tongue," although in 1890 William James called it "the tantalizing effect of the blank rhythm of some forgotten verse, restlessly dancing in one's mind, striving to be filled out with words."

23 The tip-of-the-nose phenomenon is when you recognize a scent but cannot recall its name.

24 Eidetic memory is commonly called photographic memory, though this is a misnomer. People with eidetic memory, which is more common in children than adults, can interact with the objects they remember. These objects do not appear as items in a photograph so much as a living tableau whose components people can manipulate. For example, twelve years from now, people with eidetic memory would recall this page not as a static image but as discrete words they could rearrange, enhance, and delete.

# CHAPTER FIVE

# Problem Solving

*When confronted by a difficult problem, you can solve it
more easily by reducing it to the question, How would
the Lone Ranger have handled this?*

Brady's First Law of Problem Solving

We take in and interpret sensory data through sensation and perception. We use those interpretations to build schemata that help us interact with the world through learning. We store knowledge we have learned in memory using a process called memory, and we retrieve that knowledge—Lone Ranger notwithstanding—to solve problems. A problem is a goal for which we have no attainment strategy. Users seek out your information to solve a problem; they have a goal that they want your information to help them attain—whether it is to write a Bourne shell script in UNIX, prune tea roses, understand the prescription they are taking, order merchandise from a catalog, or learn about the effects of raw sewage on whale migration.

Problem solving is creating an attainment strategy to reach a goal that we never successfully have reached before; as such, it is a response to a situation for which we have no well-established response. Consider Debbie's dilemma:

Debbie gets into the shower, pulls the handle that regulates the water, and it comes off in her hand. She looks at the handle and sees that a screw has loosened and allowed the handle to slip off its seat. All she has to do is put the handle back on its seat and tighten the screw. But she does not have a screwdriver. She does, however, have a dime and discovers that a dime makes a pretty good screwdriver. She uses the dime to screw the handle back onto its seat and enjoys a hot shower.

Debbie's problem is that she has a goal (put the shower handle back on its seat) for which she has no attainment strategy. The shower handle had never before come off in Debbie's hand, so she had no established response, but she improvised and solved the problem. By using a dime as a screwdriver, she was able to attain her goal. The next time the shower handle comes off, Debbie will reach for her handy-dandy dime. The problem-solving process has four components:

1. Conceptualizing
2. Reasoning
3. Selecting a problem-solving strategy
4. Avoiding obstacles to problem solving

Each time users employ your information to solve a problem, they go through this four-step process. Depending on how facile they are (where on the technical communication, Piaget learning, and Erikson psychosocial curves your users are), each step may take split seconds or days, may be effortful or automatic.

## Conceptualizing

Conceptualizing is forming psychological representations of objects or ideas. Conceptualizing is the foundation of thought, which is a broad, cognitive term that includes learning, memory, and problem solving. When we combine these psychological representations into groups of objects or ideas that share relationships among common, typical characteristics, we form concepts. Paper, ink, and glue are common, typical characteristics of books, but as an unrelated jumble, they do not make a book. When you put the ink on the paper and bind the paper with the glue, you form relationships among the characteristics, and these relationships form the concept of book.

Figure 5.1 shows a variety of objects that belong to one concept. Do you have any trouble recognizing the concept despite the fact that each of these objects is different?

**Figure 5.1**  Different objects belonging to the same concept.

You recognize all of these objects as cars, because you have a concept of car. Despite the fact that each is different, they share the relationships among the typical characteristics of a car, so they fit within your concept of car.

Concepts do not have to be concrete objects. Concepts run the gamut from concrete to abstract. All of the following situations are characteristic of an abstract concept. Do you have any trouble recognizing the concept despite the fact that the manifestations are all different?

- Someone gives up a Sunday golf game because a significant other wants to go to the museum.
- A child stays after school to work on a special Valentine for a grandparent.
- A parent commits a teenager to a drug rehabilitation program.
- An elderly pensioner spends hard-to-come-by cash on a trip to the veterinarian for a sick cat.
- A friend takes the car keys from a friend who has gone overboard in making the acquaintance of Jack Daniel.

You can recognize all of these situations as being manifestations of the concept of love, because they share relationships among the typical characteristics of love.

Conceptualizing is a four-step process:

1. Acquiring
2. Distinguishing
3. Combining
4. Using

## Acquiring Concepts

Acquiring is the mechanism we use to formulate concepts. There are two ways to acquire concepts:

1. Following definitional rules

   We learn a definitional rule that says a house cat is a small, furry creature with small ears and a long tail. If we were to follow this definitional rule for a cat, we would classify all of the creatures in Figure 5.2 as cats.

   As you can see by glancing at Figure 5.2, following definitional rules often leads to invalid concepts. To be useful, definitional rules must be narrow, focused, and contained. Definitional rules that work are often so narrow, focused, and contained that they are not inclusive enough to handle nontypical instances of a concept.

   For example, if you created a narrow, focused, contained definitional rule for cat, what would happen should you encounter a Rex (no fur) or a Manx (no tail)? Or a one-eyed cat or a three-legged cat? Experience leads us to build more and more concepts based on different sets of definitional rules or on sets of definitional rules with more and more exceptions.

   Following definitional rules is analogous to template-matching as a shape-recognition strategy (Chapter 2).

   Users often extrapolate very narrow definitional rules from the information they bring into their world. If rules are integral to the information you are communicating, be sure to indicate exceptions and places where users can "think outside the box." If you see that you are providing a great many exceptions, rethink your information structure. Too many exceptions is an indication that you have not created an intuitive design for your information.

**Figure 5.2** Following definitional rules to form concepts.

2. Developing prototypes

We create mental models or prototypes that share the relationships among typical characteristics of an object or idea. This model becomes our prototypical version of that object or idea and we compare new objects and ideas against the prototype to determine whether the new object or idea fits the concept.

Developing prototypes often leads to stereotypical concepts, but it is a quick and easy way to form concepts. Experience leads us to modify our stereotypical concepts until we have an enriched concept rather than a shallow stereotype. Using this way to form concepts leads us to the knowledge that only the creatures shown in Figure 5.3 are cats.

**Figure 5.3** Developing prototypes to form concepts.

Developing prototypes is analogous to prototype-matching as a shape-recognition strategy (Chapter 2).

You can help users leverage existing prototypes, evolve existing prototypes, and develop new prototypes:

- Leverage users' existing prototypes and use them as reference points for communicating new information.

  For example, your users already understand the concepts of using a mouse-driven tool palette on a canvas area to generate shapes in a draw program. Compare and contrast those concepts with your new software's ability to place nodes using a mouse-driven palette in a graphical representation of a network.

  The goal is different, but the process, tools, and environment are similar enough that you can leverage users' understanding of mouse-driven draw programs to teach them to "draw" a graphical representation of a network in your new network-management program. They take their drawing prototype and copy and save it as their network-creating prototype.

- Evolve existing prototypes by showing users how to accommodate new information to create Piaget's thesis-antithesis-synthesis process and put that information to work in their world.

  For example, say your users already know how to use the old smog analyzer to perform smog checks on cars. Map the similarities and differences between the old analyzer and the new analyzer to help users build new concepts that accommodate the new information and help them learn to use the new machine.

The goal and process are essentially the same for the old machine and the new machine, but the approach to the new equipment, the details of the procedure, and the specifics of the output are different. By comparing and contrasting the similarities and differences, you help users maintain their existing prototypes but bring them up to date with the new information.

- Develop new prototypes both by leveraging and evolving prototypes they already have and by suggesting new prototypes through problem-solving scenarios.

For example, say your users process checking account deposits and withdrawals manually. Their branch is moving to computer-aided checking transactions. Present the process information by illustrating how to solve an old problem (checking account deposit) with a new scenario (computer-aided checking account deposit).

You can leverage all of your users' existing knowledge and prototypes and illustrate a new process with a problem they solve dozens of times a day. This leads to their creating their own prototypes for using a computer to process deposits to checking accounts.

We acquire hundreds of thousands of concepts from either definitional rules, prototypes, or a combination of both. We need some way to manage all of these concepts, so, as Figure 5.4 shows, we form hierarchies to help get the job done.

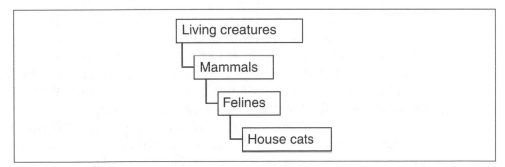

**Figure 5.4** Concept hierarchy.

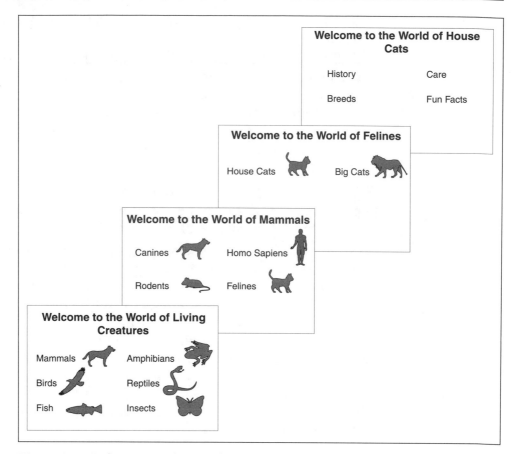

**Figure 5.5** Information hierarchy.

Help users understand concept hierarchies by mirroring those hierarchies in your information structures, that is, form following content. Suggest how users can integrate information into existing hierarchies, and show them how to create new hierarchies. It is easier to integrate information into existing hierarchies, but that is not always possible. When you must show users how to create new hierarchies, build the hierarchies slowly, layer by layer. Use graphics to illustrate the hierarchy, and always tie the hierarchy to a real-world example.

As a case in point, imagine you are creating a World Wide Web presentation on living creatures. You might structure your pages along the lines of the hierarchy shown in Figure 5.4. The presentation might have pages like those illustrated in Figure 5.5.

## Distinguishing Concepts

Acquiring a concept neither implies nor guarantees understanding of when to apply that concept and how it differs from other concepts. Distinguishing a particular concept is learning when to apply that particular concept as opposed to another concept. We rely on past experience to know when and how to apply a concept.

For example, you have a bird concept. When you see a sparrow, you have no difficulty applying the concept of bird to it. When you see a penguin, though, you may not immediately apply your bird concept to this creature, because a penguin is not as "birdy" as a sparrow; that is, a penguin is not as stereotypically a bird as is a sparrow. Your bird concept must evolve to include the exceptions as well as the rule, as Figure 5.6 shows.

**Figure 5.6** Evolution of a concept.

When helping users evolve their concepts, start with the familiar and work to the unfamiliar. The familiar is what they already know and trust in their own world, and the unfamiliar is the change to that knowledge or new knowledge that you are communicating in your information. Make the benefits of the evolution or development clear; users have absolutely no reason to change existing concepts or develop new ones until you clearly show them how they benefit from it. Give them a steady schedule of reinforcement until they have evolved the new concept, and cross-reference each phase of that evolution to one of their existing applications.

## Combining Concepts

As we acquire concepts, we begin to combine different types to form the schemata, psychological representations, or blueprints that we follow to understand and interact with the world. Going back to the stop-sign example in Chapters 2 and 3, the stop-sign schema says to stop when you see a stop sign. What are the concepts that compose this schema? Figure 5.7 shows some of the concepts you might combine to form a stop-sign schema.

The more disparate, unfamiliar, or hard-to-understand the concepts, the more important it is to help users combine concepts into serviceable schemata.

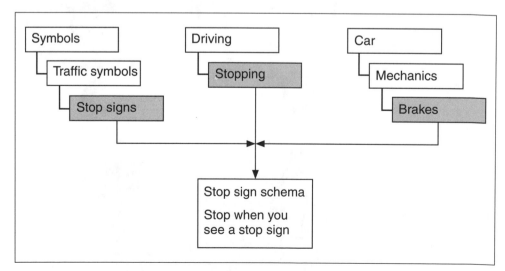

**Figure 5.7**  Combining concepts into a schema.

## Using Concepts

When we are in a situation that is identical to or similar to a situation we have faced before, the key to understanding and interacting successfully with the world is using the correct schema. When we come to a stop sign, we pull out our stop-sign schema and do what it directs us to do. We do not pull out our rice-making schema or our carburetor-fixing schema. (For situations we have not experienced before, we rely on problem-solving strategies, which are discussed later in this chapter.)

We rely on past experience to help us identify the correct schema. The first time we are behind the wheel and see a stop sign, we rely on our past experience of having seen others stop at stop signs, having read the rule in the drivers' handbook that says drivers must stop at stop signs, and having listened to our friends' stories of tickets and fines for not stopping. Thereafter, we rely on having had the experience of stopping at a stop sign and apply that experience each time we come to a stop sign.

You must ensure that your users know whether they are facing a situation in which they should apply an existing schema or a situation in which they should create a problem-solving strategy. They trust that you have made that distinction for them and that they do not have to make it. They depend on you to anticipate the problems they will encounter, to exploit the schemata they have stored, and to guide them in applying schema to a situation. Part of your user profile is to understand which situations your users have faced in the past, the experiences they may have had to facilitate identifying the correct schema to apply to a given situation, and which schemata they have stored and ready for use.

## Reasoning

Reasoning is a cognitive process that applies criteria of validity to data in order to form conclusions about that data. This is logic, which concerns only the reasoning process, not the outcome. Reasoning processes fall into two broad categories:

1. Inductive
2. Deductive

Users bring your information into their world and apply either inductive or deductive reasoning to it in order to come to some conclusions that they can use in problem solving. They may not always reach conclusions that can solve the problem because their initial assumptions about the data may be incorrect or their reasoning process may be faulty.

## Inductive Reasoning

Inductive reasoning is the logical process of inferring the general from the particular. It is a bottom-up approach to finding truth in data. When we apply inductive reasoning, we derive general truths from specific instances of concepts. If every watermelon you have ever eaten has red fruit, you infer that "watermelon has red fruit." Each instance of a watermelon with red fruit confirms your general truth; this is a positive instance, because it confirms your general truth. You feel safe in predicting that if you cut open a watermelon, the fruit will be red. Then you cut open a watermelon, and it has yellow fruit; this is a negative instance, because it disconfirms your general truth. Now you have to modify your general truth about watermelon: "Watermelon has either red or yellow fruit." Each instance of a watermelon with either red or yellow fruit is a positive instance of your modified general truth.

You use a derived general truth until a negative instance disconfirms it. There was no need to modify your "watermelon has red fruit" general truth until you experienced an instance of watermelon with yellow fruit. You will use your modified "watermelon has either red or yellow fruit" general truth until you experience a negative instance of your concept of watermelon.

Inductive reasoning is an iterative process of deriving general truths, applying them, and modifying them, as Figure 5.8 shows.

You can see that inductive reasoning is the method we use to modify schemata as depicted in Figure 5.9. (You may remember this concept from Chapter 3.)

## Deductive Reasoning

Deductive reasoning is the logical process of inferring the particular from the general. It is a top-down approach to finding truth in data. When we apply deductive reasoning, we derive particular conclusions from general truths we know or believe to be true. If the general truths and logical processing are valid, the conclusions we draw from them must be valid; the validity of the general truths and logical processing guarantees the truth of the conclusion. The only things that matter in deductive reasoning are that the general truths you start with are valid and that the steps

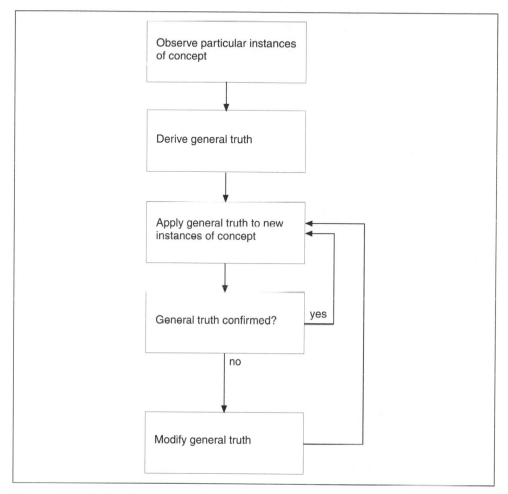

**Figure 5.8** Inductive reasoning.

you take to derive particular conclusions are valid. Remember proofs from high school geometry? They are an example of deductive reasoning.

Aristotle introduced syllogisms as the framework for deductive reasoning. A syllogism is a logical argument that contains three propositions: the first two are general truths, and the third is the particular conclusion derived from those general truths. For example:

All dogs are mammals

Hesiod is a dog

Hesiod is a mammal

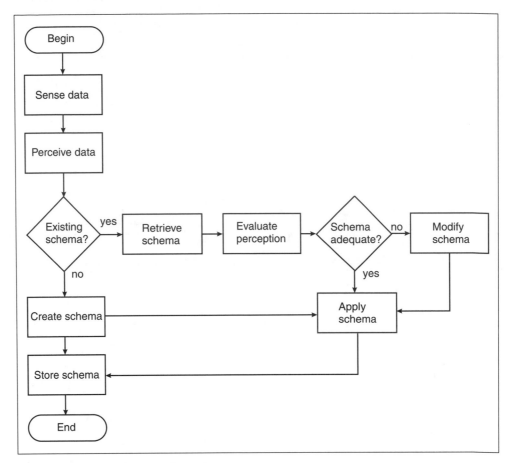

**Figure 5.9**  Experience flowchart.

There are three types of syllogisms:

1. Categorical
2. Linear
3. Conditional

### Categorical Syllogisms

Categorical syllogisms compare categories of concepts to another concept; in the preceding syllogism, we are comparing the category of the dog Hesiod to the concept of mammal.

Categorical syllogisms must contain:

- Two general truths that you know or believe to be true

  In this syllogism, the two general truths are "All dogs are mammals" and "Hesiod is a dog."

- A particular conclusion that you derive from those general truths

  In this syllogism, the particular conclusion is "Hesiod is a mammal."

- A traceable chain of relationships among the conclusion's subject, conclusion's predicate, and the general truths' middle term

  In this syllogism, the subject is Hesiod, the predicate is mammal, and the middle term is dog.

- A major premise

  A syllogism's major premise is the relationship between the predicate and the middle term. In this syllogism, the major premise is the relationship between mammal and dog.

- A minor premise

  A syllogism's minor premise is the relationship between the subject and the middle term. In this syllogism, the minor premise is the relationship between Hesiod and dog.[1]

Faulty categorical syllogisms have at their core either faulty syllogistic logic (the relationships among the subject, predicate, and middle term or between the major and minor premises are faulty) or faulty general truths (one or both of the general truths contain invalid information). What is wrong with the following syllogisms?

All birds are living creatures
All cats are living creatures
All cats are birds

All birds have feathers
All birds are living creatures
All living creatures have feathers

All living creatures have feathers
Cats are living creatures
Cats have feathers

The first two syllogisms contain faulty syllogistic reasoning; there is no traceable chain of connections. The third syllogism contains a traceable chain of connections, but the first general truth contains invalid information.

We have difficulty processing syllogisms that deal with "all," "some," and negative logic. Is this syllogism valid?

Some As are Bs

Some Bs are Cs

Some As are Cs

Figure 5.10 shows how a Venn diagram helps sort out this invalid syllogism.

Is this syllogism valid?

Some Bs are As

No Cs are Bs

Some As are not Cs

Figure 5.11 shows why this syllogism is valid.

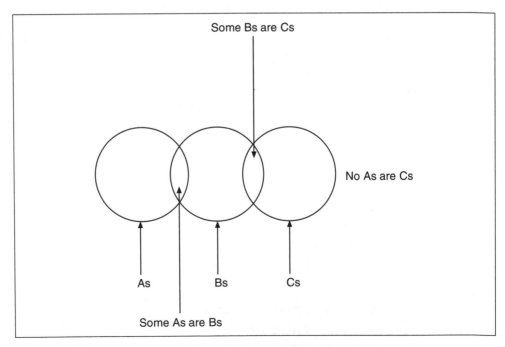

**Figure 5.10** Venn diagram showing invalidity of a syllogism.

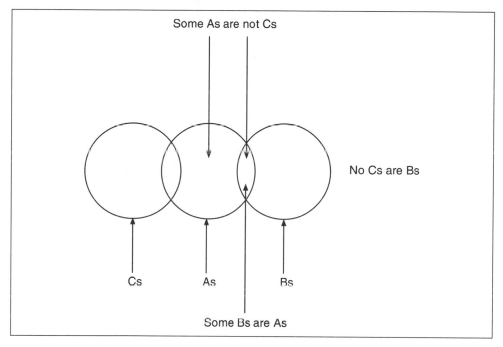

**Figure 5.11** Venn diagram showing validity of a syllogism.

### Linear Syllogisms

Linear syllogisms compare relations among concepts in a sequential fashion; in the following syllogism, we are comparing the quantity of apples each person has. We could set up this syllogism as J>M>S.

John has more apples than Mary.

Mary has more apples than Sue.

John has more apples than Sue.

Linear syllogisms must contain a series of terms that compare similar concepts. This syllogism is a three-term series that compares quantity of apples.

Two processing strategies for linear syllogisms are:

1. Visual

   Visual processing is forming a mental image to sort out the syllo gism. In this syllogism, did you form a mental picture of the number of apples each person has?

2. Verbal

Verbal processing is focusing on the linguistic content of the syllogism and not forming a mental image to sort out the syllogism. In this syllogism, did you focus solely on the words and not form a mental picture?

There are two encoding strategies for linear syllogisms:

1. Integrated

An integrated encoding strategy is abstracting information from each term in order to create a whole. In this syllogism, did you form one mental image of all three people and rank them according to the number of apples each has? This is a visual, integrated strategy for processing this syllogism.

2. Separate

A separate encoding strategy is abstracting information from each term, but not creating a whole. Did you form three separate mental images, one for each term? This is a visual, separate strategy for processing this syllogism.

We like to make wholes of parts, and we remember information better if we encode it as an image, so it is no surprise that we prefer to use visual, integrated strategies when processing linear syllogisms. However, the strategy we use depends on the problem and the circumstances.[2] As with most of our problem solving, we tend to rely on experience, past knowledge, and stored schemata when dealing with syllogistic logic.

## Conditional Syllogisms

Conditional syllogisms set up an "If A, then B" conditional relationship between concepts; in the following syllogism, there is a conditional relationship between hearing music and the radio's being on.

If you hear music, the radio is on.

You hear music.

The radio is on.

Conditional syllogisms contain:

- Two general truths

The first general truth is an implicative sentence of the form "If A, then B." In this syllogism, the first general truth is "If you hear music, the radio is on."
where:

> A is an antecedent condition.
> > In this syllogism, the antecedent condition is "music."
> B is a consequent condition.
> > In this syllogism, the consequent condition is "radio on."

The second general truth is either a:

- Confirmation of the antecedent condition
- Disconfirmation of the antecedent condition
- Confirmation of the consequent condition
- Disconfirmation of the consequent condition

> In this syllogism, the second general truth is "You hear music" and is a confirmation of the antecedent condition.

- A particular conclusion

In this syllogism, the particular conclusion is "The radio is on," which confirms the consequent condition.

Faulty conditional syllogisms have more to do with misinterpretation of the first general truth than with logic errors. Often, we mistakenly attribute a biconditional relationship to the first general truth so that "If A, then B" also implies "If B, then A." In reality, the truth of "If B, then A" is not known; therefore, "If you hear music, the radio is on" is true, but the truth of "If the radio is on, you hear music" is unknown.

## Selecting a Problem-Solving Strategy

When we face a new situation for which there is no well-established response, no prior experience, and for which we have no prior knowledge or stored schema, we must create a response. This is problem solving, and we rely on experience, prior knowledge, and stored schemata to help us create a solution to the problem.

Developing problem-solving strategies is a four-step process:

1. Identifying the problem
2. Choosing a problem-solving strategy
3. Executing the strategy
4. Evaluating whether the strategy worked

## Identifying the Problem

Most of our trouble with problem solving comes from not understanding either the problem or the desired solution. How we frame both the problem and the solution determine in large measure our success at solving the problem.

Consider this problem:

There are two boxes; one is marked "Data Center" and one is marked "Loading Dock." Each box contains 20 items that are common office supplies. The only items available are pens, rubberbands, and paperclips. Prove this sentence true with as few requests as possible to inspect items from either box: If the item is a paperclip, it belongs to the loading dock.

This problem is easier to solve if we frame it like this:

It is necessary to prove only that the Data Center's box does not contain a paperclip.

For this problem, the contents of the Loading Dock's box are irrelevant, but initial evaluation of the problem could mistakenly lead you to think that the problem hinges on its contents.

R. Mayer identifies four types of knowledge of the problem domain (the specific area of expertise in which you are solving the problem) that we must have before we can correctly identify the problem and the desired solution:[3]

1. Factual

    Basic knowledge of the rules, categories, and externalizations of that particular domain. To create a document in Microsoft Word, you must have factual knowledge of how to start the software, the types of things you can do with the software, and the interface that you manipulate to work with the software.

2. Semantic

Conceptual understanding of the problem domain. To create the document in Microsoft Word, you must have semantic knowledge of the basic concepts of word processing, using a mouse, storing and saving data, printing the memo, and understanding that what you see on the screen corresponds to what you get on paper.

3. Schematic

Infrastructural understanding of the problem domain. To create the document in Microsoft Word, you must have schematic knowledge of functionality, menus, macros, online help, and data storage and retrieval.

4. Strategic

Strategic knowledge of the problem domain is understanding how to build strategies to solve problems within the problem domain. To create the document in Microsoft Word, you must have strategic knowledge of how to put factual, semantic, and schematic knowledge together to build a strategy to use the software to accomplish the goal of creating a document. Strategic knowledge also includes understanding how to troubleshoot the problem domain.

There are differences in how we approach problem solving depending on whether we are closer to the beginner-level-user or the power-level-user end of the technical information curve in the problem domain. Table 5.1 summarizes the differences in how users approach problem solving.

Beginner-level users do not have the problem-domain experience or expertise that power-level users have. This experience and expertise is key to solving problems in a given problem domain. With enough practice, a beginner-level user acquires the experience and expertise and becomes a power-level problem solver within a given problem domain. Of course, users may choose not to become a more expert problem solver within a problem domain; they may choose to remain at one level or always to be an outsider having to relearn the fundamentals of the problem domain each time there is a problem to solve.

## Choosing a Problem-Solving Strategy

Once we have identified the problem and the desired solution, we must choose and apply one of the five problem-solving strategies:

**Table 5.1** Differences in How Users Approach Problem Solving

| Objective | Beginner-Level Users... | Power-Level Users... |
|---|---|---|
| Store domain-specific knowledge | Store in small, fragmented, disparate units, not understanding the "big picture" or how the information fits together | Store in large, solution-oriented, interconnected units that they can easily retrieve and link to other large units of knowledge |
| Apply domain-specific knowledge | Apply in a series of effortful steps | Automate their knowledge application |
| Identify problems | Identify at a surface level: observations are disjointed, out-of-context, and appearance-oriented | Identify at a structural level: observations are context-sensitive, conceptually astute, and meaningful to the principle of the problem domain |
| | Make long detailed lists of all differences | Spot differences and abnormalities quickly and easily |
| | Make several cuts at prioritizing the importance of differences | Access and prioritize the significance of differences and abnormalities almost automatically |
| | Have no integrated, functional schema of the problem domain | Create a refined, functional, and integrated schema of the problem domain |
| | Miss symptoms of the problem | Recognize symptoms automatically and correlate them to the problem |
| | Cannot relate a current problem to other possible problems in the problem domain | Possess a stockpile of similar problems and solutions to draw from that they can apply to the current problem |
| Generate and test hypotheses | Cannot detect the clues in the problem that lead to successful generation and testing of hypotheses | Detect clues |
| | Do not generate enough hypotheses or the appropriate hypotheses | Generate an adequate number of correct hypotheses |

1. Trial and error
2. Hypothesis testing
3. Algorithms
4. Heuristics
5. Insight

### Trial and Error

Trial and error is a random strategy in which we try one possible solution after another until we solve the problem. While trial and error appears more of a connectionist approach to problem solving than a Gestaltist approach, it is truly a blend of the two. J. Baron asserts that the distinction between trial and error and the Gestaltist insight is one of degree.[4] We perform trial and error in our heads as well as behaviorally. Consider this scenario:

> You buy a new blender, but when you get it home, you realize that the 12 buttons on the interface do not have labels. You want to whip up a banana-strawberry smoothie, so you need the Purée button, but you do not know which one of the 12 buttons is the right one.

What do you do? You put your banana, strawberries, and orange juice in the blender, put on the lid, and start punching buttons until you find the one you think is the right one. You do not put your ingredients in the blender and begin unscrewing the tiny rubber legs; you are able to predict that these legs do not purée the mixture. The trial and error you engaged in was a "thoughtful trial and error" comprising both cognitive understanding (Gestaltist) and behavioral experimentation (connectionist).

Connectionists theorize that we apply our habit family hierarchies when we engage in trial and error problem solving. We try the responses in our habit family hierarchies, beginning with the most effective response (called the dominant response) and working our way down to the least effective response (called the weak response).

If on your old blender, the second to last button was Purée, chances are you will try that button first on your new blender. If the second to last button on your new blender is not the Purée button, you demote that response in your habit family hierarchy, because it is not helping you solve the problem of finding the new Purée button.

Relying on the strongest response in our habit family hierarchies is called the law of exercise. Demoting responses in our habit family hierarchies because they do not solve a problem is called the law of effect.

Gestaltists call trial and error problem solving reproductive thinking, because we are reproducing solutions that worked in the past in hopes of solving a current problem.

### Hypothesis Testing

Hypothesis testing, which is generating and testing appropriate hypotheses to solve a problem, is a more purely cognitive version of trial-and-error. It requires a conceptual understanding of the problem and the problem domain to generate appropriate hypotheses. Very often, we frame hypothesis testing in a conditional relationship of the form "If A, then B, else C." We use our problem-domain knowledge to formulate hypotheses A, B, and C that we apply to the current problem.

When we generate and test hypotheses as problem solving, we are not selecting random responses that we hope will solve the problem. We are using knowledge to narrow the pool of available responses and our knowledge of the problem domain to dictate which responses are appropriate. Whereas a trial-and-error approach might involve 30 random responses, a hypothesis-testing approach could narrow the responses to ten considered responses; you could then test those ten to find the one that works. You would put those that do not work back into your mental pool of hypotheses; perhaps you would use them to solve another problem at another time.

Using the earlier example of creating a document in Microsoft Word, you would draw on your past experiences, general word-processing knowledge, and domain-specific knowledge of Microsoft Word to solve the problem of an inappropriate page break. You would not have to resort to the trial-and-error approach of punching a slew of keys or pulling down menus at random. Your knowledge would lead you to a handful of hypotheses that you would then test until you solved the problem.

### Algorithms

Algorithms are predetermined, guaranteed-success, step-by-step procedures for solving problems. Algorithms apply a set of rules that worked in the past to a similar, current problem. Because they involve verifying every step before proceeding to the next step, algorithms may be incredibly complex and time-consuming.

Consider this problem:

Use all of the letters in the word "cinerama" to form another word.

The algorithm would involve systematically trying each letter in each position, then verifying each result in a dictionary. There are 20,160 possible letter combinations. If you allow 20 seconds to verify each combination, this algorithm will take you five days to complete.[5]

## Heuristics

Unlike algorithms, heuristics do not guarantee a solution to a problem. Heuristics are rules of thumb that we have devised as a result of our experiences and knowledge.

We can apply heuristics to the "cinerama" problem and arrive at a solution without having to look up 20,160 letter combinations in a dictionary. Two heuristics we can apply are:

1. English words never start with:

   mc

   nc

   rc

   nm

2. Two As seldom come together

By applying these two heuristics and a trial-and-error approach, we should be able to solve this problem in no time.[6]

A. Tversky and D. Kahneman identified two categories of heuristics that lead to faulty problem solving:

1. Representative heuristics

   Representative heuristics enable us to make snap judgments of concepts based on how well those concepts represent a known stereotype.

   For example, which of the following more closely resembles the stereotypical technical communicator?

   A. Marti has a Master's degree in landscape design, races dirt bikes in amateur competitions, haunts swap meets looking for antique earrings, and is addicted to spy novels.

   B. Eulinda has a Master's in English, dresses conservatively, takes editing classes at night, and belongs to three software user groups.

If we apply the representative heuristic, we would say that Eulinda is a technical communicator and Marti is not. That conclusion may or may not be accurate.

2. Availability heuristics

Availability heuristics enable us to base our judgments on concepts readily available in long-term memory. If a concept comes readily to mind, we assume that it is commonplace.

For example, does the letter "k" appear more often as the first letter of English words or as the third letter? Since words beginning with the letter "k" come more readily to mind (king, knight, key, kit, keep), we might mistakenly say that words beginning with the letter "k" are more common than words that have the letter "k" as their third letter (make, take, acknowledge, ask, likely). The truth, however, is that there are far more words with the letter "k" in the third position than in the initial position.[7]

## Insight

Insight is a cognitive concept of problem solving. It is the immediate "Aha!" when the solution to a problem suddenly falls into place. Gestaltists theorize that successful problem solving involves conceptually reorganizing the problem so that we see its elements in a new light. This conceptual reorganization leads to insight.

Consider the matchstick problem, which is a classic example of cognitive problem solving:

You have six matchsticks. Arrange them into four equilateral triangles with each side of each triangle one matchstick long.

Figure 5.12 shows an incorrect solution and the correct solution. The incorrect solution is to create a square with an X, forming four triangles, but not four equilateral triangles (each triangle has a 90 degree angle, so is not equilateral). The correct solution is a three-dimensional pyramid with a triangular base.

The solution to the matchstick problem involves reorganizing the matches (the elements of the problem) in a new way (three-dimensionality). Gestaltists call this type of problem solving productive thinking, because we are producing new ways of looking at a problem.

Often, we cannot solve a problem, so we leave it and come back to it. When we return to the problem, we experience insight. This period when

**Figure 5.12** Matchstick problem.

we left the problem is called incubation, and Gestaltists say that incubation allows us to forget confusion and let insight happen.

Insight relies on our grasp of the internal organization of a problem, the relationships among the problem elements, and our ability to see problem elements in a novel way. Insight is an all-or-nothing proposition. We either get the problem solution in a moment of insight, or we do not.

Connectionists account for the phenomenon of insight by theorizing that we try out various problem solutions in our minds. This mental trial and error is not observable, so when we mentally discover the problem solution, it appears to be insight.[8]

## Avoiding Obstacles to Problem Solving

Obstacles to problem-solving are psychological blocks or mindsets that prevent successful problem solving. There are four obstacles to problem solving:

1. Problem-solving set

   Problem-solving set is our tendency to see things through the lens of our experience and our inability to see problem elements in a novel way. The inability to solve the matchstick problem is due to a problem-solving set that limits the solution pool to two-dimensional solutions.

2. Confirmation bias

   Confirmation bias is our tendency to search for solutions that confirm our ideas.[9] We are reluctant to recognize solutions that disconfirm what we believe. Not only do we avoid solutions that refute our beliefs, but once we have a belief firmly planted in mind, it is very difficult to dislodge that belief, even if it is inaccurate.

3. Functional fixedness

Functional fixedness is our inability to see the functionality of objects as flexible. Functional fixedness prohibits our using objects in novel ways to solve problems. We rely on past experience with objects to fix their functionality in our minds. If we have always viewed a dime only as a coin of the realm, we are not apt to use it as an impromptu screwdriver, despite the fact that it makes a perfectly good screwdriver.

A classic example of functional fixedness is Duncker's box problem:

> You have three matchboxes. The first one contains three candles; the second, three tacks; the third three matches. You also have a free-standing screen. The problem is to mount one of the candles vertically on the free-standing screen so as to create a candle lamp.

Figure 5.13 shows the solution to Duncker's box problem, which involves using one of the matchboxes as a stand for the candle lamp instead of as a container.

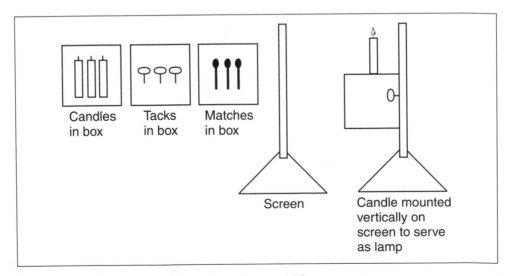

**Figure 5.13** Solution to Duncker's box problem.

4. Negative transfer

Negative transfer is the process in which our past experiences of solving problems inhibit or prevent our ability to solve current problems.[10] Gestaltists theorize that reproductive application of past experience or habit family hierarchies may be detrimental to productive problem solving. There is evidence to support the claim that past experience has a negative effect on problem solving that requires us to use problem elements in novel ways, but has a positive effect when applied to problems like those we have solved in the past.[11]

As a communicator of technical information, you can overcome problem-solving set, confirmational bias, functional fixedness, and negative transfer if you are aware that they are operating on users' ability to use your information successfully. Use examples and problem-solving scenarios to show users that they can posit and solve problems in novel ways, trust solutions that do not confirm ideas they already hold, view and apply objects in untried ways, and use negative transfer in a positive way.

## Summary

Problem solving is creating an attainment strategy to reach a goal that we never successfully have reached before. Users need your information to solve a problem; they have a goal that they want your information to help them attain. The problem-solving process has four components: conceptualizing, reasoning, selecting a problem-solving strategy, and avoiding obstacles to problem solving.

Reasoning is a cognitive process that applies criteria of validity to data in order to form conclusions about that data. Reasoning processes fall into two broad categories: inductive and deductive. Users apply either inductive or deductive reasoning in order to come to some conclusions that they can use in problem solving. They may not always reach conclusions that can solve the problem because their initial assumptions about the data might be incorrect or their reasoning process may be faulty.

Developing problem-solving strategies is a four-step process: identifying the problem, choosing a problem-solving strategy, executing the strategy, and evaluating whether the strategy worked. There are four types of problem-domain knowledge we must have before we can correctly identify a problem and the desired solution: factual, semantic, schematic, and strategic. There are five problem-solving strategies: trial and error, hypothesis testing, algorithms, heuristics, and insight.

There are four obstacles to problem solving: problem-solving set, confirmation bias, functional fixedness, and negative transfer.

## Further Reading

Adamson, R.E. "Functional Fixedness as Related to Problem Solving: A Repetition of Three Experiments," *Journal of Experimental Psychology*, 44, pp. 288–291.

Anderson, J.R. and J. G. Greeno and P. J. Kline. "Acquisition of Problem-Solving Skills," *Cognitive Skills and Their Acquisition*, R. Anderson, ed. Hillsdale, NJ: Erlbaum, 1981.

Baron, J. *Thinking and Deciding*. Cambridge: Cambridge University Press, 1994.

Bourne, L.E., Jr. "Knowing and Using Concepts," *Psychological Review*, 77, pp. 546–556.

Bower, G.H. and T.R. Trabasso. "Concept Identification," *Studies in Mathematical Psychology*, R.C. Atkinson, ed. Stanford, CA: Stanford University Press, 1964.

Ceraso, J. and A. Provitera. "Sources of Error in Syllogistic Reasoning," *Cognitive Psychology*, 2, pp. 400–410.

Chi, M.T.H. and M. Bassok, M.W. Lewis, P. Reimann, and R. Glaser. "Self Explanations: How Students Study and Use Examples in Learning to Solve Problems," *Cognitive Science*, 13, pp. 145–182.

Davis, G.A. *Psychology of Problem Solving: Theory and Practice*. New York: Basic Books, 1973.

Duncker, K. "On Problem Solving," *Psychological Monographs*, 58:5, Whole Number 270.

Egan, D.E. and D.D. Grimes-Farrow. "Differences in Mental Representations Spontaneously Adopted for Reasoning," *Memory & Cognition*, 10, pp. 297–307.

Egan, D.E. and J.G. Greeno. "Theory of Rule Induction: Knowledge Acquired in Concept Learning, Serial Pattern Learning, and Problem Solving," *Knowledge and Cognition*, L.W. Gregg, ed. Hillsdale, NJ: Erlbaum, 1974.

Erickson, J.R. "Research on Syllogistic Reasoning," *Human Reasoning*, R. Revlin and R.E. Mayer, eds. New York: Winston/Wiley, 1978.

Ernst, G.W. and A. Newell. *GPS: A Case Study in Generality and Problem Solving*. New York: Academic Press, 1969.

Evans, J. and J. Barston and P. Pollard. "On the Conflict Between Logic and Belief in Syllogistic Reasoning," *Memory & Cognition*, 12, pp. 295–306.

Farris, H.H. and R. Revlin. "Sensible Reasoning in Two Tasks: Rule Discovery and Hypothesis Evaluation," *Memory & Cognition*, 17, pp. 221–232.

Greeno, J. G. "Cognitive Objectives of Instruction: Theory of Solving Problems and Answering Questions," *Cognition and Instruction*, D. Klahr, ed., Hillsdale, NJ: Erlbaum, 1976.

Greeno, J.G. and H.A. Simon, "Problem Solving and Reasoning," *Stevens' Handbook of Experimental Psychology*, R.C. Atkinson et. al., eds., New York: John Wiley & Sons, 1988.

Hayes, J. R. *The Complete Problem Solver*. Philadelphia: Franklin Institute Press, 1981.

Holyoak, K.J. "Problem Solving," *Thinking: An Invitation to Cognitive Science*, D.N. Osherton and E.E. Smith, eds., Cambridge: MIT Press, 1990.

Johnson-Laird, P.N. and M. Steedman, "The Psychology of Syllogisms," *Cognitive Psychology*, 10, pp. 64–99.

Kintsch, W. and J.G. Greeno. "Understanding and Solving Word Arithmetic Problems," *Psychological Review*, 92, pp. 109–129.

Klayman, R. and Y. Ha. "Confirmation, Disconfirmation, and Information in Hypothesis Testing," *Psychological Review*, 94, pp. 211–228.

_____ "Hypothesis Testing in Rule Discovery: Strategy, Structure, and Content," *Journal of Experimental Psychology: Learning, Memory, and Cognition*, 15, pp. 596-604.

Larkin, J.H. and J. McDermott, D.P. Simon, and H.A. Simon. "Expert and Novice Performance in Solving Physics Problems," *Science*, 208.

Maier, N.R.F. "Reasoning in Humans I: On Direction," *Journal of Comparative Psychology*, 10

_____. "Reasoning in Humans II: The Solution of a Problem and Its Appearance in Consciousness," *Journal of Comparative Psychology*, 12.

Mayer, R.E. *Thinking, Problem Solving, Cognition*. New York: W.H. Freeman and Company, 1992.

_____. "From Novice to Expert," *Handbook of Human-Computer Interaction*, M. Helander, ed., Amsterdam: Elsevier, 1988.

Medin, D.L. and E.E. Smith. "Concepts and Concept Formation," *Annual Review of Psychology*, 35, pp. 113–138.

Myers, David G. *Psychology*. New York: Worth Publishers, Inc, 1989.

Newell, A. and H.A. Simon. *Human Problem Solving*. Englewood Cliffs, NJ: Prentice-Hall, 1972.

Wason, P. "On the Failure to Eliminate Hypotheses in a Conceptual Task," *Quarterly Journal of Experimental Psychology*, 12, pp. 129–140.

Weisberg, R. and J. Suls. "An Information Processing Model of Duncker's Candle Problem," *Cognitive Psychology*, 4, pp. 255–276.

Wickelgren, W.A. *How to Solve Problems: Elements of a Theory of Problems and Problem Solving*. San Francisco: Freeman, 1974.

## Notes

1   There are four possible ways of organizing the major and minor premises; there are 16 possible combinations of premises; there are 64 possible pairs of premises; for each of the 64 possible pairs of premises, there are four possible conclusions for a total of 256 possible syllogisms. R. Mayer (1992). *Thinking, Problem Solving, Cognition* (2nd edition). New York: W.H. Freeman and Company. (pp.118–119).

2   R. Mayer (1992, pp. 151–162).

3   R. Mayer (1992, p. 392).

4   J. Baron (1994, p. 51).

5   D. Myers (1989, p. 286).

6   The answer is "American."

7   D. Myers (1989, p. 292).

8   W. Köhler insisted that his experiments with a chimpanzee named Sultan proved that animals also experience insight. Sultan suddenly used a short stick to gain access to a long stick, which he then used to obtain a piece of fruit. Connectionists argue that Sultan's "insight" was a chain of learned responses. R. Epstein demonstrated how a pigeon could learn a series of responses leading to obtaining a piece of banana.

9   P. Wason (pp. 129–140) coined the term "confirmation bias."

10   The opposite is also true. Positive transfer is the process in which past experiences solving problems aid or promote our ability to solve current problems.

11   R. Mayer (1992, pp. 64–65).

# CHAPTER SIX

# Accessing Information

*Each information level we are forced to transcend in search of a fact lessens our desire to perform the search in an inverse square proportion.*

Goodman

Concurrent to all of the cognitive processing such as perception, memory, learning, and problem solving that comprises their world, users access the content of your information through three layers of subtext in order to cognitively process and use it. These layers of subtext are medium, navigation, and presentation. They travel through these layers to extricate the content that is relevant to them. They employ the reading process to travel through subtext and to access content. Reading is both a physiological and a cognitive process.

## Reading

Our modern English word "reading" comes from the old Anglo-Saxon "rædan," which means "to advise oneself." Reading is both a physiological process of taking in sensory data and a cognitive process of understanding that visual data. Some cultures read left to right, some right to left, and some top to bottom. The only cultural commonality is that all cultures start reading from the top of the page or screen.

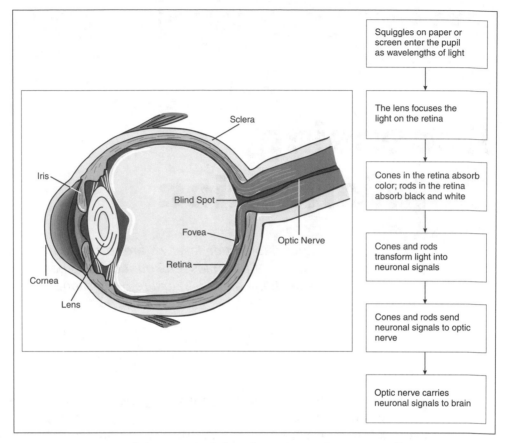

**Figure 6.1** Parts of the eye and the physiological process of reading.

## Physiological Process of Reading

Physiologically, reading is a visual process. We take in the sensory data of squiggles on paper or screen with our eyes.[1] Vision is preeminent among our senses; we take in most sensory data with our eyes. This phenomenon is known as visual capture. Figure 6.1 shows the parts of the eye and the physiological process of reading.

Our cones are most dense at the fovea, a small depression in the retina. The fovea is our area of clearest vision. When we follow a moving object, we move our head, so that we keep the object focused on our fovea. When we read, however, we keep our head still. We have to move our eyes to ensure that visual input falls on the fovea. This is called foveal vision; there are two implications of foveal vision:

1. Our eyes move along a line of text so that they can bring different parts of the line into focus on the fovea.

2. To see anything clearly, our eyes have to stop moving along a line of text for a fraction of a second so that a still image can rest on the fovea and the fovea can transmit this image to the brain via the optic nerve.

Foveal vision is not a smooth, linear process. Our eye moves along lines of text in little jumps taking in little gulps of words to focus them on the fovea. The little jumps are called saccades, and the little gulps are called fixations. The place where our eye stops to focus the fixations is called a fixation point. Our eyes jump from fixation point to fixation point, as Figure 6.2 shows.

Parafoveal and peripheral vision are two types of nonfoveal vision that act as scouts for foveal vision. As our eyes jump from fixation point to fixation point, nonfoveal vision is sending back previews of what the next words are. This enables the brain to decide what the next saccade and fixation point are. In this way, foveal and nonfoveal vision work together to take in visual data.[2]

Our eye takes in visual data in hundredths of seconds. It is never still for more than .5 second and takes .25 second to move from fixation point to fixation point. Average fixations are 2–3 words; the duration of fixations and length of saccades vary, depending on both the material and our reading skill. Our brain processes the visual data in .25–.5 second.

## Cognitive Process of Reading

Since the term "reading" means "to advise oneself," reading implies cognitive processing. It is hard to advise ourselves or anyone else if we do not

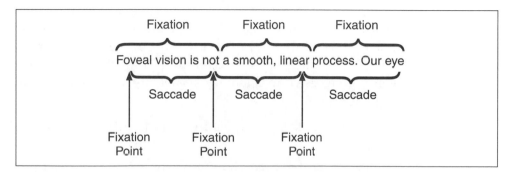

**Figure 6.2** Saccadic eye movement.

understand what we are reading, and understanding is a cognitive process that draws on other cognitive functions such as learning and memory.

The cognitive process of reading is a seven-step process:

1. Perceive visual data.

   Sensation is the purely physiological aspect of reading. Perception takes over shortly after the optic nerve transmits neuronal signals from our cones and rods to our brain. The visual sensory register deals only with sensation, but sometime between sensory register and short-term memory, perception takes place.

   Our preattentive processes help us perceive that the text is electronic or paper-bound, has boundaries, and is a separate object from ourselves. Attentive processes start to work, and we realize that those are not meaningless squiggles on paper or screen, but are words and letters and they possibly have meaning for us. Learning, memory, knowledge, and interpretation all begin to work on these squiggles.

2. Recognize words and letters or learn new words.

   The first thing we have to do is recognize the figure-ground relationship between the squiggles and the paper or the screen. Then laws of grouping begin to work to group letters into words, words into sentences, sentences into paragraphs.

   Next we begin the task of recognizing the words and letters lexically. We use the shape-recognition strategies of prototype matching, template matching, and distinctive features. Context helps us with shape recognition as do the word-superiority effect and the word-letter phenomenon. We call upon lexical memory to identify the shape of the words and letters.

   If we have not stored the word in lexical memory, we call upon procedural memory, which tells us how to look up the word in the dictionary. Once we look the word up, we either learn it and store it in lexical memory, or we retain it in short-term memory just long enough to use it to fill an immediate need (such as making sense of a sentence).

3. Understand the relationship of individual words to the whole passage.

   Once we have recognized words and letters, we call upon semantic memory to determine whether we understand the meaning of the words. If we do not have the words stored in semantic memory, we use procedural memory to look them up in a dictionary, which begins the physiological reading process again.

After we are satisfied that we understand the meaning of words, we relate individual meanings to contextual meanings until we understand the immediate chunk of text. A chunk may be a phrase, sentence, or paragraph.

As we understand the individual chunks, we combine chunks of understanding until we understand the whole passage.

4. Relate the information to a body of knowledge.

Once we understand the passage, we relate it to what we already know. We might use it to create new schemata or to refine schemata we have stored in long-term memory. Or, we might decide to throw it away. If we decide to keep it, we must integrate the new information into our existing knowledge base.

5. Encode the information.

In order to integrate the new information into our existing knowledge base, we must encode it. We encode it as a new schema or as a refinement to an existing schema. We encode it based on the type of knowledge it is, that is, whether it is declarative or procedural.

We encode it in short-term memory for storage in long-term memory.

6. Retrieve the information.

Whenever we want to use the information, we retrieve it from long-term memory into short-term memory where we use it as the foundation of thought, action, and communication.

7. Communicate the information.

To fulfill the meaning of reading as advising, we must communicate the knowledge we have gained from the act of reading. We might communicate only with ourselves, or we might share our knowledge with others. We use the communication model of saying, hearing, and feedback to communicate what we have learned from reading.

Figure 6.3 shows the cognitive process of reading.

The reading process is not linear, however; we can and do come to it at any stage. The later we come to the reading process, the more trouble we have understanding the material we are reading and the more recur-

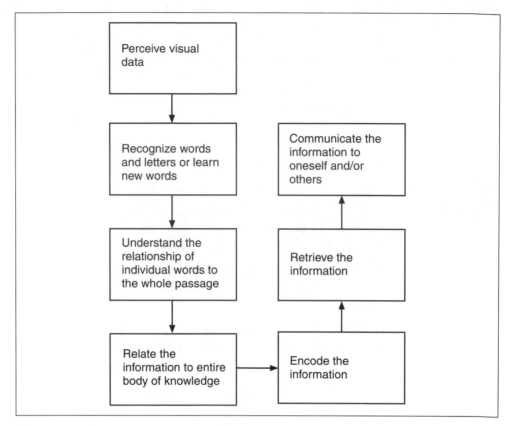

**Figure 6.3** Cognitive process of reading.

sion we experience. Recursion is having to reread information because we left parts of the information out the first time we read it.

When we read, we call upon our stored schemata to provide information not explicit in the text so that we can accurately interpret the text. Consider these sentences:

The little girl heard the ring of the ice cream man's bell. She ran inside to get her piggy bank.[3]

We have to call upon at least two schemata to fill in the gaps in the information that these two sentences present. We have to extract from our ice-cream-man schema that:

- The ice cream man sells ice cream.

- He rings his bell when he is near.

- Children like to buy ice cream from him.

We have to extract from our children-and-money schema that:

- Buying anything requires money.
- Children keep money in piggy banks.
- Children keep piggy banks in their houses.

Our schemata also provide default values that text may not provide. Consider this sentence:

Otto placed his order then sat at the counter to wait for his lunch.

We have to call upon our diner schema to interpret this sentence and to provide default values. The sentence does not indicate with whom Otto placed his order. We know that he placed his order with the waitperson, because customers, waitpeople, and placing orders with waitpeople are part of our diner schema. Our schemata help us reason correctly and infer the truth from the relationships among the words, phrases, and sentences that we read.

Our schemata provide reference points so that we can interpret text. Without a reference point, it is not easy to determine what a textual passage is saying. Consider this passage based on Bransford and Johnson:

This procedure is really very easy. First arrange the objects into different groups. One group may be sufficient depending on how much you have to do. After you complete the procedure, arrange the objects into different groups again. Then put them into their appropriate places. Eventually you will use them once more, and you will have to repeat the whole cycle.

If you knew before reading this passage that it is talking about laundry, you would have understood it. Without the reference point of your laundry schema, this is a difficult passage to interpret, but with a reference point, there is nothing difficult about it.

Schemata also provide background information, which helps us interpret text. Consider this sentence:

Mary Todd Lincoln often went blocks out of her way so as not to pass in front of Ford's theatre.

Without your Booth-shot-Lincoln schema to provide the background information that Mary Todd Lincoln was Abraham Lincoln's wife and that John Wilkes Booth shot Lincoln in Ford's theatre, this passage does not make much sense.

Some parts just are not necessary

Redundancy speeds up the reading process

We read what we expect to read

Y cn rd sntncs wtht vwls.

Y cn mt vry ffth wrd wtht lsng the mnng.

Th rdr nds nly lttl nfrmtn.

**Figure 6.4** Processing text with little lexical information.

While our schemata help us fill in the semantic gaps, we can actually process text with very little lexical data as shown in Figure 6.4.

The presence of more lexical data than we need to process text is called redundancy. Redundancy helps us read more quickly, easily, and efficiently, partly because we read what we expect to read. We do not expect bottomless sentences or sentences without vowels, so we make wholes of the parts; we add the sentence bottoms and the missing vowels. The fact that we can understand what we read without redundancy gives credence to telegraphic writing styles; however, telegraphic writing gives rise to recursion.

## Reading Strategies

Reading strategies are mechanisms we use to assimilate information from text. There are three components to a reading strategy:

1. Type

    As with learning and memory, there are two types of reading: reading to learn facts, which is declarative, and reading to perform actions, which is procedural.

    Adele is reading a mutual-fund prospectus. She wants to learn which mutual fund to invest her money in (declarative) and how to open an account with the fund she selects (procedural).

2. Access

    There are two ways to access text:

A. Sequentially

Accessing text sequentially is finding information based on what precedes and follows it. Sequential-access text is comprised of context-dependent units of information. We have to understand page 115 before we can understand page 116, and page 213 may have backward cross-referential bearing on page 116 (in this example, the pages are the units of information; a unit may be a section or a chapter).

B. Randomly

Accessing text randomly is finding information regardless of what precedes or follows it. Random access is context-independent units of information. Random-access text is modular and stand-alone.

Often, we want to be able to access text in a combination of sequential and random-access methods. We expect to be able to randomly access declarative information such as $12 \times 11 = 132$. This is a stand-alone fact that has meaning in and of itself. We expect to access procedural information sequentially within itself, such as the steps within a recipe, but we often prefer to access the units of procedural information randomly.

Lil wants to make ratatouille. She needs to access the steps in the recipe sequentially (what does she do after sautéing the onion?), but she wants the recipe itself to be a stand-alone information unit that she can access randomly in her cookbook.

3. Goal

There are five reading goals:[4]

A. Skimming

Reading for the general gist. It is a declarative reading goal and could be either sequential or random access.

B. Scanning

Reading to find specific information quickly. It is a declarative reading goal and is either sequential or random access.

C. Searching

Scanning with attention to the meaning of specific information. It is a declarative reading goal and is either sequential or random access.

D. Receptive

Reading for thorough comprehension. It is either a declarative or a procedural reading goal and, depending on the material, is either sequential or random access.

E. Critical

Reading for evaluation. It is either a declarative or a procedural reading goal and is sequential access.

## Text and Subtext

Users employ the physiological and psychological processes of reading to access the text and subtext of your communication. The text is the overt content message that you are communicating to your users.[5] The subtext is the messages you are communicating to your users' subconscious via medium, navigation, and presentation. Text is an object you consciously create and users consciously manipulate; subtext is an environment you consciously create that subconsciously manipulates users.

Figure 6.5 shows a help panel from ClarisWorks 3.0. What is the text and subtext in this example?

The text is the content the help panel is communicating, in this case, how to add text or graphics to a chart. The subtext is everything the technical communicator combines to create the medium, navigation, and presentation of this help panel:

- Choice of online help versus hardcopy
- Hyperlink and hypergraphic navigational devices
- Font and point size
- Amount of information in a paragraph
- Information chunking
- Decision not to use numbered procedure
- Use of head and subhead
- Use of inline graphics
- Panel controls such as scroll bar and sizing boxes

Both you and your users bring to the text and subtext all of your experiences, schemata, and cognitive processes. If you feel lost without your CorelDraw! reference card, for example, chances are you think

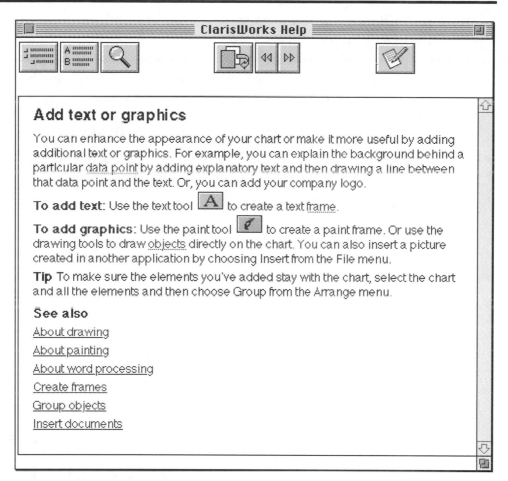

**Figure 6.5** Text and subtext.

reference cards are a good way to communicate information. If your users have had no experience with reference cards, you probably can win them over with a helpful, concise, intuitive design and content. If your users have had good experiences with reference cards, it is a match made in heaven. However, if you love reference cards and your users hate them, you are in trouble. I cannot say it often enough: if users do not choose to utilize your information, it does not exist.

In order to get to the text, users have to go through the subtext. The first contact they have with your information is the medium you have chosen. Broadly, there are two media: hardcopy and online.[6] Both you and your users have assumptions and expectations around each type of media. By choosing one medium over the other, you are communicating something in subtext.

As we move into the 21st century, more and more companies are putting information online and eschewing hardcopy altogether or at least reducing it significantly. The Internet is becoming a larger and larger player in the dissemination of information. Computers are ubiquitous in schools and in a great many homes. To some, it is only natural that they find their information online. Then there are those who pick up a mouse and try to use it like a television remote control. For these people, online information is a foreign concept. They can do it, but they have to learn how to do it, become comfortable doing it, and use the right tools to do it.

Once users access the medium of your information, they have to master the navigation of your information. In hardcopy, this usually is turning pages at the end of a page, a cross reference, or an index directive. In online information, this usually is clicking a hypermedia link, using a search engine, or an application-specific function key. Navigational cues are subtext. Consider this scenario:

> Jerry is using a software application. He wants to know how to change his password, so he calls up the help system and uses the search engine to locate information on the topic of password. There is no discrete topic called "Changing Password," so he begins to read about passwords. The introduction tells him why he needs a password and that for security reasons, he should change it often. The glossary term defines what a password is and what the constraints are when creating a password. The example shows him some sample passwords. He clicks around and finally finds how to change a password five layers down into the help system. The topic he wanted is not indexed, and the search engine does not pick it up. He stumbles upon it serendipitously.

The text of the help screen that explains how to change his password is a clear, concise, accurate five-step procedure that tells him exactly what he wanted to know. What does the subtext tell him?

After users have mastered the navigation of your information, they have to understand the presentation of it. No doubt that as a conscientious technical communicator, you had an outline or a storyboard before you began putting information on paper or screen. You probably spent a great deal of time refining your outline or storyboard. You may even have done some usability testing with a paper walk. The outline or storyboard was your tool for clarifying and focusing your vision of the information. To be successful, your presentation of the information has to clarify and focus your users' vision of the information.

For example, consider this scenario:

> Lonie wants to change the time on her answering machine. She digs the user's guide out of her kitchen junk drawer. There is no index, so she thumbs through the pages of the booklet looking for something dealing with changing the time. She finally finds a note directing her to the label affixed to the underside of the tape-compartment lid.

> She finds the label and looks for instructions on changing the time. Lonie has her answering machine on a small table next to the phone in the hallway. The light is dim, and the label has very small print and is faded. She cannot make out the instructions, so she rummages around in her pantry till she finds a flashlight.

> She shines the flashlight on the label, but the text is so small, she needs her reading glasses to make it out. She retrieves her reading glasses from her bedside table, shines the flashlight on the label, and finally is able to access the short procedure for changing the time on her answering machine.

The technical communicator had anticipated Lonie's need to know how to change the time, which is the text, but what did the subtext communicate? Was a procedure in tiny type on a label affixed to the tape-compartment lid the best presentation for this information? Was it worth the cost of Lonie's frustration?

Your information communicates its presentation via visual cues:

- Color
- Graphics
- Heads and subheads (hierarchies and heterarchies)
- Line length
- Line spacing and letter kerning
- Lists
- Margins
- Numbered procedural steps

- Online hyperlinks (textual and graphic)
- Page numbers
- Page or screen layout
- Paragraphs
- Placement
- Running headers and footers
- Text formatting (font, emphasis, point size, capitalization)

It is easy to dishonestly manipulate the subtext. You can choose a hardcopy format over an online format, elect not to index topics in the online help index or hardcopy index, use a table instead of a bar chart, use too much or too little textual emphasis, choose a heterarchy instead of a hierarchy, or literally hundreds of other potentially dishonest manipulations. It is your responsibility to create an honest, open subtext, which is the communication vehicle for the covenant of trust between you and your users.

It also is easy to overwhelm users with subtext and to create a sensory adaptation response on their part. Some hallmarks of an inappropriate subtext are:

- Too many fonts
- Too much textual emphasis
- Too many graphics
- Too much color
- Too many hyperlinks
- Too many layers of navigation or presentation

If you find any of these transgressions in your information, you need to rethink the organization and structure of your navigation and presentation. While a color-coded bar chart to represent quarterly sales figures is a powerful communicator, a colorful bar chart on every page or screen leads to sensory adaptation just as a page full of boldface or italics does.

Some heuristics you can follow to avoid overwhelming users and avoid sensory adaptation on their part are:

- Limit the number of fonts on a page to three basic fonts plus as few as are meaningful to communicate.
- Use textual emphasis sparingly. Restrict it to shorter phrases that you want to stick in the reader's mind.

- Use graphics to replace or enhance textual information.
- Never use more than six colors on a page or screen (including colors of letters and background).
- Limit the number of hyperlinks to 4 per 25 lines of textual information (including hypertext and hypergraphic links).
- Do not expect users to navigate through more than three layers to locate information.

## Graphics

Graphics are part of the subtext of your information. Choosing to use a graphic, selecting one type of graphic over another, and electing to put or not put particular data in a graphic are a powerful part of the presentation. In general, anything on a page or screen that is not words is a graphic, including white space. In fact, white space is the most widely used graphic in technical communication. Other types of graphics are:

- Drawings
- Flowcharts
- Graphs
- Hypergraphics
- Icons
- Illustrations
- Maps
- Organizational charts
- Photographs
- Schematics
- Tables

As Chapter 4, Memory, indicates, image memory is one of our most robust image stores. We can retrieve pictures and picture-evoking words more easily than we can retrieve nonpicture-evoking words. A graphic plus a label is the most potent storage and retrieval cue we have. The maxim that "a picture is worth a thousand words" is especially applicable to technical communication. Graphics should either replace or enhance words. Do not fall into the "coulda-shoulda-woulda" syndrome with graphics just because you bought a new CD-ROM with 8,000 pieces of clip art.

Choosing the right graphic is an important part of the presentation. As always, the guiding principle is transparency, ease-of-use, and intuitiveness for your users. Simplicity is the key to successful graphics. Graphics should map to your users' existing schemata. If you are introducing a new concept graphically, introduce complexity of detail in layers that users can assimilate at their own pace. Use natural mappings and vivid, robust images. If users in other cultures use your information, keep in mind the cultural aspects of graphics. Some Middle Eastern countries, for example, find graphics showing women in positions of authority unacceptable.[7] And while in a Western culture a big, slobbery dog might be the ultimate symbol of loyalty, in some Asian cultures it represents a fine meal. Historically, there are also cultural associations with left and right placement of objects. Historically, the left is evil and the right good.

We visually assimilate graphics as we do text, that is, via saccadic eye movement. The path our eyes follow is called a "scanpath."[8] For graphics of familiar objects, our schemata determine the scanpath, but for unfamiliar objects scanpaths are idiosyncratic; in fact, the same person looking at a graphic of an unfamiliar object could have several different scanpaths for that one graphic. Perceptual set plays a large part in scanpaths. We see what we expect to see. Our eyes move about a graphic trying to satisfy the expectation we hold in our minds. There is some research that suggests that the more sophisticated the user, the more sophisticated the scanpath. That is, the search path reflects a greater knowledge store and displays a tighter cycle of searching among the visual stimuli.

Refer to the perceptual illusions in Chapter 2 for more information on the role of perception and graphics.

## Color

Color is a powerful player in the presentation. It is replete with strong emotional, social, and cultural meanings. References to color permeate our daily language: "He's got the blues today. They're green with jealousy. He's a yellow-bellied coward. She's in a black mood." The meaning of color may change from culture to culture. In Western cultures, for example, white is a symbol of purity, while in some Eastern cultures, it is a symbol of mourning. The emotional effects of color have been well-documented; for example, studies show the calming effect of pink on emotionally disturbed people. Color also affects us physically; it can cause our blood pressure and body temperature to rise and make our heart beat faster.

Color has three components:

1. Hue

   Hue is what we most mean when we refer to color; red, yellow, blue, and green are hues. Hues are properties of the wavelength of light.[9] Achromatic colors (black, white, and gray) lack hue.

2. Lightness

   Lightness is the amount of black or white in a hue.

3. Saturation

   Saturation is the purity of a hue. The number of wavelengths in a hue determine its saturation—the fewer the number of wavelengths, the purer the hue. Red, for example, is more pure (more saturated) than pink.

## Color Processing

Most of us can see seven million different shades of color.[10] Most of us see these shades of color as combinations of three primary colors: red, green, and blue. People who use red, green, and blue as the primary ingredients in all of the colors they can see have normal trichromatic color vision.

The retina in a person with normal trichromatic vision has red, green, and blue cones. Each cone responds to light from a different part of the visible light spectrum. Green cones respond to light from the center of the spectrum, red cones to light from one end, and blue cones to light from the opposite end. Every light stimulus excites various combinations of red, green, and blue cones. This trichromatic color theory is also called the Young-Helmholtz trichromatic color theory.

Young-Helmholtz is only the first half of our color processing, however. Color processing is a two-stage mechanism:

1. Cones respond to light.
2. The nervous system analyzes the cones' response.

This second stage, called Hering's opponent color theory, states that our central nervous system analyzes the trichromatic color messages of the cones in terms of opponent color pairs:

- Red/green
- Blue/yellow
- Black/white

We cannot simultaneously see a color and its opponent color. We cannot see a reddish green, a yellowish blue, or a whitish black.

Eight percent of males and .4 percent of females suffer from some sort of color-vision deficiency,[11] which is a result of a genetic defect on the X chromosome. This is why so many more males suffer from color-vision deficiency than females. The extra X chromosome in females insulates them from most forms of color-vision deficiency.

There are four types of color-vision deficiency:

1. Protanopism

   Protanopes confuse red and green, because they do not have red cones.

2. Deuteranopism

   Deuternanopes confuse red and green, because they do not have green cones.

3. Tritanopism

   Tritanopes confuse blue and yellow, because they have a deficiency in the blue-light-absorbing pigment. Tritanopism is often a result of retinal disease.

4. Monochromatism

   Monochromats see only shades of gray, because they do not have cones.

Protanopism and deuteranopism are the most common forms of color-vision deficiency. Only about .005 percent of the people in the world suffer from tritanopism, and only about one in one million people suffer from monochromatism, which is the only true "color blindness."[12]

Some guidelines you can follow to help your vision-deficient users are:

- Always use color redundantly.
- Do not use red-green and blue-yellow color combinations.
- Use colors with different lightness values.
- Limit the number of colors you use (the fewer the better; never more than six).
- Put color legends close to the colors they decode.

## Using Color

Users' needs and expectations should guide you in your use of color. If you design comic book covers, it would hardly do to avoid color, since your users expect not only color, but the more lurid the better. Marketing, sales, safety, and medical information rely on color to varying degrees. Users expect color in online information. At least one study suggests that television is the reason users expect color in online information.

Although users expect color in online information, they do not necessarily expect it in hardcopy information even if it has its uses in hardcopy.[13] Hardcopy technical information is not enhanced by colorized background or letters. Users find it confusing, distracting, and tiring.[14] Hardware, software, policies and procedures, automotive, environmental, insurance, financial, and most business communications text communicates optimally as black letters on white paper.

In graphics, icons, and hyperlinks, color performs vital functions in information:

- Adds dimension
- Aids decision making
- Enhances recall
- Focuses attention
- Renders images more realistic
- Reveals organization and pattern
- Satisfies users' preference
- Speeds search[15]

If you plan to use color in a graphic, render the graphic first in black and white. Once you are certain the graphic communicates in black and white, add color. When you use color, it should always be to enhance the content. It is especially easy to dishonestly manipulate the subtext of your information by manipulating color.

If you choose to use color, there are some guidelines that make your life as a technical communicator easier:

- Use natural mappings. Users accept red, green, and yellow apples, but unless you are in Dr. Seussland, no one accepts a plaid apple. Some sample natural mappings are:

  | *Color* | *Mapping* |
  |---------|-----------|
  | blue | water |
  | brown | dead vegetation |
  | green | new vegetation |
  | red | blood, fire |
  | yellow | sun |

- Remember the cultural, social, and emotional associations of color. See Appendix A, Writing for Other Cultures, for more information on cultural associations of color. Some sample cultural associations are:

| Color | Culture | Association |
|-------|---------|-------------|
| red | Western | danger |
| red | Japanese | anger |
| red | Chinese | joy |
| yellow | Western | caution, cowardice |
| yellow | Chinese | honor, royalty |
| yellow | Arabic | happiness, prosperity[16] |

Some sample Western social associations of color are:

| Color | Meaning |
|-------|---------|
| black | evil |
| blue | male, authority |
| pink | female, helplessness |
| red | stop |
| white | good |

Some sample Western emotional associations of color are:

| Color | Emotion |
|-------|---------|
| blue | cold, calm, innocence |
| gold | richness, wisdom, honor[17] |
| orange | friendliness, pride, gregariousness |
| red | aggression, impulsiveness, shame |
| yellow | caution, cowardice, betrayal |

- Never use more than six colors on one display (page or screen). The rule of thumb is the fewer the colors the better.

- Be sure that there is adequate contrast among the colors and between the background and foreground objects. Do not pair spectrally distant pure colors, and surround colors with complementary colors.

- Red and navy create an alternating stereoscopic effect. Avoid this color combination.

- Black on white is the most legible color combination. Other acceptable combinations are blue or red on white; never use yellow on white.

White on black is the second most legible color combination. Other acceptable combinations are yellow or green on black; never use blue, red, or magenta on black.

- Always assign colors meaningfully. Never assign a color without understanding its emotional, social, and cultural associations. Do not assign colors just because your computer supports 256 million colors.

- Be sure objects are large enough to carry color. An object should be at least this big to carry color:

This is a 36-point letter O in Times font.

- Do not use color for tight patterns.

- If you must color code text, color code the **entire word**, not selected letters.

- Always test color under actual viewing conditions. Color on your screen appears much lighter than that same color appears on a printed page (due to the light behind your computer screen). Light, size, shape, angle, and texture all affect the way we see color.

- Never use color as the only code; always redundantly code color.

If you use color, you should be aware of four phenomena that affect the way we perceive color:

1. Subjective colors

   Black-and-white stimuli produce pastel afterimages. There is no one accepted explanation for this phenomenon. Some research points to a Morse-code effect of black-and-white stimuli where black-and-white flashes of certain intensities and durations signal particular colors.

2. Purkinje shift

   Our sensitivity to various wavelengths shifts toward the shorter wavelengths in poorly lit conditions.

3. Memory color

   Our perception of an object's color depends on that object's typical color.

4. Color categorization

We name and remember blue, yellow, green, and red better and faster than other colors.[18]

## Summary

Concurrent to all of the cognitive processing such as perception, memory, learning, and problem solving that comprises their world, users access the content of your information through three layers of subtext in order to cognitively process it and use it. These layers of subtext are medium, navigation, and presentation. They travel through these layers to bring the content into their world.

Our modern English word "reading" comes from the old Anglo-Saxon "rædan," which means "to advise oneself." Reading is both a physiological process of taking in sensory data and a cognitive process of understanding that visual data. There are six steps in the physical process of reading: light entering the pupil, lens focusing the light on the retina, cones and rods absorbing color and black and white, cones and rods sending neuronal signals to the optic nerve, and the optic nerve sending signals to the brain. There are seven steps in the cognitive process of reading: perceiving visual data, recognizing words and letters or learning new words, understanding the relationship of individual words to the whole passage, relating the information to a body of knowledge, encoding the information, retrieving the information, and communicating the information.

There are three reading strategies: type, access, and goal. There are two kinds of type: declarative and procedural. There are two types of access: sequential and random. There are five reading goals: skimming, scanning, searching, reading for comprehension, and reading for evaluation.

The text of your information is the overt content message that you are communicating to your users. The subtext of your information is the subconscious messages you are communicating to your users via medium, navigation, and presentation. Text is an object you consciously create and users consciously manipulate; subtext is an environment you consciously create that subconsciously manipulates users. It is easy to dishonestly manipulate the subtext. It is also easy to overwhelm users with subtext and to create a sensory adaptation response on their part.

Graphics are part of the subtext of your information. Choosing to use a graphic, selecting one type of graphic over another, and electing to put or not put particular data in a graphic are a powerful part of the presentation. We can retrieve pictures and picture-evoking words more easily than we can retrieve nonpicture-evoking words. A graphic plus a label is the most potent storage and retrieval cue we have. Simplicity is the key to successful graphics. Graphics should map to your users' existing schemata. If you are introducing a new concept graphically, introduce complexity of detail in layers that users can assimilate at their own pace. Use natural mappings and vivid, robust images. If users in other cultures use your information, keep in mind the cultural aspects of graphics.

Color is a powerful player in the presentation. It is replete with strong emotional, social, and cultural meanings. Users expect color in online information, but not necessarily in hardcopy information, though it has its uses in hardcopy. Four phenomena affect the way we perceive color: subjective colors, Purkinje shift, memory color, and color categorization.

## Further Reading

Albers, J. *Interaction of Color*. New Haven, CT: Yale University Press, 1975.

Arnheim, R. *Art and Visual Perception: A Psychology of the Creative Eye*. Berkeley, CA: University of California Press, 1974.

Barrett, E., ed. *The Society of Text*. Cambridge: MIT Press, 1989.

Berger, A.A. *Seeing Is Believing: An Introduction to Visual Communication*. Mountain View, CA: Mayfield Publishing Company, 1989.

Bransford, J.D. and M.K. Johnson. "Contextual Prerequisites for Understanding: Some Investigations of Comprehension and Recall," *Journal of Verbal Learning and Verbal Behavior*, 61, pp. 717–726.

Brockmann, R. J. "The Unbearable Distraction of Color," *IEEE Transactions on Professional Communication*, 34:3.

Charniak, E. *Toward a Model of Children's Story Comprehension*. Cambridge: MIT Artificial Intelligence Laboratory. (TR–266).

Christ, R.E. "Review and Analysis of Color Coding Research for Visual Displays," in *Human Factors*, 17:6.

Cossette, C. *How Pictures Speak: A Brief Introduction to Iconics*. Quebec: Riguil International, 1982.

Crystal, D. *The Cambridge Encyclopedia of Language*. Cambridge: Cambridge University Press, 1987.

Curtis, M.E. "Development of Components of Reading Skill," *Journal of Educational Psychology*, 72, pp. 656–669.

Daneman, M. and P. Carpenter. "Individual Differences in Working Memory and Reading," *Journal of Verbal Learning and Verbal Behavior*, 19, pp. 450–466.

Davis, E.G. and R.W. Sweezey. ""Human Factors Guidelines in Computer Graphics: A Case Study," *International Journal of Man-Machine Interaction*, 18.

De Grandis, L. *Theory and Use of Color*. New York: Abrams: 1986.

Duin, A. H. "Reading to Learn and Do," *STC Proceedings*, 1988.

_____. "How People Read: Implications for Writers," *The Technical Writing Teacher*, 1988, 15, pp. 185–193.

Dumas, J. S. *Designing User Interfaces for Software*. Englewood Cliffs, NJ: Prentice-Hall, 1988.

Durrett, H. And D.T. Stimmel. *Color and the Computer*. Boston: Academic Press, 1987.

Easterby, R. and H. Zwaga, eds. *Information Design: The Design and Evaluation of Signs and Printed Material*. Chichester, England: John Wiley & Sons, 1984.

Eckstein, H. "Four-Color Fundamentals," *Publish!* 1989, 4:5, pp. 44–49.

Felker, D.B., ed. *Document Design: A Review of the Relevant Research*. Washington, DC: American Institutes for Research, 1980.

Fischler, Martin A. and Oscar Firschein. *Intelligence: The Eye, the Brain, and the Computer*, 2nd edition. Reading, MA: Addison-Wesley Publishing Company, 1987.

Geldard, F. *The Human Senses*, 2nd edition. New York: John Wiley & Sons, 1972.

Gibson, J.J. "The Information Available in Pictures," *Leonardo*, 4.

_____. "A Theory of Pictorial Perception," *Audio-Visual Communication Review*, 1.

Gregory, R. *The Oxford Companion to the Mind*. Oxford: Oxford University Press, 1987.

Haeusing, M. "Color Coding of Information on Electronic Displays," *Proceedings of the Sixth Congress of the International Ergonomics Association*, International Ergonomics Association, 1976.

Hammet, B.F. and P.M. Illick. "Visual Literacy: A Perceptual Discipline," *Journal of Technical Writing Communication*, 1.

Horton, W.H. *The Icon Book: Visual Symbols for Computer Systems and Documentation*. New York: John Wiley & Sons, 1994.

_____. *Illustrating Computer Documentation: The Art of Presenting Information Graphically on Paper and Online*. New York: John Wiley & Sons, 1991.

_____. "Overcoming Chromophobia," *IEEE Transactions on Professional Communication*, Vol. 34:3.

Huey, E. *The Psychology and Pedagogy of Reading*. London: MacMillan, 1908. Reprint. Cambridge, MA: MIT Press, 1968.

Hurvich, L.M. *Color Vision*. Sunderland, MA: Sinauer Associates, 1981.

Iten, J. *The Elements of Color*. New York: Van Nostrand Reinhold, 1970.

Just, M.A. "Paradigms and Processes in Reading Comprehension," *Journal of Experimental Psychology: General*, 111, pp. 228–238.

————. "A Theory of Reading: From Eye Fixations to Comprehension." *Psychological Review*, 87, pp. 329–354.

Kennedy, J.M. *A Psychology of Picture Perception*. Washington, DC: Jossey-Bass, 1974.

Kohl, J.R. "Using 'Syntactic Clues' to Enhance Readability for Non-Native Speakers of English," *STC Proceedings*, 1991.

Kostelnick, C. "Visual Rhetoric: A Reader-Oriented Approach to Graphics and Design," *The Technical Writing Teacher*, 1989, 16, pp. 29–47.

————. "How Readers Perceive Pictures: Generating Design Guidelines from Empirical Research," *STC Proceedings*, 1990.

Krull, R. And P. Rubens. "Effects of Color Highlighting on User Performance with Online Information," *Technical Communication* 33 (4).

Lehner, E. *Symbols, Signs & Signets*. Cleveland: World Publishing Company, 1950.

Mandl, Heinz, Nancy L. Stein, and Tom Trabasso, eds. *Learning and Comprehension of Text*. Hillsdale, NJ: Erlbaum, 1984.

Matlin, Margaret W. and Hugh J. Foley. *Sensation and Perception*. Boston: Allyn and Bacon, 1992.

Murch, G.M. "Using Color Effectively: Designing to Human Specifications," *Technical Communication*, 32:4.

Novitz, D. *Pictures and Their Use in Communication*. The Hague: Martinus Nijhoff, 1977.

Pattow, Donald and William Wresh. *Communicating Technical Information: A Guide for the Electronic Age*. Englewood Cliffs, NJ: Prentice-Hall, 1993.

Porter, J.E. "Assessing Readers' Use of Computer Documentation: A Pilot Study," *Technical Communication*, 36:4.

Pribram, K. *Languages of the Brain*. Englewood Cliffs, NJ: Prentice-Hall, 1971.

Pugh, A. "The Development of Silent Reading," *Road to Effective Reading*. W. Latham, ed. London: Ward, Lock, 1975.

Radl, R.W. "Experimental Investigations for Optimal Presentation-Mode and Colours of Symbols on the CRT-Screen," *Ergonomic Aspects of Visual Display Terminals*. London: Taylor & Francis, 1980.

Rayner, K. "Eye Movements in Reading and Information Processing," *Psychological Bulletin*, 85.

Ruesch, J. and W. Kees. *Nonverbal Communication: Notes On the Visual Perception of Human Relations*. Berkeley, CA: University of California Press, 1956.

Russel, Peter. *The Brain Book*. New York: Plume, 1979.

Smith, F. *Understanding Reading*. New York: Holt, Rinehart, and Winston, 1971.

Spiro, R.J. "Remembering Information from Text: The 'State of Schema' Approach," *Schooling and the Acquisition of Knowledge*. R.J. Spiro, R.C. Anderson, and W.F. Montague, eds. Hillsdale, NJ: Erlbaum, 1976.

Sullivan, P. "Visual Markers for Navigating Instructional Texts," *Journal of Technical Writing and Communication*, 1989, 20:3.

Thibadeau, R., M.A. Just, and P.A. Carpenter. "Real Reading Behavior," *Proceedings of the 18th Annual Meeting of the Association of Computational Linguistics*, 1980.

Tinker, M.A. "Recent Studies of Eye Movements in Reading," *Psychological Bulletin*, 55.

Trummel, F. "Shape Concept: Color Percept...Graphics, Geometry, and Gestalt," *IEEE Transactions on Professional Communication*, 1991, 34:3, pp. 174–179.

White, J.V. *Color for the Electronic Age*. New York: Watson-Guptill Publications, 1990.

Willoughby, M. "Using Color in Technical Information Products," *STC Proceedings*, 1988.

Winn, W. "Color in Document Design," *IEEE Transactions on Professional Communication*, 1991, 34:3, pp. 180–185.

Wong, W. *Principles of Color Design*, New York: Van Nostrand Reinhold, 1987.

Wurman, R.S. *Information Anxiety*. New York: Doubleday, 1989.

_____. *Follow the Yellow Brick Road: Learning to Give, Take, and Use Instructions*. New York: Bantam Books, 1992.

## Notes

1  M. Daneman and P. Carpenter (1980, pp. 450–466). In adults, acoustic encoding supports visual encoding, so our listening abilities influence our reading ability, which is why we often sound out difficult material.

2  P. Russell (1979, p. 194) proposes that left-to-right reading is intrinsically easier, more efficient, and takes greater advantage of our left-right brain capabilities. His argument is our right visual field falls on our left retina, which transmits data to the left side of our brain. The left side of our brain is the verbal side, which processes text more easily than our nonverbal right side. In left-to-right reading, our nonfoveal vision scouts ahead to the right of our foveal vision and sends back previews of the words to come. These previews fall on our left retina, which transmits them to the left side of our brain, which then processes the text.

3  E. Charniak (1972).

4  A. Pugh (1975).

5  I am using a closely behaviorist definition of text as verbal operants that words and symbols control.

6  It necessary, I consider softcopy a subset of online information, though I try not to consider softcopy at all. For the most part, I think it utterly useless and wholly a waste of time on both the technical communicator's and user's part. I think everyone's time is better spent if the technical communicator creates intuitive online information rather than trying to find a way to dump hardcopy information online lock, stock, and barrel.

7  These same Middle Eastern countries find a woman's voice coming out of an electronic apparatus equally offensive.

8  D. Norton and L. Stark coined the term "scanpath."

9  The wavelength of light that humans can see comprises seven colors: violet, indigo, blue, green, yellow, orange, and red. The colors on this wavelength are measured in nanometers. Violet is at the low end of the wavelength, measuring 425 nanometers, while red is at the high end of the wavelength, measuring 650 nanometers.

10  F. Geldard (1972, p. 152).

11  R. Gregory (1987, p. 153).

12  M. Matlin and H. Foley (1992, pp. 230–231).

13  If you distribute information electronically, say on CD-ROM, to enable users to print information onsite, keep in mind that few users have color printers. Remember this also as you design color online information; when users print it out, and they invariably do, most of them use black-and-white printers.

14  R.J. Brockmann (1991, pp. 151–159).

15  W.K. Horton (1991, p. 161). "Overcoming Chromophobia: A Guide to the Confident and Appropriate Use of Color."

16  W.K. Horton (1994, p. 24).

17  W.K. Horton (1994, p. 125).

18  M. Matlin and H. Foley (pp. 235–241).

# CHAPTER SEVEN

# Actions

*Thought is the blossom; language the bud; action the fruit behind it.*

Ralph Waldo Emerson

Sensation and perception, learning, memory, and problem solving eventually culminate in doing something. Whatever this something is—whether it is loading a new operating system, explaining the side effects of a medication to a patient, understanding zero coupons, or balancing a cashier's till at the end of a workday—it is an action. Three things compose an action:

1. Agent—Person performing the action

2. Action structure—Physiological and psychological processes of performing the action

3. Object—Person or object receiving the action

For example, a mosquito buzzes around your ear. You reach up and swat at it. In this simple action, you are the agent; sensing the mosquito, deciding to swat at it, and raising your hand and swatting are the basic action structure; and the mosquito is the object.

In order to create intuitive, highly usable information, you must understand how users build action structures and how they interact with objects in their world. Your information should:

- Center around the agent, that is, your user
- Fully explain each phase of the action structure, including what users need in order to perform the action structure and how long the action structure takes
- Clearly identify how users interact with the object of the action structure and the effect the action structure has on the object

## Building Action Structures

Action structures are physiological and psychological processes we perform when we do things. The routine things we do have reached a point of automaticity; we do not even think about the steps involved in swatting a mosquito, flipping on a light switch, or pulling up our socks. When learning new actions, though, we consciously and sometimes laboriously go through all the phases that compose an action structure. The more unfamiliar or complex the action, the more conscious and laborious the action structure. As we gain expertise, the phases become more and more automatic until we can create exploding pie charts as automatically as scratching an itch.

Everything we do boils down to a basic three-phase action structure:

1. Evaluation—Evaluating our environment
2. Goal—Formulating a goal to change our environment
3. Execution—Performing a series of actions to achieve our goal

Figure 7.1 shows a basic action structure.

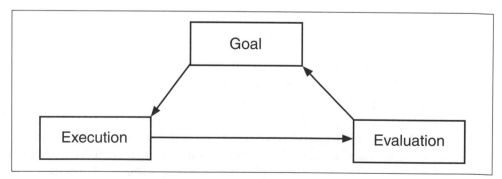

**Figure 7.1**  Basic action structure.

Consider this scenario:

Jan is driving to work on Stanford Street. There is a two-way stop sign at the intersection of Stanford Street and Beaumont Avenue. The basic action structure Jan follows is:

1. She sees the stop sign in relation to where she is on Stanford Street and where she wants to go on Stanford Street.

   This is the evaluation phase.

2. She wants to stop, wait until it is safe to cross the intersection, then cross the intersection.

   This is the goal phase.

3. She puts her foot on the brake and stops the car.

   An embedded action structure starts here:

   A. She takes in sensory input that she is stopped at the stop sign.

   B. She wants to ascertain that there are no cars on Beaumont Avenue approaching the intersection.

   C. She turns her head from side to side to see if there are any cars on Beaumont Avenue approaching the intersection.

4. She puts her foot on the gas and steers her car across the intersection.

   This is the execution phase.

During the evaluation phase, you should help your users evaluate their environment in relation to the goal they are going to attain using your information. For example, your UNIX users want to set a directory's permissions so that everyone has read permission, but only the owner has write and execute permission. Currently, only the owner has read/write/execute permission. Depending on the level of your users, you might have to:

1. Explain the concepts of directory, permission, read, write, and execute.

2. Tell them how to list directory permissions to see the current environment.

3. Explain why they want to change their current environment.

During the goal phase, you should help your users clearly understand their goal and formulate a plan to attain that goal. Continuing with the

UNIX users example, during the goal phase and depending on the level of your users, you might have to:

1. Show them the goal environment and explain how it differs from the current environment.

2. Explain the process of using a set of commands to change the directory permissions.

During the execution phase, you should help your users easily and efficiently perform steps that attain their goal. Again, using the UNIX users example, during the goal phase and depending on the level of your users, you might have to:

1. Explain how to issue the commands that change directory permissions.

2. Remind them to list the directory permissions again to ensure that they changed their environment to their satisfaction.

This last step creates the bridge to the evaluation phase and allows users to evaluate their environment once again to rate the effectiveness of their goal attainment strategy.

We can create an enhanced action structure by breaking down the first two phases into their basic components:

1. Evaluation

   This phase breaks down into:

   A. Taking in sensory input (sensation)

   B. Interpreting that sensory input based on past experience, stored knowledge, and existing concept hierarchies (perception)

   C. Integrate the perception into stored knowledge base by matching it to existing schemata, building new ones, or refining existing ones (learning, memory, and reasoning)

2. Goal

   This phase breaks down into:

   A. Forming an intention to act based on the integrated perception

   B. Designing a series of actions that carry out the intention

Figure 7.2 shows an enhanced action structure (based on D. Norman).[1]

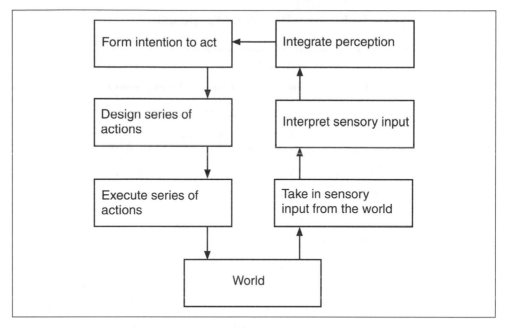

**Figure 7.2** Enhanced action structure.

Based on this enhanced action structure, we can take another look at Jan and the stop sign:

1. Jan takes in the sensory input of a large, red, octagonal sign that says "STOP" in large, white, capital letters. This sign is mounted on a pole on the right side of Stanford Street at the intersection of Stanford Street and Beaumont Avenue.

2. She mentally flips through her traffic-sign concept hierarchy and matches this particular sign to the concept of stop sign, which forms part of her stop-sign schema.

3. Her stored stop-sign schema tells her what the stop sign means; she knows she has to stop and wait until there are no cars crossing the intersection on Beaumont Avenue. Her stored stop-sign schema tells her how to form the intention to stop, design the series of actions that carry out her intention, and execute the series of actions.

4. She forms the intention to stop according to her stop-sign schema.

5. She designs the series of actions that carry out her intention to execute her stop-sign schema:

A. Remove foot from gas pedal.

B. Press brake.

C. Hold steering wheel steady.

D. Wait until there are no cars approaching intersection.

   i. Take in sensory input of being stopped at the stop sign.

   ii. Wait to ascertain whether it is safe to cross the intersection.

   iii. Turn head from side to side to see if there are any cars coming.

E. Remove foot from brake.

F. Press foot on gas pedal.

G. Steer car across intersection.

6. She executes Steps A through G in her stop-sign schema.

7. She takes in the sensory input that she has successfully negotiated the stop sign. This is an implicit validation of the action structure she used.

When we execute action structures, we are trying to change our environment. In this example, Jan changed where she was on Stanford Street.

A typical action structure has many layers of embedded action structures, and these embedded action structures could appear at any phase. What would have happened if Jan had heard a loud noise? Seen a car on Beaumont Avenue approaching the intersection? Seen a cat scurry across the intersection? Gotten midway through the intersection and seen a truck on Beaumont Avenue running the stop sign? Any of these would have created embedded action structures or could have ended the current action structure and begun a new one.

Although action structures appear linear, they are not. We come to action structures at any phase; other action structures branch off from any phase; we initiate action structures that end or delay the current action structure at any phase; action structures loop at any phase, since there is an implicit feedback loop; we form goals and subgoals, intentions and subintentions. Action structures may take a few seconds or a few days.

The phases of action structures are not as discrete as they appear. Action structures do not follow a waterfall pattern where one phase completes and hands off data to the next phase, then the next phase completes and hands off to the next. Action structures are dynamic, often unpredictable, and as simple as turning on a faucet to get a drink of water or as complex as writing algorithms that enable us to communicate with people on the moon.

If the action is one we perform with regularity, we move from a conscious action structure to an automatic one. Depending upon where we are on the user curves, we may come to an action structure with some steps already automated. We also automate different steps in an action structure on different schedules. By the time we reach power-user level for a given action structure, we have pretty much automated the entire action structure.

For some action structures, we remain outside-level users. We either do not perform the action enough to automate it, or we choose for some reason not to automate it. Practice over time moves us up the learning curves and from conscious to automatic action structures.

There are two types of actions in particular that interfere with the course of an action structure:

1. Opportunistic actions

   Opportunistic actions take advantage of circumstance rather than planning and analysis. I call these actions "go-with-the flow" actions.

   Consider this scenario:

   > Leigh is on her way to the grocery store but sees some beautiful gerbera daisies at the flower market. She stops and spends a restful half hour wandering among the buckets of bright flowers and eventually buys a large bunch of gerbera daisies.

   > Leigh had not planned to buy flowers, but took advantage of being near the flower market. Since opportunistic actions take advantage of circumstance, they require less mental effort, and are less inconvenient and more interesting than actions that rely on planning or analysis.[2]

2. Reactionary actions

   Reactionary actions are actions we take in reaction to an external force. I call these actions "best-laid-plans" actions.

   Consider this scenario:

Leigh has parked her car and is crossing the street to the flower market when an elderly gentleman on the corner clutches his chest and falls to the ground. Leigh spends the next half hour comforting the gentleman, calling for an ambulance, and waiting until paramedics arrive.

Leigh had not planned to aid someone in the throes of a heart attack, but external forces beyond her control influenced her actions. Leigh made the decision to react to the external forces, and in doing so, she tacitly agreed to build an action structure that was reactive. Once the emergency has passed, Leigh may or may not choose to continue with the interrupted action structure.

Users encounter and take full advantage of opportunistic and reactionary actions. Often, they run into a problem and turn to your information only when an action structure changes their environment in a way they do not want. Users want to explore, and in fact learn best, when they teach themselves. Take advantage of opportunistic and reactionary actions to:

- Create scenarios that let users carve out their own learning paths.
- Develop optimal troubleshooting information.
- Build navigation and presentation structures that mimic the flow of exploring and reacting.

As important as it is to let users indulge their desire for opportunistic and reactionary actions, it is as important to ensure that they do not get into trouble with these types of actions:

- Point out the pitfalls and dangers with redundantly coded cautions and warnings.
- Build tutorials that do not impact users' production environments.
- Fully explain the consequences of each action before directing users to perform it.
- Point them to recovery and fallback procedures.

## Interacting with Objects

We spend a great deal of our time interacting with objects. The part of an object that we see and interact with is called the system image. Figure 7.3 shows the system images of some common objects.

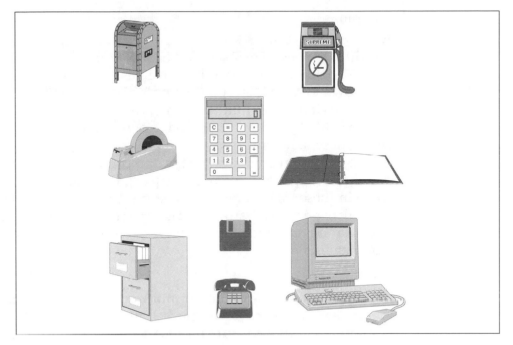

**Figure 7.3** System images of common objects.

An object's system image comprises four components, collectively called its clues, that help us interact with that object. A well-designed object has all four clues, but in reality, many objects have a combination of only some of these crucial components.

1. Affordances

    An object's affordances are its actual and perceived properties that determine what we can do with it and that invite us to interact with that object. A chair's affordance, for example, is its "sitability."

2. Constraints

    An object's constraints are its actual properties that limit what we can do with it. While a chair's affordance is certainly its "sitability," we can also use it to stand on to reach a cookbook on top of the refrigerator. A chair does not have any constraints that prevent our using it as a step stool. Our functional fixedness may prevent our using it as a step stool, but the chair does not have a constraint that does so. We cannot, however, use it as a pot to boil water; it does have constraints that prevent our using it as a pot.

3. Mappings

An object's mappings are its properties that suggest natural relationships between the object and how we can use it successfully. A car's electric window control that we push up to lower the window and down to raise it is a poor mapping. When we think of raising the car's window, we think up; when we think of lowering the car's window, we think down. The design of the control should function along these same lines.

Mappings often involve shape and color; a red, pale yellow, or pale green apple is a natural mapping, because apples naturally come in those three colors. A blue, orange, or plaid apple is not a natural mapping. A sparrow that is larger than a penguin is likewise not a natural mapping, because sparrows are not naturally larger than penguins.

4. Visibility

An object's degree of visibility is the degree to which crucial parts are obvious and convey the correct affordances, constraints, and mappings. How do you turn on and off the calculator and computer in Figure 7.3? There is no obvious power button on these objects. They do not have a high degree of visibility, since being able to power them on is crucial to being able to use them.

Users of your information interact with two levels of system image:

1. System image of noninformation objects such as the objects receiving the action structure and the objects they manipulate to evaluate their environment, formulate their goal, and execute their action structure.

2. System image of information objects such as the hardcopy and online information they consult. Hardcopy and online information have affordances, constraints, mappings, and visibility.

For example, Figure 7.4 shows the log-on screen for eWorld. How would you rate its clues as a help-system graphic?

Some of the things to consider when evaluating the clue of this graphic are:

• Affordances

This is a screen capture of a dynamic object rendered in a static environment. In the product, you enter your eWorld name and password and click Connect (or press Enter). In the information

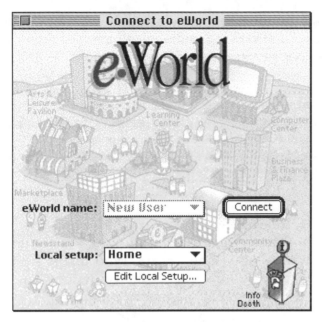

**Figure 7.4** Clues to an information object.

object, this is a static graphic that fraudulently invites users to manipulate it. The perceived and actual properties are not the same. As a graphic in a help system, this object has poor affordances. You can improve the affordances by sizing the graphic so it does not appear as large as the full size of the real log-on screen, reproduce it in grayscale, or add a disclaimer that it is a nonfunctioning reproduction. The optimal affordance would be to program the graphic to accept data, start the program, pass the data to the program, and take the users to the logical next place in the program.

- Constraints

In the product, there are only four things you can do at this screen:

1. Log on
2. Edit local setup
3. Get information
4. Exit

All but number 4 are obvious, and number 4 is obvious to experienced Macintosh users (or users of almost any Graphical User Interface [GUI]).

In the information, you can discuss these four possibilities and none other, so it effectively limits the scope of the information. As such it has good constraints.

- Mappings

  Since this is a screen capture, it is faithful in its dimensions and color (although this book uses only grayscale). It looks exactly like the real log-on screen. While this is a positive, it could be a negative if users try to manipulate this object in the expectation that it accepts data and passes that data to the program.

- Visibility

  Without annotation or explanatory text, the graphic has no visibility. How do users know what the crucial parts are? What the affordances, constraints, and mappings are? With annotation or explanatory text, the graphic has good visibility; without annotation or explanatory text, the graphic has poor visibility.

As you design and develop your information, remember its clues and use the medium, navigation, and presentation to create well-designed information objects with strong affordances, constraints, mappings, and visibility.

In addition to clues, feedback helps us successfully interact with objects. Feedback is any indication of what we have done with an object. Positive feedback indicates that we have successfully used an object. Phone buttons that play different tones when we press them, touch screen buttons that appear to be three-dimensional and look as if we have depressed them after touching them, and crayons that leave a colorful trail across the paper as we scribble all provide positive feedback.

It is important to build feedback into your information. Users lower on the curves need consistent reassurance, and they depend on feedback in the information to reassure them that they are performing correctly. Some ways of building feedback into information are:

- Show process and screen flows
- Illustrate what happens after an action
- Preview an environment change

Negative feedback indicates that we have not successfully used an object. Computers that "boing" when you press an invalid key, a pen that scratches the paper but leaves no ink, and a button that does not depress are examples of negative feedback. Always give users recovery and fallback procedures in the event they receive negative feedback. There are three categories of feedback:

1. Auditory

   Auditory feedback is feedback that we can hear, such as the tones phone buttons play, the reassuring chord when our Macintosh starts, or the adrenaline-producing crack when our Louisville Slugger meets a fastball.

2. Visual

   Visual feedback is feedback that we can see, such as the brilliant trail crayons make, the way pseudo-three-dimensional buttons look depressed, or the red glow of an electric stove's burner coils.

3. Tactile

   Tactile feedback is feedback we can feel, such as the way our keyboard keys lower and raise as we type, the way homemade bread that is ready to come out of the oven springs back at a touch, or the way a sharp pair of scissors opens and closes.

We determine the usefulness of an object by measuring two gulfs, which are the differences between what we want to do with an object and what we can do with it:[3] The more narrow the gulf, the better the object is designed.

1. Gulf of execution

   The gulf of execution is the difference between how we intend to use an object and what that object allows us to do with it. For example, the diskette in Figure 7.3 allows us to put it into the computer only right-side up and right-side in. It only fits in such a way that it is useful; we cannot make a mistake with it. There is no gulf of execution between our intention to store data on the diskette and what the diskette allows us to do with it. This is a well-designed object.

2. Gulf of evaluation

   The gulf of evaluation is the amount of effort we expend trying to figure out how to use an object. The calculator in Figure 7.3 does not have an obvious power button, so there is a wide gulf of evaluation, because we cannot figure out how to turn it on. This is not a well-designed object.

When we cannot use an object successfully—for whatever reason— we tend to blame ourselves. This tendency to blame ourselves when we cannot use objects successfully goes hand-in-hand with two types of helplessness:

1. Learned helplessness

   Learned helplessness occurs when we repeatedly fail at using an object successfully. We begin to think that we are helpless in the face of that object and we "learn" that we cannot use it.

   For example, Doris cannot set the clock on her new VCR; she tries and tries and fails and fails. She finally gives up and is content to live with "12:00" flashing at her for the duration of her relationship with that particular VCR.

2. Taught helplessness

   Taught helplessness occurs when the poor instruction we receive in using one part of an object "teaches" us that we cannot use any part of that object.

   For example, Doris cannot understand the instructions for setting the clock on her new VCR. This "teaches" her that she cannot use this VCR, so she gives up, puts it back in its box, and continues to use her old one.

The more complex the action, the easier it is for us to fall into learned and taught helplessness. Regardless of the reality, we perceive that we are to blame, especially as we watch others use these same objects with no difficulty.

If users cannot perform an action as your information directs them, if they do not get the feedback your information tells them to expect, or if an object malfunctions, they blame themselves. Once they begin this cycle of blame, they fall into learned and taught helplessness, and your information becomes useless.

Test users in their environment to understand where the gulfs occur and build into your information antidotes to the gulfs and the types of helplessness they engender. Understanding the gulfs is especially critical with poorly designed objects. While your information cannot remedy an object's bad system image, you can use your information to enable users to derive optimal performance even out of the most poorly designed object. Developing particularly good user-centered information is vital when objects are badly designed:

- Make the hidden obvious with annotated graphics—schematics, charts, cutaway and exploded diagrams
- Use end-to-end, cross-task problem-solving scenarios that fully exercise the system image
- Leverage users' schemata of other objects that function similarly but may have different system images
- Provide clear, concise troubleshooting information
- Point to recovery or fallback procedures
- Use redundantly coded cautions and warnings

## Summary

Ultimately, users turn to your information because they want to do something. The something they want to do is an action. Three things compose an action: agent, action structure, and object.

Action structures are physiological and psychological processes we perform when we do things. The routine things we do have reached a point of automaticity; we do not even think about the steps involved in them. When learning new actions, though, we consciously and sometimes laboriously go through all the phases that compose an action structure. The more unfamiliar or complex the action, the more conscious and laborious the action structure. As we gain expertise, the phases become more and more automatic.

A basic action structure has three phases: evaluation, goal, execution. An enhanced action structure has six phases: receiving sensory data, interpreting sensory data, integrating the interpretation, intending to act, designing a series of actions, and executing the series of actions. A typical action structure has many layers of embedded action structures, and these embedded action structures could appear at any phase.

Action structures are not linear. We come to action structures at any phase; other action structures branch off from any phase; we initiate action structures that end or delay the current action structure at any phase. Action structures may loop at any phase, since there is an implicit feedback loop. Making action structures even more circuitous, we form goals and subgoals, intentions and subintentions. Action structures may take a few seconds or a few days.

The phases of action structures are not discrete. Action structures do not follow a waterfall pattern where one phase completes and hands off data to the next phase, then the next phase completes and hands off to the next. Action structures are dynamic and often unpredictable. There are two types of actions in particular that interfere with the course of an action structure: opportunistic actions and reactionary actions.

We spend a great deal of our time interacting with objects. The part of an object that we see and interact with is called the system image. An object's system image comprises four components, collectively called its clues, that help us interact with that object: affordances, constraints, mappings, and visibility.

In addition to clues, feedback helps us successfully interact with objects. Feedback is any indication of what we have done with an object. Positive feedback indicates that we have successfully used an object. Negative feedback indicates that we have not successfully used an object. There are three categories of feedback: auditory, visual, and tactile. We determine the usefulness of an object by measuring two gulfs: the gulf of execution and the gulf of evaluation.

When we cannot use an object successfully, we blame ourselves. Two kinds of helplessness enable this self-blame: learned helplessness and taught helplessness. The more complex the action, the easier it is for us to fall into learned and taught helplessness.

## Further Reading

Caplan, R. *By Design: Why There are no Locks on the Bathroom Doors in Hotel Louis XIV and Other Object Lessons.* New York: St. Martin's Press, 1982.

Forty, A. *Objects of Desire: Design and Society from Wedgewood to IBM.* New York: Pantheon Books, 1981.

Greenbaum, J. and M. Kyng. *Design at Work.* Hillsdale, NJ: Erlbaum, 1991.

Hollan, J., E. Hutchins, and D. Norman. *User Centered System Design: New Perspectives on Human-Computer Interaction.* Hillsdale, NJ: Erlbaum, 1986.

Miller, G.A. et al. *Plans and the Structure of Behavior.* New York: Holt, Rinehart & Winston, 1960.

Miyake, N. "Constructive Interaction," *Cognitive Science* 10.

Norman, D. A. *The Psychology of Everyday Things.* (Later edition renamed to the *Design of Everyday Things*) New York: Basic Books, Inc., 1988.

Papanek, V. and J. Hessessey. *How Things Don't Work.* New York: Pantheon Books, 1977.

Reason, J.T. and K. Mycieslka. "Actions Not as Planned," *Aspects of Consciousness*. G. Underwood and R. Steven, eds. London: Academic Press, 1979.

Schank, R.C. and R.P. Abelson. *Scripts, Plans, Goals, and Understanding*. Hillsdale, NJ: Erlbaum, 1977.

Shaw, R.E. and J. Bransford, eds. *Perceiving, Acting, and Knowing*. Hillsdale, NJ: Erlbaum, 1977.

## Notes

1  D. Norman (1988, p. 48) identifies these seven steps in an action structure: forming the goal, forming the intention, specifying the action, executing the action, perceiving the state of the world, interpreting the state of the world, and evaluating the outcome.

2  D. Norman (1988, p. 49).

3  J. Hollan, E. Hutchins, and D. Norman. (1986).

# CHAPTER EIGHT

# User Partnerships

*Food without wine is a corpse; wine without food is a ghost; united and well matched they are as body and soul, living partners.*

Andre Simon

Building user partnerships is the bridge between human factors theory and human factors application in technical communication. It is through building partnerships with your users that you test your understanding of their cognitive processes of sensation and perception, learning, memory, problem solving, accessing information, and acting. And it is in building partnerships with you that your users teach you about their cognitive processes and help you understand and meet their needs and expectations.

It is impossible to create user-centered information without having an ongoing, dynamic relationship with users. The biggest problem technical communicators face is not in the areas of tools, technology, or source material; it is in the area of active partnership with their users. Often, sales, marketing, support, field personnel, and developers have access to users, whereas technical communicators do not. Technical communicators frequently find themselves writing in a vacuum, hoping they are providing easy-to-use, intuitive, transparent information for users but never really knowing.

The first thing technical communicators learn is "Know Thy Audience," but rarely do they learn how to create opportunities to do so. Too often, technical communicators accept second- or third-hand information about their users. This chapter looks at ways you can build first-generation technical communicator–user partnerships. These partnerships enable you to create robust user profiles that serve as blueprints of user psychology. You use these blueprints as foundations for your choice of medium, and your design and development of navigation, presentation, and content. Ideally, you would use this chapter as an integrated approach to building partnerships with your users. The reality rarely matches the ideal, however, and you may find that some components of this approach work in your environment and some do not (or cannot for various reasons such as budgets, deadlines, and unresponsive management).

## Connecting with Users

Consider the following:

- In a software house where I worked for several years, technical communicators might have eliminated 63 percent of the customer support calls if they had had access to users while designing and developing the information. Sixty-three percent of the time, the call involved information that was in the manual or online information, but the user either could not find it or did not recognize it. Ninety percent of those information-related calls were about installation and configuration of new or upgraded software.
- R. Bailey indicates that information development impacts 30 percent of human error in computer systems.[1]
- J. Sugarman, president of a mail-order firm specializing in high-tech items, says, "Very often, items with the highest rate of return are those where the customers are frustrated with the instructions."[2]
- Coleco lost $35 million in the fourth quarter of 1983 with its Adam computer. Coleco blamed the financial disaster on "manuals which [sic] did not offer the first-time user adequate assistance."[3]

In each of these instances, if technical communicators had been in active partnership with their users, the information would have been better, the users happier, and the companies richer. These are compelling financial arguments for technical communicator–user cooperation that you can use to help management see the wisdom of these crucial partnerships.

When beginning a new project, locating users who are willing to be design partners should be one of the first things you do as a technical communicator. Some ways you can connect with users are:

- Marketing-test groups

  Cultivate relationships with the marketing folks and get to know the people they use to test the market. Get copies of any marketing literature that your organization has distributed. Good marketing material presents a product as a market-driven solution. You can present these same solutions in your information (as examples or problem-solving scenarios, for example). This affords consistency with the market material and a thread of familiarity that users can trace through all communication—marketing or technical.

- Sales personnel

  Form alliances with sales personnel and ask for personal interaction with some of their contacts. Get copies of any sales literature that your organization has distributed. Salespeople directly support the bottom line; learn what they are telling users to make the sale. Use those same points in your information (as examples or problem-solving scenarios, for example).

- Field personnel

  The field personnel often know the users better than anyone. They usually spend more time with those users who are "in the trenches" with the product. Users with the most problems usually have the most to say about what they need in information, and they are not shy about voicing these needs to the people in the field.

- Customer-support representatives

  When users have problems, they call customer support. Sit in on customer-support calls and get to know the customers who call in and the types of problems they are having.

- Customer advisory councils

  Many organizations have CACs (customer advisory councils), whose members are prerelease or early customers (but often not users) who are willing to advise developers of their needs and to evaluate prototypes. Involve these people at the earliest stages of information design. If your corporation does not have CACs, talk to management about starting them.

- User groups

  Become a regular member of user groups who use your product. These people are all "in the trenches" users of the product and often have shortcuts and workarounds that you would never find. If your corporation does not have user groups, talk to management about starting them.

- Focus groups

  Attend as many focus groups as you can to get an idea of the areas your organization is concentrating on now and for future development. Bring the information-development perspective to these meetings, and question everyone you can about their needs and expectations in information.

- Former alpha, beta, and usability test subjects

  Feedback from alpha, beta, and traditional end-of-cycle usability testing is usually too late to help you develop current information. At best, you build a stockpile of information to include in the next version of a piece of information. However, contact with these test subjects provides users who have a vested interest in easy-to-use, intuitive, transparent information, and they usually are eager to join your brainstorming, mind mapping, and storyboarding sessions. These users often agree to review drafts and test information prototypes.

- Established customer base

  Excellent sources to help you determine your established customer base are: sales, marketing, field, and customer-support personnel; returned questionnaires, product evaluation cards, and registration materials; and trade-show attendees. Modify your customer response cards to include a checkbox users can mark if they are willing to:

  - Participate in information brainstorming, mind mapping, and storyboarding sessions
  - Review drafts
  - Test information prototypes
  - Participate in early, iterative usability testing
  - Allow you to conduct site visits

These sources provide a pool of diverse users you can involve as partners in your information design and development.

## Involving Users in Information Design and Development

The user-involvement portion of your work is where your understanding of human factors theory becomes important. Information rooted in human factors theory concentrates on the psychological and physiological needs and expectations of users. Approach the design and development of your information from the solutions-provider perspective. Your users want to solve a problem, and they turn to your information to help them do it.

Once you connect with users who are willing to become information-design partners, involve them in person, by phone, by videoconferencing, by e-mail, by snail mail, or by smoke signals, if necessary in:

- Site visits
- Competitive benchmarking
- Brainstorming
- Mind mapping
- Storyboarding
- Paperwalks
- Draft and Prototype Reviews
- Usability testing

You are probably already familiar with these tools as information-development tools, but they are also means by which you can build user partnerships, and they enable you to create truly user-centered information. You can combine the use of these tools into a systematic human factors approach to building user partnerships such as Figure 8.1 shows. Or, you can use these tools individually. The ideal is to use them as a systematic approach; the reality of the contemporary workplace is that you use them when and where you can.

### Site Visits

Site visits are a great way to strengthen your commitment to user partnerships. They allow your users to play host to you, enable you to see your users' true working conditions, and give you some insight into the formal and informal organization in which your users work. You come away with knowledge of your users' physical and psychological environment.

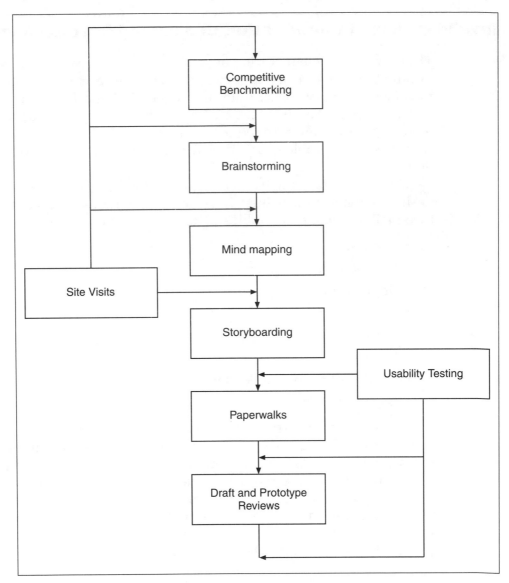

**Figure 8.1** Systematic human factors approach to building user partnerships.

Often, management balks at site visits, which can be costly and can also interrupt your users' workday. Management also worries that most technical communicators are not trained to be corporate representatives. Obviously, remote site visits are more expensive than local site visits. If you are lucky enough to live close to some of your user community, you can take advantage of economical site visits. The more insight you have into both how your users work in their daily environment and what the physical and psychological challenges of that environment are, the better your information meets the needs and expectations of your users. And the better your information meets those needs and expectations, the happier your users are and the richer your company is in dollars and goodwill.

Site visits are politically sensitive issues. They are not sight-seeing junkets for technical communicators. They are professional opportunities for you to gather invaluable facts and impressions. Some guidelines to help you conduct successful site visits are:

- Conduct site visits as formal meetings that have approval from your management and your users' site management.

- Research your corporation's legal liabilities regarding transportation to and from site visits as well as their liability for your actions during the site visit. Part of the approval should be concurrence from your legal department.

- Make all arrangements through a liaison at your site and your users' site. Let these liaisons handle all site visit-related communications.

- Limit the number of people participating in a site visit.

- Limit the number and duration of site visits.

- Limit the focus of your site visit. You cannot see everything that impacts your users in one site visit. Select a well-defined area to investigate and prepare specific questions relating to that area.

- Remember that you are an official representative of your organization.

- Respect the people who have to "work through" your site visit and do not do anything that is disruptive to the normal work flow.

- Ask ahead of time whether video cameras or tape recorders would intimidate anyone.

- Respect the site's mores. If everyone wears suits, do not show up in jeans.

- Honor the site's security requirements.

- Do a post-visit reality check with the users you observed. Hold a conference call and share the facts and impressions you gathered with the users at the site.

## Competitive Benchmarking

"Competitive benchmarking is the continuous process of measuring our products, services, and practices against our toughest competitors or those companies renowned as industry leaders," says D. Kerns of Xerox Corporation.[4] Involve your users in competitive benchmarking of your competition's information. Let your users tell you what works and what does not work in the competition's information. You can learn from the competition's failures and successes.

Competitive benchmarking includes examining the following aspects of information:

- Medium
- Navigational infrastructure
- Presentation
- Organization
- Subtext
- Production
- Production costs
- Distribution
- Support and maintenance

There are several techniques you can use to arrive at a list of competitors you would like to benchmark:

- Ask your users which information they like and why.
- Use professional organizations and journals to acquire information about the competition.
- Question new employees who have worked for the competition.
- Contact the competition.

Figure 8.2 shows the competitive benchmarking process that you can use in partnership with your users.

## Brainstorming and Mind Mapping

Brainstorming and mind mapping are group problem-solving sessions. Brainstorming is a verbal free-for-all during which someone (the scribe) writes down every idea anyone throws out. Nothing is forbidden in brainstorming. The goal is to get as many ideas on paper as possible. The

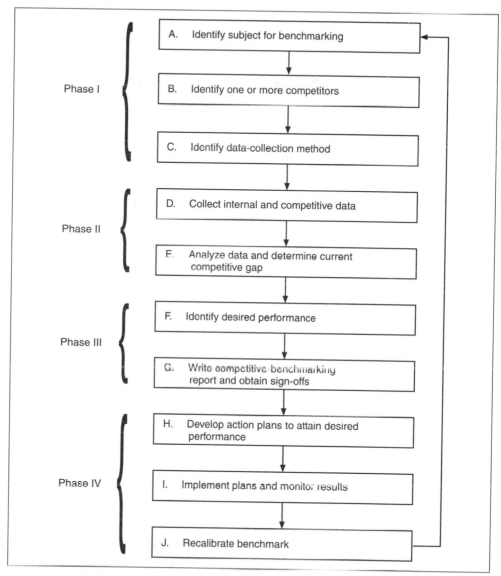

**Figure 8.2** Competitive benchmarking phases.

only rule is that everything is valid. Figure 8.3 shows what a scribe's brainstorming sheet might look like for making a cup of coffee.

It is a good idea to start brainstorming sessions with something fun to get the creative juices flowing. For example, what would chairs look like if our knees bent the other way? I have also used games such as

---

### Making a Cup of Coffee

| | |
|---|---|
| coffee maker | measure coffee |
| water | measure water |
| pot | put filter in basket |
| electricity | put basket in coffee maker |
| pot is hot | put water in coffee maker |
| cup | turn on coffee maker |
| filter | put pot on burner |
| coffee grinder | robbing the pot |
| decaf | coffee beans or ground coffee |
| sugar | spoon |
| cream | measuring spoon |
| | using timer |

---

**Figure 8.3** Brainstorming sheet.

Mother May I? and Simon Says to loosen people up, get them in a team frame of mind, and get them thinking with the creative sides of their brains. Some sort of play is a good way to set the stage for a successful brainstorming session.[5]

Mind mapping is the second stage of brainstorming. It is the phase of combining ideas, identifying and eliminating redundancies, classifying hierarchies and heterarchies, and throwing away ideas that do not fit. Figure 8.4 shows a mind map of the brainstorming sheet from Figure 8.3.

In this mind map, participants have grouped topics into three main categories: prerequisites, procedure, and warnings. They have numbered the procedural steps and done away with some topics altogether.

During brainstorming and mind mapping, people's ideas reflect their perceptions, perceptual sets, concepts, and schemata. You get a peek into their associative memory network and into whether they are right or left brain dominant. Their ideas help you get a bead on where they fit on the user curves and some insight into their motivations and approaches to

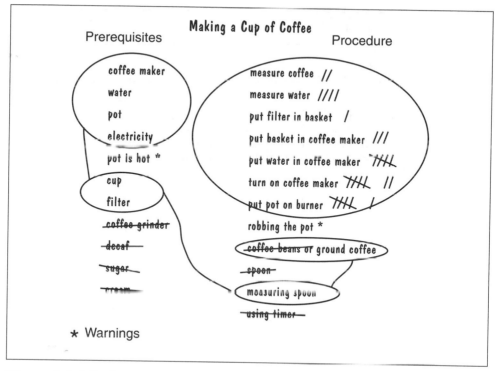

**Figure 8.4**  Mind map.

problem solving. Brainstorming and mind mapping reveal what problems users want to solve and give you an idea of the tasks they need to perform in their daily environment.

## Storyboarding

Storyboarding is the phase in which you use the idea-centered mind map to map out your information both logically and physically. A storyboard is a visual blueprint of information content and layout. You can storyboard one information module at a time or an entire documentation set, including hardcopy and online information. Figure 8.5 shows a sample storyboard for popping corn.

I advocate using storyboards instead of outlines. Outlines are flat, nondynamic, hierarchical structures that do not reflect the ways users access information. Storyboards force you to take adequate planning time up front, design your information and graphics (including white space), build your navigation and presentation infrastructures, and design an

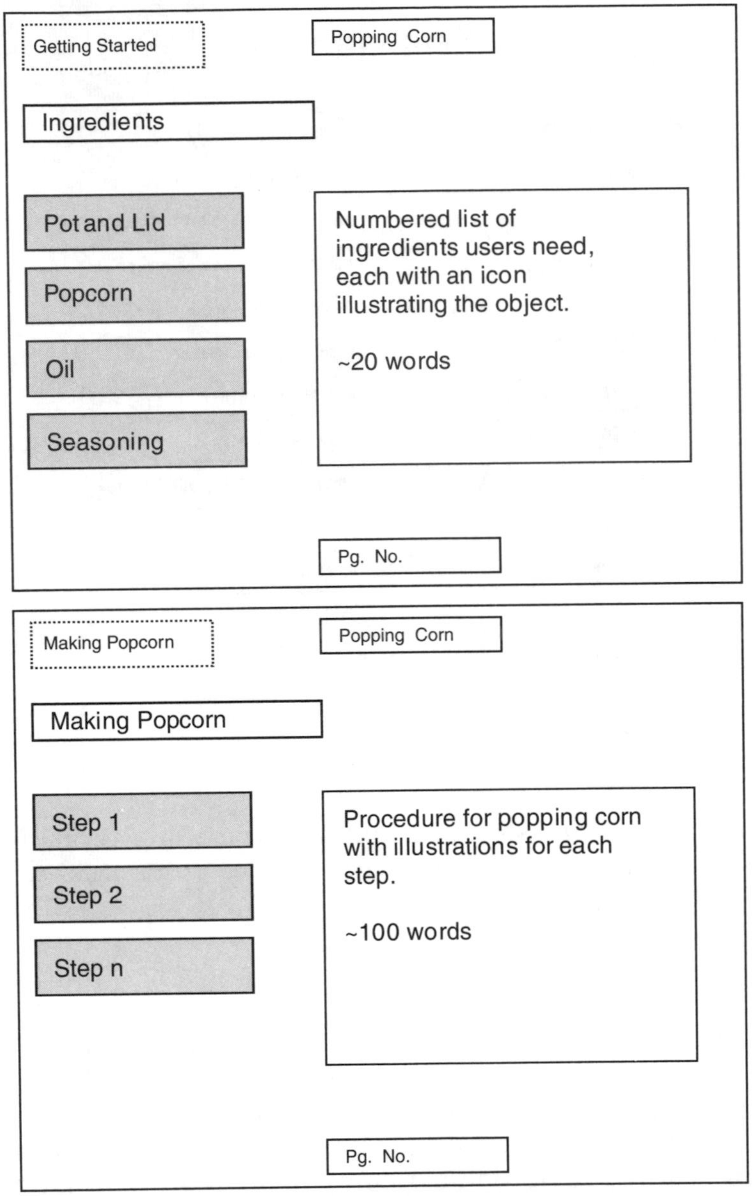

| Getting Started | Popping Corn |
|---|---|
| **Ingredients** | |
| Pot and Lid | Numbered list of ingredients users need, each with an icon illustrating the object. |
| Popcorn | |
| Oil | ~20 words |
| Seasoning | |
| | Pg. No. |

| Making Popcorn | Popping Corn |
|---|---|
| **Making Popcorn** | |
| Step 1 | Procedure for popping corn with illustrations for each step. |
| Step 2 | |
| Step n | ~100 words |
| | Pg. No. |

**Figure 8.5** Storyboard.

intuitive information flow. Outlines are especially useless in designing online information; storyboards are much better suited to the nonlinear, random access world of online information.

Your storyboards should:

- Force preparation and discipline by enforcing up-front planning, preparation, and design
- Ease ownership and editorial problems of multi-writer documentation
- Enable stand-alone information modules
- Help pinpoint missing information and weak transitions
- Show where information flow breaks down
- Promote consistency
- Create a paper trail that technical communicators, management, and users can sign off at every step
- Engender a "lead-with-graphics" approach
- Result in task-oriented, multi-user documents

Most important, storyboards let users work alongside you to build concrete information navigation and presentation infrastructures. Involving users in storyboarding enables information structures that users can easily and intuitively access. When they are your partners in storyboarding, you gain insight into their learning styles, text and subtext access mechanisms, and problem-solving approaches.

The storyboarding process is essentially a six-step process:

1. Transfer information components and subcomponents from the mind map to the storyboard.
2. Create heads for components and subheads for subcomponents.
3. Write a one-sentence abstract of each component and subcomponent.
4. Identify one or more graphics for every component and subcomponent that lends itself to graphic communication.
5. Paperwalk the storyboard.
6. Get signoffs for the storyboard (technical communicator, management, and user).

Seven guidelines for using storyboards are:

1. Design both content and layout.
2. Design at the most granular subcomponent level.
3. Use iterations of storyboards to move from "sketch stage" to "final stage."

4. Review the storyboard with and get sign off from writers, management, and users at every stage.

5. Change, tweak, and massage the information at the storyboard level.

6. Paperwalk the storyboard.

7. Write according to the storyboard.

## Paperwalks

Paperwalks are the validation of your storyboard. During a paperwalk, you take over a large conference room or rarely used corridor, pin up your storyboards, and walk potential users through the information. Use video taping, tape recording, or note taking to capture everything users say during paperwalks.

During a paperwalk, your goal is to validate the human-factors decisions you have made regarding the medium, navigation, presentation, and content of the information and to ensure that you have taken into account your users':

- Perceptual sets
- Perceptions
- Concepts
- Schemata
- Learning styles
- Place on user curves
- Motivational needs
- Memory processes
- Text-access needs
- Action structures

You can easily tell what works and what does not work during a paperwalk. Pay particular attention to places where users:

- Ask questions
- Seem confused
- Appear hesitant
- Make a wrong navigational turn
- Do not understand the subtext's messages
- Find processing the information difficult

- Do not know how to navigate among information modules
- Become frustrated at the information's pace

## Draft and Prototype Reviews

Drafts of hardcopy information and prototypes of online information[6] are users' first peek at the information as they ultimately will use it. If they have been involved in the brainstorming, mind mapping, storyboarding, and paperwalk, the draft and prototype review should hold few surprises.

Users always want information as soon as possible, sometimes even before they have the product. Users often evaluate a product based on their advance review of the information. Guidelines for user reviews do not differ markedly from peer or internal reviews:

- Select representative users.
- Choose one person per site to be the gatekeeper; this person receives the copy, distributes it, and returns it to you.
- Give users adequate time to review the material; they need more time for new material than they do for reissue material.
- Send a gentle reminder two days before the review material is due back to you. Send another two days after it was due back to you.
- Encourage users to review online information online; it does both you and the information a disservice to print out online information and review it in hardcopy format. This is not the way most users are going to use it most of the time. Ask reviewers of online information either to use a screen capture program that allows them to capture an online panel and annotate it or hold a conference call and have an oral review of the material panel by panel.
- Be sure to use some mechanism such as change bars to denote new material in hardcopy information and asterisks in online information so that reviewers spend their time strictly on new material.
- Encourage dialogue among reviewers and between you and the reviewers. You might want to hold an oral review so reviewers can hear each other's comments.
- Always express gratitude for users' time and input.

Remember that the more feedback you receive and implement from users during the draft and prototype reviews, the happier they will be with the final information. This saves you time and frustration and saves your company money. If you choose not to use reviewers' feedback, be sure to explain to them why you have not incorporated it. Users do not want to spend their time helping you improve the product, only to have you discard their input.

## Usability Testing

Historically, usability testing is when technical communicators and users come together; it is most technical communicators' first brush with human factors. Usability testing traditionally comes near the end of an information cycle. By the time users get involved with testing a product and its information, it is too late to change either one. Human factors is an approach, not a phase of the information cycle. It is an approach that permeates how you think about your users and your information. The human-factors approach to usability testing is an iterative approach that begins with requirements gathering and repeats throughout the information cycle.

When you involve your users as design partners, you create a partnership of ongoing usability testing throughout the information cycle. Both you and your information benefit from systematic, organized, formal usability testing at one or more junctures of the information cycle. There are, then, two types of usability testing: the informal "reality checks" that naturally spring from your partnership with your users and the formal testing methodology, which is a fully documented, statistical evaluation of how well your information meets your users' needs and expectations.

Your first insight into your users' needs and expectations is during site visits. You gain an initial understanding of their environment, daily work habits, and common tasks. Your next insight into user psychology is during brainstorming. The ideas they offer originate in their needs and expectations. How they begin formalizing those needs and expectations with a mind map is your next insight into their psychology. Site visits, brainstorming, and mind mapping allow you to begin your requirements gathering.

As you and your users transfer ideas from a mind map to a storyboard, you gather insight into the chunking, layout, graphics, pace, navigation, subtext, and relationships that your users require. Both you and your users slip into a common rhythm and develop a language of shared metaphors that you translate into the information. The paperwalk confirms the validity of what you have done with the storyboard, and the draft and prototype reviews ensure that users' needs and expectations have not been lost in the transition from storyboard to prose.

Each of these points—brainstorming, mind mapping, storyboarding, paperwalk, and draft and prototype review—is a reality check with users; each is an informal usability test. In partnership with your users, you need to take full advantage of each of these opportunities.

You also need formal usability testing, and you need it early enough in the information cycle to be of use in your finished product. You must build it into your schedule and repeat it as often as you can during your information cycle. Be sure to usability test your hardcopy indexes; these are often overlooked in usability testing, and they are critical to users.

At its skeletal level, an information usability test must test three things:

1. Locating the information

   Users must:

   - Understand what they are looking for
   - Employ an information schema that they either have, create, or modify
   - Employ a search schema that they either have, create, or modify
   - Recognize the information when they find it

2. Understanding the information

   Users must:

   - Understand the medium, navigation, presentation, and content of the information
   - Use their cognitive processes of sensation, perception, learning, memory, and reading

3. Successfully using the information

   Users must:

   - Design and execute one or more appropriate action structures
   - Store new or modified schemata based on the action structures

When you design your usability tests, test at the task level. Do not test the interface or the product functions; test tasks that span the spectrum of interface and functionality.

For example, asking a test subject to archive a copy of FileA under the name FileB on a diskette would be a useful usability test question. Asking a test subject to turn on the computer, issue the cd command to switch to the test directory, issue the ren command to rename FileA to FileB, insert a diskette, issue the copy command to copy FileB to diskette, issue the A: command to switch to the diskette drive, issue the dir command to ensure FileB was copied, issue the C: command to switch back to the C drive, and issue the del command to delete the copy of FileB on the C drive would not be a useful usability test question.

Limit your usability tests to no more than one hour and prepare specific questions for your test subjects. You cannot test everything you want to test in one session, so do not even try. For an accurate test, have a variety of test subjects from all levels of the user curves.

There are several types of usability testing; individual circumstances at your site, your users, and the information itself determine which type or combination of types of usability testing is right for you. Table 8.1 summarizes some types of usability testing and the advantages and disadvantages of each. Keep in mind that these types of usability testing are not mutually exclusive; in fact, you probably want to create a series of test suites that touch on most if not all of these types of testing.

Some issues to consider in determining which type of usability testing to use are:

- Cost

  Usability testing costs dollars, but in the long run, it saves even more dollars, and that is its attraction for management. You can do usability testing on a grand scale, with dedicated laboratories, machines, technical communicators, and audio and video equipment. You can also do it on an economical scale with the technical communicator sitting with a potential user and asking questions and taking notes. And you can do it on a medium scale somewhere between these two options (perhaps a dedicated room without a great deal of expensive equipment). Regardless of the initial monetary outlay, usability testing results in bottom-line savings by:

  - Determining design problems before you release the information
  - Increasing customer satisfaction
  - Reducing the number of calls to customer support
  - Reducing training costs
  - Avoiding possible legal action

**Table 8.1** Types of Usability Testing

| Type | Description | Advantages | Disadvantages |
|------|-------------|------------|---------------|
| Silent User | Video- and audiotape users as they use the information. | You do not have to be present.<br><br>It more closely simulates the real work situation.<br><br>You have a video and audio audit trail. | Equipment is expensive.<br><br>The participant may feel uncomfortable being audio- and/or videotaped.<br><br>You have to spend time reviewing the tapes.<br><br>If the participant runs into a show-stopper problem, the usability testing is over. |
| Structured Interview | Sit with users as they use the information and ask them questions. | It is the least expensive real-time method of doing usability testing.<br><br>There is a great deal of interaction between participant and technical communicator.<br><br>If the participant encounters a show-stopper problem, you can work through it together.<br><br>You can gauge the participant's frustration level and intervene as necessary. | You have to be present during the testing.<br><br>You may inadvertently impart bias to the participant.<br><br>You have only a handwritten audit trail.<br><br>It is not a real-time interview.<br><br>The participant's memory may be faulty. |
| Verbal Protocol | Ask users to think aloud as they use the information while video- and audiotaping them. | You can intervene in the event of a show-stopper problem or if you see the participant's frustration level rising.<br><br>You have an audio and video audit trail. | Many people are unable to perform tasks and think aloud at the same time.<br><br>Participants may feel insecure about thinking aloud, especially when being audio- and videotaped. |

*(continues)*

**Table 8.1** Types of Usability Testing (*Continued*)

| Type | Description | Advantages | Disadvantages |
|---|---|---|---|
| | | You gain insight into the inner workings of the participant's mind. | It is expensive. |
| | | It allows you insight into the various levels of participant-motivation. | |
| | | You have a videotape trail whose highlights you can show to management and developers. | |
| Post-Test Interview | Ask users questions about the information after they have used it. | It is not expensive.<br><br>You have face-to-face interaction with the participant.<br><br>You can prod and poke the participant to provide feelings and details. | You have only a handwritten audit trail.<br><br>It is not a real-time interview.<br><br>You may inadvertently impart bias to the participant.<br><br>You are not present in the event of a show-stopper problem or a high frustration level. |
| Validation Laboratory | There are several possibilities for validation laboratories: dedicated laboratory at your corporate site, shared laboratory at a consultant site, or shared laboratory at a friendly corporate or educational site. | It produces good public relations for your corporation.<br><br>You have the ability to do a large quantity of usability testing.<br><br>You have a videotape trail whose highlights you can show to management and developers. | It is the most expensive method of usability testing.<br><br>You are not present to intervene in the event of a show-stopper problem or a high frustration level. |

- Deadlines

  The information time frame has a great deal to do with which method of usability testing you select. The real-time methods are more time-efficient than the videotape methods, because the ratio for reviewing videotapes is 3:1, that is, it takes three hours to review one hour's worth of videotaped testing, with a gain in usable data of only 10 percent.[7]

  However, most usability testers rely on the video tapes as a backup or a way to show usability-testing highlights to management and developers.

- Acceptable ranges of usability scores

  Before beginning usability testing, you must decide on your performance metrics. You must set up a mechanism to quantify the data you get from usability testing and determine which score range is acceptable to you so that you will be able to analyze numerically the usability scores and decide if indicated changes are significant enough to make. It is important to distinguish between statistical significance and practical significance. Usability testing loses its credibility when you use it to justify statistically significant changes that are not practically significant.

- Audit trails

  It is historically important to have an audit trail of all usability testing. This is an obvious advantage of audio- and videotaping, though a written audit trail is acceptable. You will find that senior management and marketing representatives especially like audit trails, and you will find that you refer to them over and over when maintaining documentation as well as when creating new documentation.

- Availability of appropriate users

  You must maintain the integrity of test subjects. For example, if you are testing entry-level subjects and break at 5 pm on Thursday, when you begin testing on Friday morning, those participants are no longer entry-level subjects. On the other hand, you now have two subjects for the price of one, because the participant who was an entry-level subject on Thursday is a beginning or intermediate-level subject on Friday.

- Number of test subjects

  A statistically valid usability test should have no fewer than ten test subjects. You can, however, learn significant information from a test with fewer than ten test subjects.

- Legal issues

  Some of the legal issues surrounding usability testing are:

    - Consent forms for audio- and videotaping
    - Access to confidential documents
    - Corporate nondisclosure policies

- Hawthorne Effect

  The Hawthorne Effect refers to the fact that test subjects outperform their capabilities by virtue of being test subjects.

- Negative Hawthorne Effect

  Negative Hawthorne Effect refers to the fact that test subjects are nervous, stressed, or shy and do not perform up to their capabilities by virtue of being test subjects.

- Forced-pace versus self-paced results

  Deadlines may dictate that you have to impose a forced-pace on your test subjects. When this happens, remember that the testing was done in a less than optimal environment and judge the results accordingly.

For sources containing a thorough discussion on designing and administering formal usability testing, see the Further Reading section at the end of this chapter.

## Creating User Profiles

The goal of building user partnerships is to give you insight into your users' psychology so that you can design and develop user-centered information. The psychological blueprint you use to create this information is the user profile. Traditionally, technical communicators do not spend enough time developing an effective user profile. The result is information that does not meet the users' needs and expectations. If information does not meet their needs and expectations, users do not use it. If users do not use your information, all of your time and effort is for nothing.

The loudest argument I hear against creating robust user profiles is that it takes too much time. Technical communicators and managers say that deadlines do not permit the luxury of thoroughly profiling users. My answer is that user profiling is not a luxury; it is the foundation of information design and development. If you invest time in user profiles, you design and create human factors-oriented information that meets your users' needs and expectations. This ultimately saves time, effort, money, and frustration. If you do not invest time in user profiles, your information, your users, your corporation, and you suffer the long-term consequences.

Technical information development is not a shot in the dark. Technical communicators must understand the psychology of their users. User profiles give you that understanding. Begin with individual user profiles of target users, then combine that data into a general user community profile.

User profiles should answer the questions that follow. None of these questions has a straightforward black-and-white answer. For all of these issues, your user community has a variety of responses, but you need to know what the averages are, what the two extremes are, and where the bulge in the Bell curve is for your users.

- Schemata

  - Can your information leverage existing schemata?
  - Are existing schemata universal enough that you can abstract references, examples, and problem-solving scenarios?
  - Do you need to help users change existing schemata or build new ones?
  - How open are users to changing or building new schemata?
  - What are the experiences, perceptions, and concepts feeding into users' schemata?
  - Are there special cultural considerations?

- Learning style

  - What are your users' habits that impact the information you are designing and developing?
  - How strong are these habits?

- Do you have to help users change or create new habits?
- How open are your users to changing or creating new habits?
- What negative and positive interference issues do your users have?
- Is the learning goal declarative or procedural?
- Are your users doing, imagining, reasoning, or theorizing learners?

- Place on user curves

  - Where are your users on the technical users curve?
  - Where are your users on Piaget's developmental curve?
  - Where are your users on Erikson's psychosocial curve?

- Place on motivation pyramid

  - Where are your users on the motivation pyramid?
  - Do your users expect to climb the motivation pyramid using the information?

- Feedback needs

  - What are your users' feedback needs?
  - How must these needs evolve over time using the information?

- Problem-solving strategies

  - What existing concepts can your information leverage?
  - Do you have to help users evolve or create new concepts?
  - Do your users use definitional rules or prototypes to form concepts?
  - What existing concept hierarchies can your information leverage?
  - Do you have to teach users new ways of combining concepts?
  - Do your users apply inductive or deductive reasoning to data?
  - What are your users factual, semantic, schematic, and strategic expertise in the problem domain?
  - Do your users use trial and error, hypothesis testing, algorithms, heuristics, or insight to solve problems?

- Obstacles to problem solving

    - What are your users' perceptual sets?

    - What are your users' problem-solving sets?

    - What are your users' confirmation biases?

    - Do your users suffer from functional fixedness?

    - Is negative transfer an issue for your users?

- Reading goal

    - Is your users' reading type declarative or procedural?

    - Do your users want to access information sequentially or randomly?

    - Are your users skimming, scanning, searching, reading for comprehension, or reading for evaluation?

    - How are these reading goals going to change over time using the information?

- Subtext expectations

    - What do your users expect in the way of media, navigation, presentation, structure, graphics, and color?

    - Do your users suffer from color-vision deficiency?

    - Do your users have cultural preconceptions about color and graphics?

Always profile as broad a range of target users as possible. Even if you are writing for a very narrow audience, your users do not fall into neat categories and uniform slots on curves. Most products have a user community that stretches from extreme to extreme with a little of everything in between. After you complete your individual user profiling, you can create a general user profile for your entire user community.

## Summary

It is impossible to create user-centered information without having an ongoing, dynamic relationship with users. It is essential to build user partnerships with your user community. Some contacts for building these partnerships with your users are: marketing test groups; sales personnel; field personnel; customer support representatives; customer advisory councils; user groups; focus groups; alpha, beta, and usability test subjects; and your established customer base.

You can use a systematic human factors approach to building user partnerships; this approach comprises: site visits, competitive benchmarking, brainstorming, mind mapping, storyboarding, paperwalks, draft and prototype reviews, and usability testing. You can also use these components individually if the reality of your workplace situation is that you cannot institute a systematic human factors approach.

The results of each phase of building user partnerships gives you the input to create individual user profiles, which you combine into user community profiles. Individual and community profiles address these issues: schemata, learning style, place on user curves, motivation, feedback needs, problem-solving strategies, obstacles to problem solving, reading goals, and subtext expectations.

## Further Reading

Amada, R.E. "Using Customer Feedback As a Writing Tool," *STC Proceedings*, 1990.

Anderson, A. and G. Mahan. "Usability Testing: What It Is and What It Can Do for Your Documentation," *STC Proceedings*, 1991.

Andriole, S.J. *Storyboard Prototyping: A New Approach to User Requirements Analysis.* Wellesley, MA: Q.E.D. Information Sciences, 1989.

Asahi, T. and H. Miyai. "A Usability Testing Method Employing the 'Trouble Model'," *Proceedings of the Human Factors Society*, 1990.

Atkinson, J.M. "Usability Testing: Online and Under Budget," *STC Proceedings*, 1990.

Barkman, P. "Storyboarding and Writing," *STC Proceedings*, 1982.

Baroudi, J. et al. "An Empirical Study of the Impact of User Involvement on System Usage and Information Satisfaction," *Communications of the ACM*, 29:3, 1986.

Benel, D.C.R. and R.F. Pain. "The Human Factors Usability Laboratory in Product Evaluation," *Proceedings of the Human Factors Society*, 1985.

Benyon, D. et al. *A Guide to Usability: Human Factors in Computing.* J. Preece, ed. Wokingham, England: Addison-Wesley, 1993.

Berger, P.R. and L. Harris. "Using Storyboards to Test Documents," *STC Proceedings*, 1990, 1991.

Bergfeld Mills, C. "Usability Testing: User Reviews," *Technical Communication*, Fourth Quarter, 1985.

Bergfeld Mills, C. et al. "Usability Testing in the Real World," *CHI 86 Proceedings*, 1986.

Bethke, F.J. "Measuring the Usability of Software Manuals," *Technical Communication*, Second Quarter, 1983.

Bias, R.G. and D.J. Mayhew, eds. *Cost-Justifying Usability*. Boston: Academic Press, 1994.

Brockman, R.J. *Writing Better Computer User Documentation: From Paper to Online*. New York: John Wiley & Sons, 1990.

Brown, D. "How to Get Started in Usability Testing," *STC Proceedings*, 1989.

————. "Training Writers in Usability Testing: A Step-by-Step Approach," *STC Proceedings*, 1991.

Burnham, K. "Marketing Usability: How to Sell Usability Testing to Your Company or Clients," *Common Ground*, 2:2, 1992.

Casey, B. "An Information Developer's View of Usability Testing," *STC Proceedings*, 1984.

Chaboya, N.L. and M.A. Bolden. "Usability Testing and You: Improving Your Product for Your Customer," *STC Proceedings*, 1988.

Coe, M.A. "Is Usability Testing Worthwhile?" *STC Proceedings*, 1991.

Cummings, M. And K. Kolesar. "Testing the Product: Usability and Liability," *STC Proceedings*, 1991.

Dieli, M. "A Problem-Solving Approach to Usability Test Planning," *Proceedings International Professional Communication Conference*, 1988.

Dieli, M. et al. "Training for Usability Testing: Giving Writers a Tool They Can Use," *STC Proceedings*, 1991.

Dorazio, P.A. and F.Y. Winsberg. "Usability Testing of Online Information," *STC Proceedings*, 1988.

Dreyfus, H.L. and S.E. Dreyfus. *Mind Over Machine: The Power of Human Intuition and Experience in the Era of the Computer*. New York: The Free Press, 1986.

Dumas, J.S. "On Usability Testing," *Common Ground*, 1:2, 1991.

————. "Stimulating Change Through Usability Testing," *SIGCHI Bulletin*, 1989, pp. 37–42.

Dumas, J.S. and J. C. Redish. *A Practical Guide to Usability Testing*. Norwood, NJ: Ablex, 1993.

Eason, K.D. "Towards the Experimental Study of Usability," *Behavior and Information Technology*, 3:2, 1984.

Ericsson, K.A. and H.A. Simon. *Protocol Analysis: Verbal Reports as Data*. Revised edition. Cambridge, MA: MIT Press, 1993.

Evans, J.P. "Using Visual Techniques to Enhance Usability," *STC Proceedings*, 1993.

Fisher, J.R. and C.E. Wilson. "Starting and Sustaining Usability Activities in a Company," *STC Proceedings*, 1995.

Gillihan, D. And J. Herrin. "Evaluating Product Manuals for Increased Usability," *Technical Communication*, 35:3, 1985.

Gould, J.D. and C. Lewis. "Designing for Usability: Key Principles and What Designers Think," *Communications of the ACM*, 2:3. 1985.

Greenwald, J. "How Does This #%$@! Thing Work?" *Time*, June 18, 1964.

Grice, R. "Considering Product Usability Along with Information Usability," *STC Proceedings*, 1993.

──────. "Get Real! Planning Tasks and Activities for Your Usability Test," *STC Proceedings*, 1995.

Grice, R. and L.S. Ridgway. "A Discussion of Modes and Motives for Usability Evaluation," *IEEE Transactions on Professional Communication*, 1989, pp. 230–237.

──────. Usability and Hypermedia: Toward a Set of Usability Criteria and Measures," *Technical Communication*, 40:3.

Grimball, N. "Using a Validation Laboratory To Create, Test, and Update Computer Documentation," *STC Proceedings*, 1990.

Hasslein, V. "Get In Touch With Your Readers Through Site Visits," *STC Proceedings*, 1990.

Hewett, T.T. and C.T. Meadow. "On Designing for Usability: An Application of Four Key Principles," *CHI 86 Proceedings*, 1986.

Hix, D. *Improving the Human-Computer Interface*. UCLA Course, 1990.

Hubbard, S.E. and M. Willoughby. "Testing Documentation: A Practical Approach," *STC Proceedings*, 1985.

Jacobs, V. "Conducting the Test—Who Does What?" *Proceedings International Professional Communication Conference*, 1987.

Knodel, E.L. "Reading to Decide: Designing for Usability with a Needs, User, and Learnings (NUL) Analysis," *STC Proceedings*, 1995.

Land, R.K., ed. *The Art of Human-Computer Interaction*. Reading, MA: Addison-Wesley, 1990.

Lass, L.W. and W.L. Reed. "Improving Document Quality Through Customer Visits," *STC Proceedings*, 1993.

Lau, B. "Mind Mapping." *Working Woman*, June 1984, pp. 84–85.

Martin J. *Information Engineering*. Vols. 1, 2, and 3. Englewood Cliffs, NJ: Prentice-Hall, 1993.

Mills, C.B. and K.L. Dye. "Usability Testing: Users Reviews," *Technical Communication*, 32:4, 1985.

Murphy, D.J. "Performing Information Requirements Analysis: A View From the Top," *STC Proceedings*, 1995.

Navarro-Boomsliter, M.L. "Usability Testing—Expectations Versus Reality," *STC Proceedings*, 1992.

Neal, A.S. and R. M. Simons. "Playback: A Method for Evaluating the Usability of Software and Its Documentation," *IBM Systems Journal*, 23:1, 1984.

Neilsen, J. "Finding Usability Problems Through Heuristic Evaluation," *Proceedings CHI 92*, 1992.

_____. *Usability Engineering*. Boston: AP Professional, 1993.

Neilsen, J. and R.L. Mack, eds. *Usability Inspection Methods*. New York: John Wiley & Sons, 1994.

Nichols, M.C. et al. "Usability is Everybody's Business," *STC Proceedings*, 1993.

Nisbett, R. and T. Wilson. "Telling More Than We Can Know: Verbal Reports on Mental Processes," *Psychological Review*, 84.

Planeta, L.S. "Major Issues in Usability Testing," *STC Proceedings*, 1992.

Preece, J. and L. Keller, *Human-Computer Interaction: Selected Readings: A Reader*. Hertfordshire, England: Prentice-Hall in association with Open University, 1990.

Ramey, J. "Broadly Applicable Information from Product-Specific Usability Testing," *IEEE Transactions on Professional Communication*, 1986, pp. 113–116.

Redish, J. "Comparing Assessment Techniques," *STC Proceedings*, 1993.

Rosenbaum, S. "Usability Evaluations Versus Usability Testing: When and Why?" *IEEE Transactions on Professional Communication*, 1989, pp. 210–216.

Rubens, P. et al. "A Hypertext Prototype: From Design, Through Code, To Usability Testing," *STC Proceedings*, 1990.

Rubin, J. *Handbook of Usability Testing*. New York: John Wiley & Sons, 1994.

Scanlon, T. and A. Flanders. "You Want to Do What? Convincing Your Management to Support Usability Studies," *STC Proceedings*, 1993.

Schell, D.A. "Overview of a Typical Usability Test," *IEEE Transactions on Professional Communication*, 1987, pp. 117–125.

_____. "Testing Online and Print User Documentation," *IEEE Transactions on Professional Communication*, 29:4, 1986.

_____. "User Friendly Documentation: What Writers Need to Know About Usability Testing, *IEEE Transactions on Professional Communication*, 1986, pp. 117–120.

Schneiderman, B. *Designing the User Interface: Strategies for Effective Human-Computer Interaction*. Reading, MA: Addison-Wesley, 1987.

Schriver, K.A. "Plain Language Through Protocol-Aided Revision," *Plain English Principles and Practice*, E.R. Steinberg, ed. Detroit: Wayne State University Press, 1991.

Skeleton, T.M. "Testing the Usability of Usability Testing," *Technical Communication*, 3, 1992, pp. 343–359.

Stertzbach, L.A. "Rethinking User-Centered Information Development," *STC Proceedings*, 1995.

Stovall, J.C. and J.R. Fisher. "Usability Testing with a Vendor," *STC Proceedings*, 1992.

Sutherland, A. and M. Weiss. "A New Look at Audience Analysis," *STC Proceedings*, 1995.

Trapasso, L.S. "Storyboarding and Collaboration," *STC Proceedings*, 1993.

Vogt, H. "Designing the Test—Writing the Scenarios," *Proceedings International Professional Communication Conference*, 1987.

von Oech, R. *A Whack on the Side of the Head: How to Unlock Your Mind for Innovation*. New York: Warner Books, Inc., 1983.

Werner, M.J. "Documentation Testing: Principles for Designing a Sound Experiment," *STC Proceedings*, 1990.

Wharton, C. et al. "Applying Cognitive Walkthroughs to More Complex User Interfaces: Experiences, Issues, and Recommendations," *Proceedings CHI 92*, 1992.

Winsberg, F.Y. "How To Find Out What Your Readers Want When They're Too Busy, You Don't Know Enough, and Your Boss Doesn't Want You To," *STC Proceedings*, 1990.

Xerox Corporation. *Competitive Benchmarking Guide*. Rochester, NY: Xerox Corporation

Zirinsky, M. "Usability Testing of Documentation," *IEEE Transactions on Professional Communication*, 1986.

## Notes

1   R.J. Brockmann (1990, p. 16).

2   J. Greenwald (June 18, 1984, p. 64).

3   J. Greenwald (p. 64).

4   Xerox Corporation (1988, p. 1).

5   R. von Oech's *A Whack on the Side of the Head: How to Unlock Your Mind for Innovation* is an excellent source of creativity-loosening exercises.

6   If you are sending a review copy of a help system, which in the final product is an integral part of the product, and the product is not ready for user review, you can compile the help system as a stand-alone manual or compile it into a dummy product interface.

7   D. Hix (1990).

# CHAPTER NINE

# Choosing a Medium

*The medium is the message—because it is the medium that shapes and controls the search and form of human associations and actions.*

Marshall McLuhan

The first layer of information subtext users encounter is your information's medium. A medium has two components: type and subtype. The type is the gross categorization, that is, whether the medium is hardcopy or online.[1] The subtype is the finer categorization within the type. Some subtypes of hardcopy are reference card, data sheet, spiral-bound 8 ½ x 11-inch report, brochure, and fanfold product insert. Some subtypes of online are online manuals, searchable help topics, pop-up footnotes, and context-sensitive help. Users' needs and expectations should drive the choice of media type and subtype.

Users expect information that gives them what they need and want when they need and want it, in a medium that makes the information most usable. As you build your user partnerships, pay special attention during site visits to the information media they are using and how they are using it. During brainstorming, pay attention to users' complaints or compliments about media. You can also gauge their response to your comments about media. For example, perhaps your organization is thinking about moving its reference material online. During a brainstorming session, mention moving reference material online and gauge users' reactions. You can also see how they follow through with the suggestion during mind mapping. If users let the idea get through storyboarding, you can assume they are going to give the new idea a fighting chance.

On the other hand, if they howl and cry, you need to find out why. Is it merely a resistance to change, or are there substantive issues that design and training would address?

Site visits are an excellent way of gathering input on media type and subtype. For example, consider this scenario:

> Karen works for an electrical contractor and is visiting a construction site, because her boss has had complaints about the instructions for installing a particular switch box. Karen has tested and tested the instructions, so she knows they are technically accurate.

> At the site, she finds that electricians wire this switch box overhead. They use one hand to hold open the box door and one hand to connect the wires. That leaves no hands for holding the instructions. She also finds that construction sites are dirty, damp, and exposed to the elements; the standard-stock reference card gets dirty, gets wet, tears, or blows away.

> The electricians tell her that they do not have a problem with the technical accuracy of the instructions. The medium, however, is another story. She holds an impromptu brainstorming session with the electricians, and they tell her they need a laminated reference card with a reinforced hole at the top so they can tack the reference card to the wall while they wire the switch box.

In this scenario, Karen's decisions about media type and subtype were accurate. However, her execution of the subtype did not meet the users' needs.

Early, iterative usability testing is another good way of gathering input on media type and subtype. For example, consider this scenario:

> Quoc has designed an online operator's manual for a new network-monitoring software. Operators watch a graphical representation of a network with shape and color-coded icons that represent network nodes. The default shape and color representing an OK node state is a green rectangle. When one of these icons turns into a red circle, there is a problem with that node.

> When operators detect a problem node, they double-click the icon to open a problem-determination panel that gives them two codes: the first indicates the problem domain such as communication, stor-

age, or security; and the second indicates the problem type such as communication line down, disk full, or unauthorized entry.

Quoc has a series of tables in the online manual that map the first and second codes. All the operators have to do is open the online manual and look up the code. They can either use the search engine to locate the code or scroll through the tables manually. When Quoc usability tested a prototype of the manual, users liked having the code information online at their fingertips. They liked not having to flip through a hardcopy manual to find the information they needed.

They did not, however, like having to go to a separate piece of information for the codes and then having to either use the search engine or hunt for the codes manually. They wanted to double-click the code on the problem-determination panel and get a pop-up explanation of the code.

Because Quoc tested the design early enough in the development cycle, she was able to ask the code developers to code in help hooks. This way, she could take the code information out of an online manual and put it in context-sensitive help pop-up panels.

In this scenario, Quoc's decision about media type was correct, but her decision about subtype was not. If Quoc had brainstormed, mind mapped, and storyboarded in partnership with her users, they might have told her at an earlier stage what they wanted. Sometimes, though, it is not until users usability test a prototype and see the implementation in action that they realize the choice of media does not meet their needs. This is why iterative usability testing that begins with requirements gathering at initial site visits and continues throughout the information cycle is critical.

Competitive benchmarking is another good means of insight into users' needs and expectations regarding media type and subtype. You can use your competition's successes as blueprints for your own success, while avoiding their failures.

## Media Types

Often, the choice of media is not in your hands, but in the hands of decision-makers higher on the totem pole. Frequently, these decision-makers are not technical communicators and do not make decisions with the best interests of user-centered information at heart. Trends, whims, rush to market, and competition can all be factors in the decision to go online, for example. However, if you are the person who makes the media type decision or influences that decision, here are some questions to research beforehand:

- What media type are users using now?

  The media type users are using now is not necessarily the correct choice for the particular piece of information you are designing, but it does give you some insight into what users are used to. If you are going to change the media to a type users are not familiar with, building effective user partnerships becomes extremely important. Users who feel enfranchised with the information process are more likely to be satisfied users of the information.

  If you make a change in media type, build in some user training time. Users do not like surprises in their information.

  For example, your company has previously provided mutual fund prospectuses exclusively in hardcopy format and now is going to make them available also on the Internet with a goal of eventually eliminating the hardcopy version. Start weaning users away from hardcopy; train them to get the information from the Internet, and involve them in the design and development of the information on the Internet.

- What advantages does this media type have over the other media type?

  There are clear-cut advantages and disadvantages to both types of media as Table 9.1 shows.

  Ideally, when weighing the advantages and disadvantages of media type, you should look at the issue from the users' perspective. What are the advantages and disadvantages to your users? Let them tell you. Realistically, organizations make media type decisions based on their immediate bottom line without taking into account the need to train users to a new media type and the long-term bottom-line impact of user frustration if the training is not adequate.

- Where and how are users going to use the information?

  If, for example, you are designing a gardening manual, most if not all of your users need a hardcopy media type for this type of information. Computers are not yet standard gardening equipment.

**Table 9.1**  Advantages and Disadvantages of Media Types

|  | *Advantages* | *Disadvantages* |
|---|---|---|
| *Hardcopy* | Has a long history so users know what to expect and have strong hardcopy schemata in place | Incurs costly production work |
|  |  | Requires long information development cycles |
|  | Is instantly portable, so users can take it home or on a plane | Is not easy to update in the field |
|  | Does not rely on hardware and software at users' sites |  |
|  | Is the only practical medium for some information |  |
|  | Allows users to annotate information |  |
| *Online* | Is less expensive to produce, distribute, and maintain | Most users do not have online schemata that are as efficient as their hardcopy schemata |
|  | Is instantly accessible |  |
|  | Ensures in-the-field currency | Requires more technically sophisticated technical communicators and users |
|  | Assumes a legitimacy because it is an integral part of the product | Requires specific hardware and software at users' sites |
|  | Enables context-sensitive information | Users must make their own hardcopy versions by printing out the online information |
|  | Takes advantage of search engines for quick information searches | Users are "chained" to the computer in order to view the information unless they print it out, and online information is not structured for optimal hardcopy use |

Unless your users are large landscape companies, they do not have even a palm-top computer among their trowels, clippers, and fertilizer.

If your users are in the field and do not have access to a computer, obviously hardcopy is the only practical media type. If your users either work at a computer or have access to a computer, online becomes an option.

If your users' work is computer-intensive, they probably welcome the availability of online information and are glad to say good-bye to the days of hunting for the manual then balancing it on their lap.

- What are users telling you they want?

Listen to what your users tell you. Sometimes, they are explicit about the media type they want. Sometimes, their needs regarding media type are more implicit.

For example, if they are having trouble finding information, they may be having a problem with more than just the organization of the information. Moving to online allows users to do key word searches. This might solve their problem with finding information. Or, if users are asking for more realistic applications in a tutorial, moving to an interactive online tutorial that allows users to create real-time applications of the information may be the answer.

There is a major paradigm shift when technical communicators choose an online medium: they become interface developers. A product's online information is part of its interface, a critical and widely used part of the interface. Technical communicators must become more "programmer-like." Online information development demands that technical communicators deal with issues such as screen design and response time—areas that once were the exclusive domain of code developers.

## Media Subtypes

Technical communicators make the media subtype decisions more often than they make the media type decisions. Working in close partnership with your users tells you all you need to know about media subtype. For example, consider this scenario:

Michael is documenting a new release of a proprietary language for creating ATM screens. This new release moves from being structured code-based to being object-oriented code-based. His audience is a group of programmers at the R&D site of an international financial corporation.

Michael knows that his audience is not used to working on PCs, using a mouse, or manipulating objects on the screen. They are used to pounding out thousands of lines of code using text editors and compilers at dumb terminals connected to huge mainframes.

His audience is used to hardcopy manuals and softcopy manual pages (man pages).

During brainstorming, Michael sees how attached the programmers are to their man pages. This is a strong schema for them, so strong it has reached the point of automaticity. Michael throws out an idea: what if he designs the PC-based help information like man pages?

The programmers help Michael mind map and storyboard the information in the subtype of online man pages. Michael has a successful project, and the programmers have information that meets their needs and expectations.

In this scenario, Michael leveraged his users' existing schemata, soothed their anxiety over something new, and used positive interference to his advantage. He can still take full advantage of all the "bells and whistles" of PC-based information while maintaining an environment that is familiar and comfortable for his users. Using this guise of familiarity and comfort, the programmers are learning the PC more quickly, easily, and eagerly than they would if forced into a media subtype that they did not trust. In this instance, both the information and the technical communicator enjoy stature among the users.

Keep in mind that subtypes are finer distinctions than media types and information that works well in one subtype does not necessarily work well in another. For example, a command summary and a tutorial could work well in either hardcopy or online media types, whereas a reference card is an appropriate media subtype for a command summary, a tutorial is not.

Here are some questions to research before making the media subtype decision:

- What media subtype schemata do users already have in place?

  It is easier on you and on your users to leverage the schemata they already have. If your users are used to and happy with a HyperCard stack to track their font inventory, for example, there is no need to change the subtype.

On the other hand, if you are moving from another subtype such as a poster to a HyperCard stack, you have to help your users create new schemata. Their level of expertise with the new subtype determines the schemata you have to help them build. If they are Hyper-Card experts, you have to help them understand and use your stack—a relatively easy task. If they have never used a Macintosh, HyperCard, or a relational database, you have a much larger task at hand, and you may want to rethink the wisdom of your plan. Leverage positive interference and transfer as much as possible when you help users build new schemata or change existing ones.

• Is the information itself concept, process, procedure, or reference information?

The type of information itself can help you determine the media subtype. Some information lends itself to several subtypes. Procedures, for example, work well in manuals, reference cards, and online help systems. However, if the procedure is a once-in-the-product-lifetime procedure, you probably do not want to put it in a reference card. And if it is a troubleshooting procedure, you may not want to put it in an online help system that users cannot access when the product is down (unless you provide an alternate means of accessing the online information).

Partnerships with users give you insight into which type of information particular users are looking for. Because most executives are interested in conceptual information, procedural information may be wasted on them as they may not perform procedures. Whereas a high-level overview in brochure format might satisfy your executive users, operators who need the detailed procedures could not get what they need out of such a brochure.

Partnerships with users give you insight into what users' expectations are for each type of information. They may want to do key word searches on reference material, for example, which limits the online subtypes you can use, since search engines currently do not function on some online subtypes, such as pop-up footnotes.

• What is the users' reading goal for the information?

Do your users want to skim, scan, search, read for content, or read for evaluation? Do they want to access the information randomly or sequentially? Some media subtypes lend themselves more easily to one reading goal than to another.

For example, if users want to read for evaluation, chances are they want a hardcopy subtype such as a manual or report. They do not want a HyperCard stack.

- How often do users access the information?

Is the information something users need to look up occasionally, or is it something they need to have in front of them continuously as they perform tasks? An arcane piece of reference material that few users need could survive quite well in an appendix of a reference guide. A list of the rules for naming an object in a particular application is something users need when creating an object. It is a good candidate for context-sensitive help. Beginning-level users can use it until they have learned the rules. Once they know the rules, they will complete the name field and not invoke the context-sensitive help.

- Where are users on the user curves?

Users lower on the user curves need a great deal of conceptual explanation, directed procedures, and feedback. Tutorials—either hardcopy or online—provide all of these things. A brochure does not. Likewise, reference cards are pretty much lost on beginner-level users who are not yet in a position to appreciate the information they contain.

Once again, make the subtype decision from your users' perspective. Involve them as design partners and let them tell you what subtype best meets their needs.

Before you put words on paper or screen, you should map out the media types and subtypes for your information. An information set may contain mixed media types and certainly mixed media subtypes. When working with users to determine media types and subtypes, keep in mind that an information set contains many pieces and kinds of information. Often users suffer from tunnel vision during brainstorming, mind mapping, storyboarding, and usability testing and focus too heavily on just one component in the information set. One of the skills you bring to the user partnership is an ability to see and understand the entire information set and to communicate that vision to your users.

## Converting from Hardcopy to Online Information

There is a pervasive move to deliver information in online formats. For some corporations, this merely means softcopy delivery in a format such as CD-ROM. While I understand that there are some uses for softcopy, I am not a proponent of the format and do not address it as a viable medium for information. This section deals with the hardcopy information you currently have, sometimes called "legacy" information, that you want to redesign and deliver in an online format such as a help system or an online manual.

A truism to which everyone pays lip service, but hardly anyone supports with time, effort, empowerment, and dollars is, "Online information is not hardcopy information made electronic." Technical communicators design, develop, test, think about, and relate to hardcopy differently than they do online information. Users also think about, relate to, and use online information differently than they do hardcopy. There are tremendous psychological adjustments that technical communicators have to make to create online information successfully and that users have to make to use it successfully.

There certainly are some advantages to moving information from hardcopy format to online format:

- It is less expensive to produce, distribute, and maintain.

   There is virtually no production work in online information. The compiling and debugging are integral aspects of its development. No printers, paper, ink, bindings, or covers.

      There are also no huge UPS bills to distribute it. You can distribute tremendous amounts of online information electronically, on diskette, on tape, or on CD-ROM. Help systems are built into the product, so there is no distribution for them at all.

      There is no shelf stock to inventory and maintain. The most current versions are always available online.

- It is easier to keep current in the field.

   All you have to do to update online information is send users a new file. They overwrite their existing one, and they have current information.[2]

- It eliminates the need for change packages and errata sheets.

Technical communicators and users alike can say good-bye to change packages and errata sheets, because all you have to do is send users a new file.

- It virtually eliminates time-consuming production work.

  Technical communicators realize more design, development, and testing time, because there is little if any production time.

- Turnaround time for updates is a fraction of the turnaround time for hardcopy.

  Once again, with little or no production time and being able to distribute a new information file, you can handle updates with lightning speed.

- Users do not have to have a set of manuals at each workstation (some companies charge for manuals, so not having to buy them is quite a savings).

  No more hunting for the manual. Everyone with a workstation has the information at a key or mouse click. Sites can even put the information on a server and let clients point to it, so that each PC does not have to have an information object resident on its hard drive.

- Users do not have to balance an unwieldy manual on their lap or at their desk; online information appears right on their desktop.

- Users do not have to relinquish space to shelves and shelves of manuals.

  Online information affords information on demand right on the users' desktop. Some online environments even support book-marks, giving users the ability to mark and return to specific places in online information.

- Users have the best of both worlds: online information at their fingertips and the ability to print it out should they ever need the hardcopy version.

  Online information does not necessarily mean the end of hardcopy, it just means that if users want a hardcopy version, they must print it themselves. Users can print out the entire online information set, or they can print out just those sections they want.

- Customer sites can run entire manual sets on a server.

A server system administrator can update an information object, and the entire corporation has the most current version of the information.

So with all these wondrous and cost-effective reasons to move hardcopy online, why do users, management, and technical communicators resist it? Because there are also some disadvantages:

- It is new.

Users, management, and technical communicators do not have schemata to help them deal with new experiences. They are faced with building new schemata or changing existing ones, and this is often a frightening prospect.

Two things help people make the psychological leap to accepting new schemata or changing existing schemata: benefits and training. You must posit the change as a beneficial one, and you must provide the training necessary to make it a comfortable one.

- There is no shrink-wrapped security blanket sitting on the bookshelf.

Many users never open the manual but derive great comfort and satisfaction from the fact that it is sitting in all its shrink-wrapped glory on their bookshelf. The manual truly is the last place users go for information. First they try trial and error, then they go to their colleagues, then they consult the manual. For users who are used to hardcopy, that manual on the shelf is a safety net.

They can derive just as much security from online information, but you have to prove that to them. Involving them in user partnerships is a great start.

Once you gain their trust with online information, few, if any, users want to go back to hardcopy.

- It requires a more technically sophisticated creator and user.

The production side of online information is more akin to computer programming than to word processing. You have to use a tagged language and compiler. You have to debug your tagging syntax, and you have to build your information objects.

Users have to understand search engines, controls, and hyperlinking. For users born and bred to hardcopy, this is a daunting task, but once they have mastered online information, most users love it and would not return to hardcopy.

- Users cannot gauge the depth and breadth; there is no "thwack factor"[3] (this can, however, also be an advantage).

Some users derive comfort from a nice, thick manual, though most would just as soon prefer not to have to wade through it. Users have no way of gauging the amount of information when the information is online. This could be either an advantage or a disadvantage. Either way, you can exploit the advantage or obviate the disadvantage by engaging your users as design partners. Then they feel enfranchised with the information and feel they have an emotional ownership stake in it.

- Management does not see and cannot hold a physical object representing the payoff for the time, effort, and money spent developing it.

This is a matter of your training management to gratifications other than hardcopy manuals. Giving presentations showcasing the online information is a good way to give management a preview of what they are paying you for. Have some users present to ooh and aah, and management soon learns the gratification online information can bring.

- Users feel entitled to it as part of the cost of the product.

To some users, a wheelbarrow full of manuals is part and parcel of what they pay for, and if the product arrives without the manuals, they feel shortchanged.

To get beyond this "bang-for-the-buck" mentality, you have to start early in training users to accept online information. Once again, The best way to do this is by involving them as design partners.

- It becomes part of the software product, an integral part of the interface. To technical communicators, this is an advantage; to some programmers and managers, this is a disadvantage.[4]

Online information is a very visible, highly used piece of the product interface. Some old-fashioned programmers and managers see this as a threat. They feel the interface is their exclusive domain. Just as you train your users to online information, you have to train your programmers and managers to online information.

Since everyone has to at least pay lip service to wanting the best product for the users, this is the tack to take to convince corporate dissidents of the benefits of online information. Let the users tell them. If you build strong partnerships with your users, you have all you need to convince the threatened members of your organization. A little tact and diplomacy help, too, of course.

Not one of these disadvantages, however, is a reason not to move to online format. If you take a human-factors approach and keep your users at the center of information development, you and your users can overcome each and every one of these disadvantages.

The key to overcoming these disadvantages is understanding their root causes and effecting psychological changes at that level. One of the greatest challenges in moving hardcopy information online is understanding what the real issues are. Because these issues have to do with expectation, schemata, motivation, learning, memory, perceptual sets, problem-solving strategies, and security, it is often difficult to understand what really is driving the resistance to moving online. Users, technical communicators, and management recite a litany of time, money, training, and tools as reasons not to embrace online information; these are all smokescreens hiding deeper psychological resistances that grow out of the "unknownness" of something new.

The biggest obstacle to moving from hardcopy to online information is the hardcopy baggage technical communicators and users bring to online information. Because they do not know what else to do, technical communicators and users approach online information as if it were hardcopy information. Too often technical communicators try to port their hardcopy skills to the online information and users try to use their hardcopy schemata to access online information. Neither works very well.

Areas of special concern when converting hardcopy information to online information are:

**A screen is not a page.**

A screen is not a page, though some technical communicators and users try to use it as such. Screens are a different medium, size, and appearance. Screens have light behind them and may have several windows open on the same desktop. Users can size screens.

Screens have glare, reflection, and flicker. Many monitors are color and so have color screens. Hyperlinks stand out on screens and draw users' attention to them.

Users do not move among information units on a screen as they do on a page. Whereas it is not possible to become lost on a page, hyperlinking makes it possible to become lost on a screen.

### Book schemata do not apply.

From a very early age, most of us develop book schemata; these schemata have reached the stage of automaticity. Very few of us (at least those of us who were born before Reagan was president) grow up with online information schemata. Accessing online information is more conscious and effortful than accessing hardcopy information.

While many online information units do have an index and a table of contents, they function differently than their hardcopy counterparts. Online indexes and tables of contents are dynamic; one click of a mouse, and a specific topic appears. Online indexes and tables of contents are more specific and have fewer nested layers than hardcopy indexes and tables of contents.

Users do not navigate in a piece of online information by turning pages. They navigate by hyperlinking, scrolling, and keystroking.

Users cannot annotate or dog-ear a screen as they can a page. Some online environments support notes and bookmarks, however.

The organization of online information is not as readily apparent as the organization of hardcopy information. There are no chapters or sections. There are panels and related panels.

Users generally do not become lost among the pages of a book, whereas it is quite possible to become "lost in hyperspace" among the screens of an online information unit.

There is no pagination in online information. Even when users print out online information, it is not paginated.

There are no running headers and footers in online information.

There is no inherent linear progression in online information.

Online information is wholly random access in a way that hardcopy can never achieve.

Online information is not portable. Users are pretty much chained to their computers when accessing online information unless they print it out.

### Online information requires more white space and chunking.

In hardcopy information, the rule of thumb is 25 to 40 percent white space. In online information is it 40 to 60 percent white space.

Users of online information expect the information at their fingertips. Users lower on the user curves tend to use the index, while users higher on the user curves tend to use the search engine to find specific information. Whatever method they use, users want the information to stand out. They do not want to be confronted with screens and screens of text that they have to pick through.

Lists, tables, and graphics as ways of gaining more white space and chunking are especially important in online information.

### Online information enables hyperlinking.

The good news is online information enables hyperlinking. The bad news is online information enables hyperlinking. Too few hyperlinks (text or graphics) and the information does not flow well and the organization fails. Too many hyperlinks and users become sensory adapted to them.

The rule of thumb is four hyperlinks (either text, graphics, or both) per panel (each panel is 25 lines of online text).

Users, especially users lower on the user curves, tend to get lost in the hyperlinking and often are unable to get back to where they started. Hyperlinking lets users explore opportunistic actions more than hardcopy does, and there are more chances for reactionary actions in online information than there are in hardcopy.

Hyperlinking allows you to structure information in a truly random access fashion and take full advantage of our associative memory processes. The imposed linear structure of hardcopy information is not a player at all in the online world.

### Online information enables key word searches.

If you anticipate users' needs correctly, in seconds users can call up specific topics using the search engine. You must anticipate the key words under which your users search for topics and index topics by key words as well as build a robust synonym file into your information object.

Users come to rely on key word searches the higher they move up the user curves.

### Users have less stamina and patience when reading online information.

Conventional wisdom has it that users do not like drilling down more than three layers in online information or scrolling through more than three panels to get the information they seek.

The way you chunk and organize your information is of paramount importance in online information. Most help systems fail not because the information is not available, but because users give up before they can find it. Users should not have to go on safari to find online information. White space, chunking, indexing, hyperlinking, and using a synonym file all facilitate users' ease-of-use in online information.

### Color is "free."

Whereas color is costly in hardcopy information (from two to five times more expensive than black and white), it is virtually free on color monitors. This sometimes leads technical communicators to go "color wild" when converting information from hardcopy to online. The rule of thumb is: no more than six colors on one screen, including the color of the background, text, and hyperlinks.

### Screen captures look real.

In a hardcopy manual, no one assumes that the screen captures are real; users do not try to enter information in a field on a screen capture in a hardcopy manual. Online screen captures look so much like the product interface, however, that users become terribly frustrated because they try to interact with the screen capture as they would the interface itself.

This is not to say you should not use screen captures in online information. You should, but you should make it obvious that they are captures and not the real thing. You can use borders, size, and color to indicate captures.

### You have to design to the smallest amount of screen real estate your users have.

When users receive a unit of hardcopy information, the size of that information is not determined by an apparatus they use to view it. An $8\frac{1}{2} \times 11$-inch page, for example, never changes its size.

If some of your users have 20-inch monitors and some have 14-inch monitors, how do you design the size of your online information panels? As with all technical communication, you design to the lowest common denominator, so you design to the 14-inch monitor.

In addition, users can size help windows as they wish. While you cannot take into account all the variables of users' sizing windows, you must take into account the small screen size your users have.

Screen size impacts mainly tables and graphics. Users should not have to scroll horizontally to see all of a table or graphic. When you develop your online tables and graphics, test them on the small screen your users have.

As you can see, converting from hardcopy to online information is not merely a matter of retagging legacy information or of sending it through a "black box." It is a matter of restructuring it, and most of the time, rewriting it to fit the ways users approach online information. The key to the success of online information is training technical communicators how to create it and users how to use it. And as with any information decision, the users' needs and desires should fuel the conversion to online.

## Summary

The first layer of information subtext users encounter is your information's medium. A medium has two components: type and subtype. Users' needs and expectations should be the driving force behind the choice of media type and subtype. Users expect information that gives them what they need and want when they need and want it in a medium that makes the information most usable.

Answer these questions before choosing a media type: What media type are users using now?, What advantages does this media type have over the other media type?, Where and how are users going to use the information?, and What are users telling you they want?

Answer these questions before choosing a media subtype: What media subtype schemata do users already have in place? Is the information itself concept, process, procedure, or reference information? What is the users' reading goal for the information? How often do users access the information? Where are users on the user curves?

Before you put words on paper or screen, you should map out the media types and subtypes for your information. An information set may contain mixed media types and certainly mixed media subtypes. When working with users to determine media types and subtypes, keep in mind that an information set contains many pieces and kinds of information. Often, users suffer from tunnel vision during brainstorming, mind mapping, storyboarding, and usability testing and focus too heavily on just one component in the information set. One of the skills you bring to the user partnership is an ability to see and understand the entire information set and to communicate that vision to your users.

There is a pervasive move to change hardcopy information into online information, but there are both advantages and disadvantages to each media type. Good online information is not hardcopy information put in a new media type. You must design and develop online information as online information, not as recycled hardcopy.

## Further Reading

Al-Awar, J. et al. "Tutorials for the First-Time Computer User," *IEEE Transactions on Professional Communication*, 1982, pp. 30–37.

Alper, S. "Providing Documentation Over the World Wide Web—Pros and Cons," *STC Proceedings*, 1995.

Alschuler, L. "Hand-Crafted Hypertext: Lessons from the ACM Experiment," *Society of Text, Hypertext, Hypermedia, and the Social Construction of Information*, E. Barrett, ed. Cambridge, MA: MIT Press, 1989.

Arnheim, R. *Visual Thinking*. Berkeley, CA: University of California Press, 1972.

Barber, R.E. and H.C. Lucas. "System Response Time, Operator Productivity and Job Satisfaction," *Communications of the ACM*, 26:11.

Barfield, W. et al. "Information Retrieval with a Printed User's Manual and with Online HyperCard Help," *Technical Communications*, 37:1, 1990.

Bates, M.P. and C. Cooper. "Juggling or Struggling: The Art of Managing Online and Hardcopy Documentation," *STC Proceedings*, 1995.

Berstein, M. "Hypertext: New Challenges and Roles for Technical Communicators," *STC Proceedings*, 1988.

Bevan, N. "Is There an Optimum Speed for Presenting Text on a VDU?" *International Journal of Man-Machine Studies*, 14.

Bloomer, C.M. *Principles of Visual Perception*. New York: Design Press, 1990.

Boggan, S. et al. *Developing Online Help for Windows*. Indianapolis, IN: Sams Publishing, 1993.

Bolt, R. *The Human Interface: Where People and Computers Meet*. Belmont, CA: Lifelong Learning Publications, 1984.

Bond, S.J. and B. F. McLaughlin. "From Handbook to Hypertext: Is it Worth It?" *STC Proceedings*, 1991.

Borestein, N.S. "The Design and Evaluation of On-Line Help Systems," Ph.D. dissertation, Carnegie Mellon University, 1985.

Bork, A. "A Preliminary Taxonomy of Ways of Displaying Text on Screens," *Information Design Journal*, 3:3, 1983.

Bradford, A.N. "A Planning Process for Online Information," *Effective Documentation: What We Have Learned from Research*, S. Doheny-Farina, ed. Cambridge, MA: MIT Press, 1988.

Bradford, A.N. and B. Rubens. "A Survey of Experienced User and Writers of Online Information," *Transactions of the IEEE Professional Communication Society*. New York: IEEE, 1985.

Brockmann, R.J. *Writing Better Computer User Documentation: From Paper to Online*. New York: John Wiley & Sons, 1986.

Brooksbank, P.L. "Rhetorical Analysis of a Quick Reference Aid," *STC Proceedings*, 1993.

Brown, J. and S. Cunningham. *Programming the User Interface: Principles and Examples*, New York: Wiley-Interscience, 1989.

Card, S. et al. "Window-Based Computer Dialogues," *INTERACT 84*, 1984.

_____. *The Psychology of Human-Computer Interaction*. Hillsdale, NJ: Erlbaum, 1983.

Casey, B. "In Search of the Most Amazing Computer Interface," *Transactions of the IEEE Professional Communication Society*. New York: IEEE, 1985.

Chapanis, A. "Words, Words, Words," *Human Factors*, 7, 1965, pp. 1–7.

Christ, R.E. "Review and Analysis of Color Coding Research for Visual Displays, " *Human Factors*, 17:6, 1975, pp. 542-570.

Christie, B., ed. *Human Factors of the User-System Interface: A Report on an ESPRIT Preparatory Study*. Amsterdam: Elsevier Science Publishing Company, 1985.

Cloud, M.R. et al. "Putting Service and Support Documentation Online—Avoiding the Perils and Pitfalls," *STC Proceedings*, 1995.

Cohen, N. et al. "Designing an On-Line Interactive HELP System," *STC Proceedings*, 1989.

Cohill, A.M. and R.C. Williges. "Computer-Augmented Retrieval of HELP Information for Novice Users," *Proceedings of the Human Factors Society*, 1982.

Conklin, J. "Hypertext: An Introduction and Survey," *IEEE Computer*, 20:9, 1987.

Cote, J. et al. "Paper to CD-ROM: A Case Study in Converting from Paper to Online Documentation," *STC Proceedings*, 1995.

Dannenbring, G. "The Effect of Computer Response Time on User Preference and Satisfaction: A Preliminary Investigation," *Behavioral Research Methods and Instrumentation*, 15.

Duffy, T.M. et al. *Online Help: Design and Evaluation*. Norwood, NJ: Ablex, 1992.

Dwyer, B. "Programming for Users: A Bit of Psychology," *Computers and People*, 30.

Evans, J.P. "Issues in Designing, Implementing, and Evaluating a Help System," *STC Proceedings*, 1993.

Fernandes, T. *Global Interface Design: A Guide to Designing International User Interfaces*. Boston: AP Professional, 1995.

Fraser, B.P. and D.A. Lamb. "An Annotated Bibliography on User Interface Design," *SIGCHI Bulletin*, 21:1, 1989.

Frost, T. "Documentation Is Documentation—or Is It? A Writer Looks At Online Documentation," *STC Proceedings*, 1990.

Gale, J. et al. "Balancing Paper and Online: Integrating CD-ROM into Document Libraries," *STC Proceedings*, 1995.

Galitz, W.O. *Handbook of Screen Format Design*. Wellesley, MA: Q.E.D. Information Sciences, Inc., 1982.

Gardiner, M.M. and B. Christie, eds. *Applying Cognitive Psychology to User-Interface Design*. Chichester, England: John Wiley & Sons, 1987.

Gerrie, B. *Online Information Systems: Use and Operating Characteristics, Limitations, and Design Alternatives*. Arlington, VA: Information Resources Press, 1983.

Girill, T.R. et al. "Reading Patterns in Online Documentation: How Transcript Analysis Reflects Text Design, Software Constraints, and User Preferences," *STC Proceedings*, 1987.

Grice, R.A. "Producing and Using Online Information: The Display Screen as an Extension of the Printed Page," *Proceedings of the 1984 IEEE Professional Communication Society Conference*. New York: IEEE, 1984.

_____. "Advice to the Online: Try and Try Again," *STC Proceedings*, 1991.

Haas, C. and J.R. Hayes. *Effects of Display Variables on Reading Tasks: Computer Screen Versus Hardcopy*. Pittsburgh: Carnegie Mellon University, 1985.

Hansen, W.J. et al. "Why an Examination Was Slower On-Line Than on Paper," *International Journal of Man-Machine Studies*, 10.

Hayhoe, G.F. "Online Triple Play: Three Tools for Implementing Multiplatform Online Documents," *STC Proceedings*, 1995.

Heckel, P. *The Elements of Friendly Software Design*. New York: Warner Books, 1982.

Helander, M.G. et al. "An Evaluation of Human Factors Research on Visual Display Terminals in the Workplace," *Human Factors Review*, 1984.

Hicks, M.B. "Choices, Challenges, and Constraints: Putting Documentation on the World Wide Web," *STC Proceedings*, 1995.

Horton, K. and W. Horton, "Converting Documentation to Multimedia," *STC Proceedings*, 1995.

_____. "No Dumpling Allowed: The Right Way to Put Documents Online," *STC Proceedings*, 1995.

Horton, W. "Myths of Online Documentation," *STC Proceedings*, 1988.

_____. *Designing and Writing Online Documentation: Help Files to Hypertext*. New York: John Wiley & Sons, 1990.

Huckle, Barbara. *The Man-Machine Interface: Guidelines for the Design of the End-User/System Conversation*. Carnforth, Lancashire, UK: Savant Research Studies for Savant Institute, 1981.

Humphreys, G. and V. Bruce. *Visual Cognition: Computational, Experimental and Neuropsychological Perspectives*. Hove, UK: Erlbaum, 1989.

Hyman, F.N. and J.R. Price. "Moving Beyond Help," *STC Proceedings*, 1995.

Jedlicka, L.B. et al. "Put Your Documentation Online—From Conception to Delivery," *STC Proceedings*, 1995.

Jensen, S.M. "Online, Paper, or Both?" *STC Proceedings*, 1995.

Jonassen, D.H., ed. *The Technology of Text: Principles for Structuring, Designing and Displaying Text*. Englewood Cliffs, NJ: Educational Technology, 1982.

Jones, P.F. "Four Principles of Man-Computer Dialog," *IEEE Transactions on Professional Communication*, 4, 1978, pp. 197–202.

Jong, S. "Approaching Hyperspeed," *STC Proceedings*, 1990.

Kantowitz, B.H. and R.D. Sorkin. *Human Factors: Understanding People-System Relationships*. New York: John Wiley & Sons, 1983.

Kearsley, G. *Online Help Systems: Design and Implementation*. Norwood, NJ: Ablex, 1988.

Kloiber, D.J. and L. Taylor. "Making the Hypertext Decision: Guidelines for the Information Developer," *STC Proceedings*, 1990.

Knapp, J. "Hypertext: Not Just Another Pretty Interface," *STC Proceedings*, 1991.

Koubek, R. J. and C.G. Janardan. "A Basis for Explaining the Conflicting Results in Performance on CRT and Paper Displays," *Proceedings of the Human Factors Society*, 1985.

Magers, C. "An Experimental Evaluation of On-Line HELP for Non-Programmers," *Proceedings CHI 83*, 1983.

Marr, D. *Vision: A Computational Investigation into the Human Representation and Processing of Visual Information*. New York: Freeman, 1982.

Martin, J. *Design of Man-Computer Dialogues*. Englewood Cliffs, NJ: Prentice-Hall, 1973.

Mayhew, D. J. *Principles and Guidelines in Software User Interface Design*. Englewood Cliffs, NJ: Prentice-Hall, 1992.

McKim, R.H. *Experiences in Visual Thinking*. Monterey, CA: Brooks/Cole Publishing Company, 1972.

Mehlmann, M. *When People Use Computers: An Approach to Developing an Interface*. Englewood Cliffs, NJ: Prentice-Hall, 1981.

Miller, L.H. "A Study in Man-Machine Interaction," *Proceedings of the National Computer Conference*, 46. Montvale, NJ: AFIPS Press, 1977.

Moskel, S. et al. "Proofreading and Comprehension of Text on Screens and Paper," University of Maryland computer science report, June 1984.

Muter, P. and R. Kruk. "Reading of Continuous Text on Video Screens," University of Toronto Department of Psychology, 1983.

Muter, P. et al. "Extended Reading of Continuous Text on Television Screens," *Human Factors*, 24, 1982.

Neilsen, J. "Hypertext II," *SIGCHI Bulletin*, 21:2, 1989.

_____, ed. *Coordinating User Interfaces for Consistency*. Boston: Academic Press, 1989.

_____. "The Matters that Really Matter for Hypertext Usability," *Hypertext 89 Proceedings*. ACM, 1989.

_____. *Multimedia and Hypertext: The Internet and Beyond*. Boston: AP Professional, 1995.

Norman, D.A. "Stages and Levels in Human-Machine Interaction," *International Journal of Man-Machine Studies*, 21.

Pace, B.J. "Color Combinations and Contrast Reversals on Visual Display Units," *Proceedings of the Human Factors Society*, 1984.

Pakin, S.E. and P. Wray. "Designing Screens for People to Use Easily," *Data Management*, July 1982.

Palme, J. "A Human-Computer Interface Encouraging User Growth," *Designing for Human-Computer Communication*, M.E. Sime and M.J. Coombs, eds. London: Academic Press, 1983.

Patterson, D. "Online Documents: Haystacks or Building Blocks," *STC Proceedings*, 1981.

Preece, J. et al. *Human-Computer Interaction*. Wokingham, England: Addison-Wesley, 1994.

Quesenbery, W. "Designing the Interface for an Electronic Document," *STC Proceedings*, 1995.

Radecki, S.L. "Practical Hypermedia: Using Hypertext and Multimedia in the Real World," *STC Proceedings*, 1993.

_____. "Developing Help for OS/2 Applications," *STC Proceedings*, 1993.

Ray, E.J. "Choices, Challenges, and Constraints: World Wide Web-Based Information Delivery," *STC Proceedings*, 1995.

_____. "Choices, Challenges, and Constraints: Documentation and Newsletters Over the World Wide Web," *STC Proceedings*, 1995.

Relles, N. and L.A. Price. "A User Interface for Online Assistance," *Proceedings Fifth International Conference on Software Engineering*, 1981 (available from IEEE).

Relles, N. et al. "A Unified Approach to Online Assistance," *Proceedings AFIPS National Computer Conference*, 50, 1981.

Reynolds, L. "Designing for New Communications Technologies: The Presentation of Computer-Generated Information," *The Future of the Printed Word*, P. Hills, ed. Westport, CT: Greenwood Press, 1980.

Ridgeway, L. "Information Display Screens," *STC Proceedings*, 1983.

Ridgeway, L. and R. Grice. "Advice to the Online: Tried and True," *STC Proceedings*, 1991.

Rockley, A. "Putting Large Documents Online," *STC Proceedings*, 1993.

_____. "Going Online: Making the Right Decisions," *STC Proceedings*, 1995.

Roemer, J.M. and A. Chapanis. "Learning Performance and Attitudes as a Function of the Reading Grade Level of a Computer-Presented Tutorial," *Proceedings Human Factors in Computer Systems*, 1982.

Rubin, M.L., ed. *Documentation Standards and Procedures for Online Systems*. New York: Van Nostrand Reinhold, 1979.

Rubinstein, R. and H. Hersh. *The Human Factor: Designing Computer Systems for People*. Burlington, MA: Digital Press, 1984.

Sandberg-Diment, E. "A Tool Box for On-Screen Tutorials," *New York Times*, September 7, 1986, p. F11.

Santarelli, M. "It's Not the Same Old 'Help' Anymore," *Software News*, April 1984, p. 45.

Schneiderman, B. and G. Kearsley. *Hypertext Hands On: An Introduction to a New Way of Organizing and Accessing Information*. Reading, MA: Addison-Wesley, 1989.

_____. *Designing the User Interface; Strategies for Effective Human-Computer Interaction*. Reading, MA: Addison-Wesley, 1987.

_____. *Software Psychology: Human Factors in Computer and Information Systems*. Boston: Little, Brown and Co., 1980.

Schwartz, D.M. "Preparing Text for Online Display," *STC Proceedings*, 1993.

See, E. "Advice to the Online: Tried and Untrue," *STC Proceedings*, 1991.

Shirk, H. "Guidelines for Selecting Hypertext as a Medium for Technical Communication," *STC Proceedings*, 1991.

Smart, K.L. "Moving Documentation Online: Challenges and Opportunities," *STC Proceedings*, 1995.

Thimbleby, H. "User Interface Design," *Fundamentals of Human-Computer Interaction*, A. Monk, ed. London: Academic Press, 1984.

Titta, C.M. and J.E. Johnson, "Seven (Plus or Minus Two) Things to Remember About Producing Online Documentation," *STC Proceedings*, 1993.

Tombaugh, J.W. et al. "Multi-Window Displays for Readers of Lengthy Texts," *International Journal of Man-Machine Studies*, 26, 1987.

_____. "The Effects of VDU Text-Presentation Rate on Reading Comprehension and Reading Speed, *Proceedings CHI 85*, 1985.

Traub, D. "The Potential of Hypermedia," *Microsoft CD-ROM 1989–1990*.

Treisman, A. "Perceptual Grouping and Attention in Visual Search for Features and for Objects," *Journal of Experimental Psychology: Human Perception and Performance*, 8:2.

Tullis, T. "An Evaluation of Alphanumeric, Graphic, and Color Information Displays," *Human Factors*, 23.

Vogt, H.E. "Some Hard Questions About Soft Copy Documentation," *STC Proceedings*, 1990.

Weiss, R.H. "Hypermedia: Is It the Right Choice for Technical Documentation?" *STC Proceedings*, 1991.

Wenger, M.J. "Hypertext and the Challenge of Creating Meaning," *STC Proceedings*, 1991.

Wright, P. and A. Likorish. "Proof-Reading Texts on Screen and Paper," *Behaviour and Information Technology*, 2:3, 1983.

Zetie, C. *Practical User Interface Design*. New York: McGraw-Hill, 1995.

## Notes

1  I have purposely confined myself to information users read; therefore I am not addressing video and audio media types.

2  If your help environment supports bookmarks, be sure to explain to users that their old bookmarks probably will not work with the new information.

3  I once worked with a misguided R&D director who evaluated hardcopy manuals by dropping them on a conference room table. The resulting sound was the "thwack factor." Too loud a thwack factor or too soft a thwack factor, and the director vetoed the manual—without ever having opened it.

4  There is an often repeated disadvantage that opponents of online information like to play as if it were a trump card: Users have to have the product in order to have the information. This is not true. You can create stand-alone online information that users can view and print with commands even if they have not yet purchased the product or the product is down.

# CHAPTER TEN

# Building the Navigational Infrastructure

*I have an existential map. It has 'You are here' written all over it.*

Steven Wright

Your information's navigational infrastructure is the second layer of subtext users encounter. The navigational infrastructure is the skeleton on which you hang your information. It provides the paths users use to move around in your information. Page numbers and hyperlinks are examples of hardcopy and online information navigational cues. Once you have determined the medium for your information, you must build the framework that enables users to get around in your information.

Most users have well-established hardcopy navigational schemata. They come to a unit of hardcopy information fully expecting the table of contents at the front of the book and the index at the end. They have reached automaticity in turning page 6 to get to page 7 and going from Chapter 1 to Chapter 2. The physical nature of hardcopy imposes a familiar, linear progression through the information. Just about all users could tell you that Chapter 8 follows Chapter 7, regardless of whether they have read either chapter and regardless of whether they need to read Chapter 7 before reading Chapter 8. They know the order of chapters, pages, and components, because it is part of their hardcopy navigational schema.

There are built-in navigational clues in hardcopy information that are not present in online information. The physical order of pages, the presence of page numbers, the arrangement of sections and chapters, the conventions of front and back matter—all of these are hardcopy navigational clues that technical communicators and users take for granted.

Online information has different navigational needs than hardcopy information. Because by nature online information must be wholly random-access, stand-alone modules of information, and the hardcopy structural clues of pages, chapters, and front and back matter do not apply. This is especially challenging for technical communicators and users alike, because users still need and expect to be able to easily, quickly, and intuitively navigate among the modules of online information.

In building your navigational infrastructure, you should leverage your users' existing schemata as much as possible. Working with users during storyboarding gives you a great deal of insight into their navigational needs. During paperwalks, pay close attention to how users are navigating through your information. Exploit what is working well for them, and ask them for suggestions on how to correct what is not working well. As always, if you have to help users build new schemata or modify existing ones, do so slowly, layer by layer, always positing the new schemata as beneficial to their problem-solving experience.

## Hardcopy Schemata

With minor cultural variations[1], there is a universal technical communication manual schemata much like the one Figure 10.1 shows.

Of course, you could break down each of the components into even more concepts, and you might add some components like appendixes. Users have a schema for each hardcopy media subtype they have used such as reference cards, brochures, product inserts, and prospectuses. During brainstorming and mind mapping, you can get some insight into users' hardcopy navigational schemata. Both the good experiences they have had as well as the bad become part of their various schemata.

Consider this scenario:

Barbara bought a packet of shipping labels for her ink-jet printer. The labels come with a brochure explaining how to set up a one-column table for printing 2 inch × 4 inch labels in Microsoft Word.

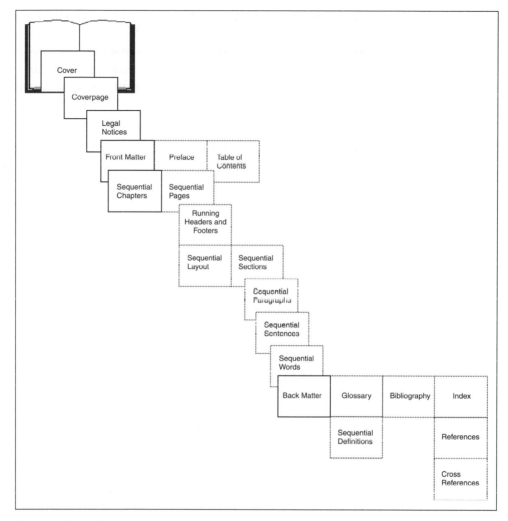

**Figure 10.1** Manual schemata.

The brochure comprises two 8½ inch × 11 inch sheets of paper folded length-wise to achieve eight half-size pages. The outer piece of paper has pages 1, 2, 7, and 8, while the inner piece of paper has pages 3, 4, 5, and 6.

When Barbara pulled the brochure out of the package, she got only the outer piece of paper. Because the two pieces of paper composing the brochure were not stapled together, it was easy to leave one behind in the package.

At first, Barbara thought the one piece of paper was the entire brochure, but the procedure for setting up the table was incomplete. Then she began to look at the page numbers and noticed that pages 3, 4, 5, and 6 were missing. She rooted around in the wastebasket and came up with the label package containing the missing brochure pages.

The navigational infrastructure of this label brochure violated Barbara's brochure schema, which says that pages of a brochure are stapled together. For one staple that costs a fraction of a cent, the label company could have saved Barbara some frustration. What if Barbara had tossed some used tea bags into the wastebasket before realizing that she was missing some brochure pages? How much goodwill would the label company generate by asking her to dig around among the used tea bags to find a piece of paper that should have been stapled to its partner in the first place? This frustrating experience now becomes part of Barbara's brochure schema.

Consider this scenario:

Otto has purchased an automotive guide to help him maintain a vintage Volkswagen Beetle that he has just acquired. In particular, he wants to adjust the valves on his new car. He looks up "valves" in the index and finds an entry for "adjusting," which points him to the entry for "routine maintenance." When he looks up "routine maintenance," he finds an entry for "valves, adjusting," which points him back to "valves."

When Otto wanted to look up something in his automotive guide's index, he hauled out his index schema. Prior to this incident, circular cross-references were not part of his index schema. He modifies his index schema to include particularly bad indexes, a hallmark of which is circular cross-references. Even though you create the most edifyingly clear index for Otto, your index meets with some skepticism, because Otto's frustrating experience with the automotive guide is part of the index schema that Otto uses for all indexes.

The easiest way to leverage users' hardcopy schemata is to imitate all that is good in their schemata and help them modify all that is bad. The distinct advantage to leveraging users hardcopy schemata is that users already know their way around hardcopy. They understand how pages and tables of contents and indexes work. In your partnerships with users, determine what they like about their hardcopy schemata and what they dislike. Imitate what they like and create navigation that helps them modify what they dislike.

For example:

> Gail is updating a quick-start brochure for a new release of her company's morphing software. The layout of the brochure calls for the verso page always to show the resultant screen capture and the recto page always to show the procedure for installing and configuring each component of the software.
>
> The human-factors justification for this layout is that it takes advantage of the image and text processing capabilities of our left and right brain hemispheres. Gail found that her users like the idea of showing the resultant screen captures but feel that by making them smaller and putting them inline, Gail could reduce the page count of the brochure.
>
> The users helped Gail storyboard several pages using the inline graphic approach instead of the recto-verso approach. Gail realized that she could reduce the total number of pages in the brochure by 30 percent. This helps her company, because the brochure becomes less expensive to produce, and it helps her users, because it is what they want. It is also easier for her to develop and maintain.

While Gail had a perfectly good human-factors reason for the recto-verso layout (and one that many corporations use), she found that her users were more concerned with the page count of the brochure than the recto-verso layout. Users are always the final arbiter in terms of what they do. You may have the best navigational infrastructure that human-factors engineers can produce, but if users do not use it, the point is moot.

This is not to say that you always should take what users say as gospel. There are numerous examples of users who say a product is fine in principle, then reject it in fact. This is why you must perform iterative informal and formal usability testing throughout the documentation cycle.

Consider the following:

> Pat is updating a UNIX command reference for a group of programmers who maintain the UNIX kernel at her site. One member of the group wants a permuted index at the front of the manual instead of the table of contents.
>
> Pat can see the advantage of a permuted index instead of a table of contents for this particular manual, since all the table of contents

does is list the command name and page number. She agrees with the programmer that a traditional table of contents is useless for this manual and that a permuted index is a much better idea. Because these are UNIX programmers, they are used to permuted indexes anyway, since much of the UNIX system information contains permuted indexes.

Pat still has to sell the idea to the rest of the programmers, however. At the brainstorming session, the programmer who wants a permuted index brings up the idea, and the other programmers immediately squash it. They do not see the advantages; they are more interested in documenting some new switches than in changing the infrastructure of the manual. So Pat creates a prototype and has the group of programmers review it. She points out the advantages of the permuted index over the table of contents and shows the programmers how it gives them more information in less time. Now they like the idea, and she goes on to replace the table of contents with a permuted index in the final manual.

The key to changing any schemata is to make the change slowly and to explain how the change enhances users' problem-solving abilities. Had Pat just redone the manual without getting the buy-in of the users, she might have had a technically superior manual, but her users would have been unhappy—and the manual would have been worthless.

Some guidelines for leveraging users' hardcopy information schemata are:

- Do not violate the universally accepted hardcopy schema unless you have a compelling reason.

- If you must change the hardcopy schema, introduce the change slowly, posit it as a boon to users' problem-solving experience, always get users' buy-in, and train users in the new schema.

- Do not cut corners when producing hardcopy information if it is at the expense of users' ease-of-use.

- Check and double-check your cross-references.

## Online Information Schemata

While there is a good deal of online information in the world and online environments like the Internet (especially the World Wide Web) are growing prodigiously each day, users do not have the history with online information that they have with hardcopy information. When they exist, their online information schemata are apt to be muddled, incomplete, or very narrowly applicable to specific units of online information. This is due in large part to the fact that there is no established online paradigm that technical communicators adhere to. Can you imagine a technical communicator creating a unit of hardcopy information in which page 17 is after page 84 or the graphic for page 4 is on page 28? While there are acknowledged standards of hardcopy information infrastructure, there are none for online information. Online information in a Windows environment is different from online information in an OS/2 environment, which is different from online information in a Macintosh environment. While the concepts are in the same ballpark (information appears on a screen, there is a search engine and index, and there are hyperlinks), the implementation of them in an online infrastructure is anyone's ball game.[2]

It is no wonder that users cannot create universal online information schemata. And it is no wonder that some users resist online information.

## Online Navigational Components

The ten navigational components that compose a unit of online information are fairly standard:

1. Index
2. Contents
3. Panels
4. Hyperlinks (textual and graphical)
5. Recent feature
6. Bookmark feature
7. Search engine
8. Help options
9. Controls
10. Synonym file

### Index

The index is one of the five primary entry points to the online information infrastructure. It is the first encounter with online information for many users low on the user curves. The more experienced users become, the less they use the index as a navigational tool.

The index is a gateway to individual pieces of information, but not necessarily to all of the pieces of information users need to perform an end-to-end task. For information that is oriented to end-to-end tasks and that may span multiple pieces of information, users turn to online information contents.

Most online information environments do not allow more than three levels of index entries, and some do not allow more than two. Figure 10.2 shows an example of an online information index. This particular sample is part of the help index for Microsoft Word.

## Contents

The contents is one of the five primary entry points to the online information infrastructure. It is a grosser categorization of information than

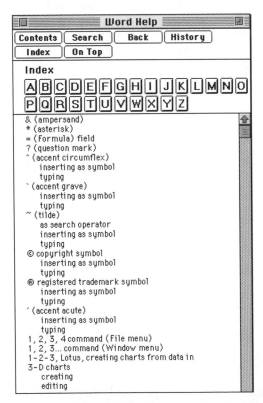

**Figure 10.2**  Online information index.

the index is and is usually task-centered. Low- and middle-level users on the user curves use the contents to gain an overall understanding of the end-to-tend tasks they can perform with the product.

Users traditionally use the contents when they need multiple pieces of information that compose one end-to-end task or when they need an overview of the types of tasks they can perform. When they need a particular piece of information that is not necessarily end-to-end task-oriented, users use either the index or the search engine.

In a tutorial, for example, the contents is an important navigational component.

Figure 10.3 shows an example of an online contents. This particular sample is part of the online help for Quicken.

## Panels

The panels of online information are analogous to hardcopy pages in that they hold the information and display the formatting, layout, and navigational clues. Unlike pages in a unit of hardcopy information, there is nothing binding together the panels in online information. The "glue" that is a natural by-product of the hardcopy environment is a conscious, effortful task for the technical communicator in the online environment.

Figure 10.4 shows an example of some online panels. These particular samples are part of the online help for Quicken.

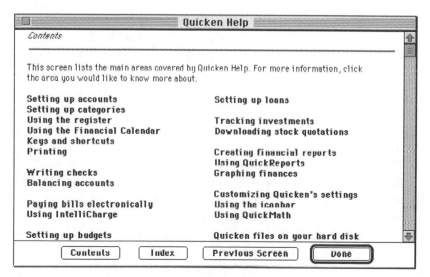

**Figure 10.3** Online information contents.

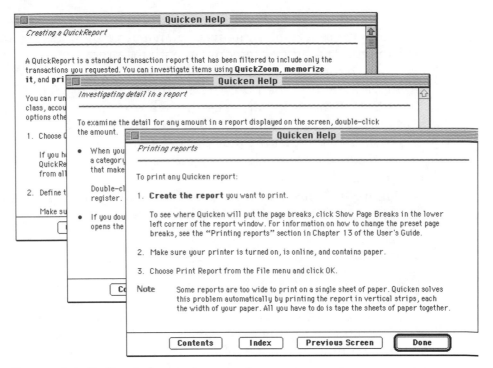

**Figure 10.4** Online information panels.

## Hyperlinks (Textual and Graphical)

My favorite definition of a hyperlink is one a student told me some years ago when I was teaching a course in HyperCard: "It's magic."

While hyperlinks are not magic, the successful creation and use of them sometimes seems like prestidigitation. A hyperlink is merely an entry point to further information. For example, in Figure 10.4, the words "Create the Report" in boldface are a hyperlink. When users click their mouse on these words, a new panel that contains information on creating reports appears.

There are two types of textual hyperlinks (hyperlinks, which bring up another panel that overlays the current panel, and footnotes, which bring up a small pop-up panel that overlays only a portion of the current panel) and one type of graphical hyperlink (also called a hypergraphic).

The hyperlink "Create the Report" in Figure 10.4 is an example of a hyperlink. Figure 10.5 shows an example of a footnote. This particular sample is part of the online information for Microsoft Word. Footnotes usually, but not always, contain definitional information.

**Annotation**

A note or comment an author or reviewer adds to a document. Each annotation has an identifying mark, usually the annotator's initials and a number. Annotations appear in a separate annotation pane; double-click the annotation mark to open the annotation pane and read the comments.

**Figure 10.5**  Footnote.

The advantages to using footnotes are that they do not overlay the online information panel and users do not have to navigate away from their current panel to get further information. The disadvantages are that some footnotes themselves do not support hyperlinks and some search engines do not search footnote text.

Figure 10.6 shows several examples of hypergraphics. When users click their mouse on any one of the graphics on this Home card, a new HyperCard stack containing information about that topic appears. This particular sample is a portion of the Home card for HyperCard.

You can also segment hypergraphics. When you segment hyper-graphics, you divide them into zones, and each zone becomes an individual hyperlink to a different panel. This is particularly helpful in illustrating exploded diagrams and cross-sectional diagrams and in providing more detail or definition about a particular part of a graphic.

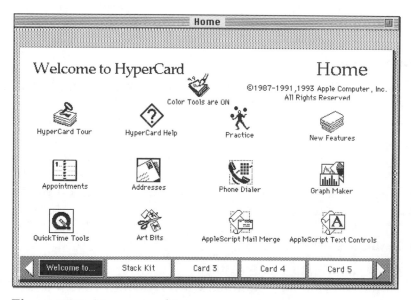

**Figure 10.6**  Hypergraphics.

Since most online information environments support only bitmaps or metafiles, search engines do not search the text in online graphics or hypergraphics.

The navigational danger in hyperlinks is that users become lost in hyperspace. They merrily click their way through panels until they are lost and unable to return to their starting point. Controls such as Next, Previous, and Back are of some help, but often produce unexpected results. Users can always return to the index and retrace their steps to their starting point, but this is cumbersome and time-consuming. The best rescue plan for users who are lost in hyperspace is a Recent feature (also called a History feature) or a Bookmark feature.

Some online information environments do not support Recent and Bookmark features. If you are developing in one of these environments, you have to build in navigational clues that help users when they are lost. One example of a navigational clue you can build in is a Return to Main Panel hypergraphic. Another is a split-screen design that lists the main and related topics as hyperlinks in one of the panels so that users can always navigate back to particular panels.

The challenge in both of these examples is that you must design your main and related topics in such a way as to anticipate how your users navigate among them. Working in close partnership during site visits, brainstorming, mind mapping, storyboarding, paperwalks, prototype reviews, and usability testing can give you insight into how to build this component of your navigational infrastructure.

## Recent Feature

The Recent or History feature is one of the two secondary entry points to the online information. A Recent or History feature gives users a list or map of topics they have already visited. Each topic on the Recent list or map is a hyperlink that takes users back to that particular topic.

Figure 10.7 shows an example of a Recent or History list. This particular sample is part of the online information for Microsoft Windows. All users benefit from a Recent feature, but users lower on the user curves particularly need it.

## Bookmark Feature

The Bookmark feature is the other of the two secondary entry points to the online information. Bookmark features allow users to build lists of

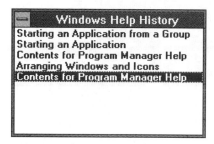

**Figure 10.7** Recent feature.

information topics they visit frequently. Instead of using the index or the search engine, they can select a topic from the Bookmark list. The higher users are on the user curves, the more they use the Bookmark feature.

Figure 10.8 shows an example of a Bookmark feature with a list of three entries. This particular sample is part of the online information for Microsoft Windows.

### Search Engine

The search engine is one of the five primary entry points to the online information. The search engine is a shortcut users can take advantage of to perform key-word searches. The higher users are on the user curves, the more apt they are to use the search engine.

Figure 10.9 shows a typical GUI search-engine panel. This particular sample is part of the help system for Microsoft Word.

In Figure 10.9, the user has entered the key words "file formats," and the application has returned a list of topics that contain that word either in the text, head, or index entry.

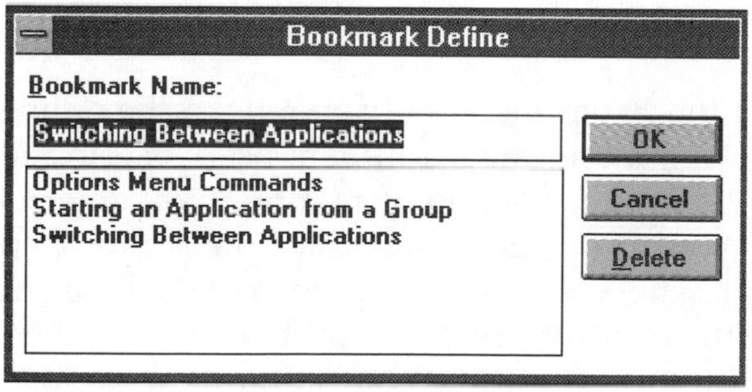

**Figure 10.8** Bookmark feature.

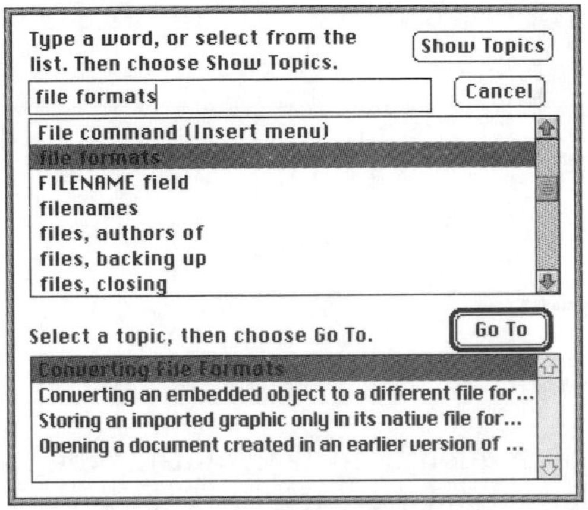

**Figure 10.9** Search engine.

### Help Options

Some environments allow Help buttons, Help pull-down menus, and Help pop-up menus. These buttons and menus are collectively one of the five primary entry points to the online information. Help buttons and pop-up menus are usually context sensitive. For example, if you highlight a particular object and select Help from a pop-up menu, you get help for that particular object.

Help pull-down menus can be either general to the application, in which case its options take you to the information contents and index, or specific to an object, in which case its options take you to information for the object you have highlighted. General-level help is usually available from the highest layer of the interface, while object-level help is usually available from lower layers within the application.

### Controls

Controls are one of the five primary entry points to the online information. Controls are the buttons and scroll bars users employ to navigate through your GUI-based information. Sometimes you determine which controls appear to your users, and sometimes the controls are defaults you cannot alter unless you alter the source code of the help engine itself.

In Figure 10.9, the controls are the scroll bars and the Show Topics, Cancel, and Go To buttons. In Figure 10.3, the controls are the Contents, Index, Previous Screen[3], and Done buttons as well as the panel dismissal box in the upper left corner of the panel.

Other examples of controls in various environments are Search, Print, Next Screen, and Example buttons. Be careful when using Previous Screen and Next Screen controls, as these sometimes produce unexpected results. Be sure to test them frequently and vigorously.

### Synonym File

Synonym files are source files you compile into your online information object file to facilitate keyword searches for users who use the search engine. Synonym files map keyword synonyms to keywords that appear either in the information text, heads, or index entries. Synonym files allow you to anticipate all the variations of keywords under which your users search.

For example, in Figure 10.10, the word "begins" is mapped as a synonym for the word "activate." In this instance, the technical communicator used the word "activate" in the text, heads, and index entries. Users, however, can do keyword searches for the pertinent information using the keyword "begins" instead of "activate."

If you anticipate your users' synonyms correctly, their keyword searches are always successful. If not, they might get either information they really did not want or an error message saying the information could not be found.

Brainstorming and mind mapping are excellent opportunities to capture users' synonyms. You can also prepare lists of key words and ask users to provide synonyms. Be sure to usability test your synonym file early and often with a variety of users at all levels on the user curves.

Figure 10.10 shows part of a sample synonym file coded in Information Presentation Facility (IPF), the tagging language for creating online information in an OS/2 environment.

```
.*****************************************************************************
:isyn root='access'.access accesses accessed accessing
.*****************************************************************************
:isyn root='activate'.activate activates activated activating start starts
started starting begin begins beginning began
.*****************************************************************************
:isyn root='activity'.activity activities
.*****************************************************************************
:isyn root='add'.add adds added adding insert inserts inserted inserting
.*****************************************************************************
```

**Figure 10.10** Synonym file.

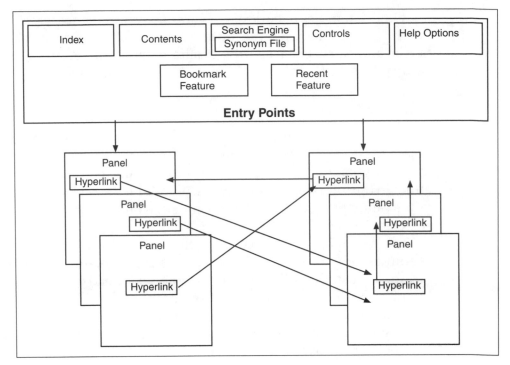

**Figure 10.11** Online information schema.

## Building Online Navigational Infrastructures

As Figure 10.11 shows, online information schemata are webs very much like our associative memory.

The challenge in building the infrastructure for this web is understanding the relationships among the navigational components and knowing which associative tags to use as navigational keys to access the components. You must take all of these navigational components and weave an easy-to-use, intuitive web that gives users information quickly as well as helps them build online information schemata.

Consider this classic human-factors scenario:

David is usability testing a unit of online information that he wrote. He gives his test subject this question: Move the second paragraph of ReportA to the end of the report.

His audience is administrative entry-level users who are making the transition from typewriters to PCs. They know only the rudiments of the application they are using.

His test subjects eventually locate and open ReportA, then they begin looking for a Move option. They pull down all of the menus, but they cannot find a Move option. They pull down the Help menu and select Contents. They scroll through the contents, but do not find a Move topic. They go back to the Help menu and select Index. They scroll through the index, but do not fine a Move topic.

They become frustrated and ask David if this is the correct usability test question. He assures them it is. Eventually, one of the test subject hits upon the idea of using the search engine. This person calls up the search engine and enters the word "move." An error message indicating that the topic could not be found appears.

Not one of the test subjects is able to complete the usability test.

This was a navigational error on David's part. The information the test subjects needed was in the online information. It was under "Cut and Paste." This is not a term these users knew. He should have mapped the familiar term ("move") to the new term ("cut and paste") in a synonym file. If his online environment does not support synonym files, he should have used a cross-reference in the index entry. When the test subjects selected "Move" from the index, an informational panel saying "See Cut and Paste" should have appeared. David modifies his creating-online-information schema to include mapping familiar and unfamiliar terminology. Of course, had David brainstormed, mind mapped, and storyboarded in partnership with his users, this discrepancy in terminology probably would have surfaced much earlier.

Consider this scenario:

Marti has constructed a piece of online information for her company's new network-heartbeat software. This software resides on a network server and polls client nodes at user-defined intervals to ensure that the client nodes are up and running. If the software does not detect a client node heartbeat, it sends a message to an operator's message queue.

Marti is doing a usability test with some of her user partners. She notices that every one of the users is confused on how to define the heartbeat interval. Eventually, they all get to the information, but they do so more slowly and with more confusion than she had anticipated.

She discovers that the problem is that users have to hyperlink to three different panels from the panel containing the procedure on defining the heartbeat interval to get all of the definitional information they need. Then, because the environment does not support either a Recent or a Bookmark feature, they do not know how to get back to the main panel. They keep having to go back to the index and select the main panel topic from the index. By the time they do this, they have forgotten some of the definitional information to which they hyperlinked.

Marti takes the definitional information out of panels and puts it in footnotes so users do not have to navigate away from the main panel. When she retests her information, users sail through the usability test with the ease she had hoped for the first time.

This navigational problem is one that may not have cropped up during earlier work with Marti's users. But now that Marti has had this experience, she has modified her hyperlinking-to-definitional-information schema. The next time she builds a unit of online information, she knows to consider that even experienced users can get lost in hyperspace.

Consider this scenario:

Leigh has designed an online tutorial for a new ATM screen-generation utility. This utility allows users to build object-oriented ATM screens by selecting objects from palettes and functions from pop-up menus.

Leigh has designed a set of end-to-end scenarios that allows users to build a working ATM screen in their own environment. She has a robust synonym file that maps terms users are familiar with to those that the new utility uses. She has presented realistic problem-solving scenarios that show how the new utility saves screen designers time and effort.

She has included optional problem-solving scenarios users can attempt if they feel the need for more instruction. She has exploited all of the navigational components and worked closely with her user partners through brainstorming, mind mapping, and storyboarding.

She is conducting her paperwalk and notices users time and again walking back down the hall to the contents sheet that is tacked to the wall. Finally she asks them why they keep going back to the contents.

They tell her that they do not know what task to perform next, so they go back to the contents to see what they are supposed to do.

Leigh addresses this problem by creating a bitmap that looks like a button that says "Continue." At the end of each tutorial task, users click the hypergraphic Continue button, and the next module of information appears.

In a hardcopy environment, Leigh would have made the next task the next section or the next chapter. Users would have known to go to Chapter 5 after Chapter 4. That progression is not obvious in online information. You have to make it obvious. Leigh modifies her transition-in-online-information schema to include the necessity of pointing the way for users.

Another way around this problem would have been for Leigh to include the Next Screen control. Often, however, the Next Screen control takes users to the next module of information in your source (the precompiled text that you write), which may not be the next module of information you want them to go to in your object (the compiled text that users see on their screens). Before using the Previous Screen and Next Screen controls, be sure you rigorously test them.

Some navigational guidelines for helping users build online information schemata are:

- Map familiar terminology to new terminology through a synonym file or index cross-references.

- Use robust synonym files to capture likely synonyms and all variations of synonyms.

- Exploit all the navigational components that your online environment supports.

- Use pop-up footnotes wherever possible so users do not have to navigate back to their starting point (be sure you understand the limitations of footnotes).

- Help users avoid being lost in hyperspace by using Recent or History features, Bookmark features, hyperlinked cross-references, hyperlinked related topics, split-screen designs, and navigational hypergraphics.

- Make navigational relationships easy, quick, and intuitive.

- Do not require users to navigate more than three panels from their starting point or scroll more than three panels to view a module of information.

## Summary

Your information's navigational infrastructure is the second layer of subtext users encounter. The navigational infrastructure is the skeleton on which you hang your information. It is the way users move around in your information.

Most users have well-established hardcopy navigational schemata. They come to a unit of hardcopy information fully expecting the table of contents at the front of the book and the index at the end. They automatically turn page 6 to get to page 7 and go from Chapter 1 to Chapter 2. The physical nature of hardcopy imposes a familiar, linear progression through the information.

There are built-in navigational clues in hardcopy information that are not present in online information. The physical order of pages, the presence of page numbers, the arrangement of sections and chapters, the conventions of front and back matter—all of these are hardcopy navigational clues that technical communicators and users take for granted. Online information has different navigational needs than hardcopy information. Because by nature online information must be wholly random-access, stand-alone modules of information, hardcopy structural clues of pages, chapters, and front and back matter do not apply.

In building your navigational infrastructures, you should leverage your users' existing schemata as much as possible. Working with users during storyboarding gives you a great deal of insight into their navigational needs. During paperwalks, pay close attention to how users are navigating through your information.

Users' actions are always the final arbiter. You may have the best navigational infrastructure that human-factors engineers can produce, but if users do not use it, the point is moot.

### Further Reading

ACM. *Hypertext 87 Proceedings*. New York: ACM, 1987.

ACM. *Hypertext 89 Proceedings*. New York: ACM, 1989.

ACM. *Proceedings of the ACM Conference on Hypertext*. New York: ACM, 1991. ACM Order Number 614910.

ACM. *Proceedings of the ACM Conference on Hypertext*. D. Lucarella et al, eds. New York: ACM, 1992. ACM Order Number 614920.

ACM. *Proceedings of the ACM Conference on Hypertext.* C. Kacmar et al, eds. New York: ACM, 1993. ACM Order Number 614930.

Anderson, D. and J.R. Huntington. "Using What You Have to Write Help," *STC Proceedings*, 1995.

Barrett, E., ed. *The Society of Text.* Cambridge, MA: MIT Press, 1989.

Basara, D. et al. "A Case Study of Online Information: Second Generation Systems Design," *IEEE Transactions on Professional Communication*, 4, 1986.

Bell, L. "The Design and Implementation of Online Specifications," *STC Proceedings*, 1987.

Beren, W.G. "Tutorial-Gate: An Under-the-Covers Workshop on Online Tutorials," *STC Proceedings*, 1995.

Berk, E. and J. Devlin, eds. *Hypertext/Hypermedia Handbook.* New York: McGraw-Hill, 1991.

Berry, R.R. and M.C. Nichols. "Windowing the World of Online Information," *STC Proceedings*, 1995.

Billingsley, P. "Navigation Through Hierarchical Menu Structures: Does It Help to Have a Map?" *Proceedings of the Human Factors Society*, 1982.

Bolter, J. D. *Writing Space: The Computer, Hypertext, and the History of Writing.* Hillsdale, NJ: Erlbaum, 1991.

Borenstein, N.S. "Help Text vs. Help Mechanisms: A New Mandate for Documentation Writers," *Proceedings of the SIGDOC 85*, 1985.

Bresko, L.L. et al. "Hyper-Help: Uniting Humans and Machines," *STC Proceedings*, 1991.

Brockmann, R.J. *Writing Better Computer User Documentation: From Paper to Online.* New York: John Wiley & Sons, 1990.

Brockmann, R.J. and W. Horton. "From Database to Hypertext: An Information Odyssey," *Society of Text: Hypertext, Hypermedia, and the Social Construction of Information.* Cambridge, MA: MIT Press, 1989.

Brooks, R.M. "Principles for Effective Hypermedia Design," *Technical Communication*, 40:3.

Brown, H., ed. *Hypermedia/Hypertext and Object-Oriented Databases.* London: Chapman & Hall, 1991.

Bush, V. "As We May Think," *Atlantic Monthly*, July 1945, pp. 101–108.

Caldanaro, R.M. and M.C. Corbin Nichols. "The Evolution of a Help System," *STC Proceedings*, 1995.

Carlson, P.A. "Hypertext: A Way of Incorporating User Feedback into Online Documentation," *Text ConText, and HyperText: Writing with and for the Computer.* Cambridge, MA: MIT Press, 1988.

Charland, D.A. "Online Documentation Promises and Problems," *STC Proceedings*, 1984.

Charney, D. "Comprehending Non-Linear Text: The Role of Discourse Cues and Reading Strategies," *Hypertext 87 Papers*. Chapel Hill, NC: University of North Carolina, 1987.

Chavarria, L.S. "More Online Computer Documentation in the Future—Are You Ready?" *STC Proceedings*, 1983.

Cherry, J. et al. "Do Formats for Presenting Online Help Affect User Performance and Attitudes?" *STC Proceedings*, 1988.

Cohen, N. et al. "Designing an On-Line, Interactive, Help System," *STC Proceedings*, 1986.

Collier, G.H. "Thoth-II: Hypertext with Explicit Semantics," *Hypertext 87 Papers*. Chapel Hill, NC: University of North Carolina, 1987.

Dansereau, M.E. "Creating an Online Index," *STC Proceedings*, 1987.

Davis, S.A. "A Simplified Look At Practical Hypertext," *STC Proceedings*, 1990.

Delany, P. and G.P. Landow, eds. *Hypermedia and Literary Studies*. Cambridge, MA: MIT Press, 1991.

Dorazio, P.A. "Helping Out Help," *STC Proceedings*, 1986.

_____. "Help Facilities: A Survey of the Literature," *Technical Communication*, 35:2, 1988.

Evans, J.P. "Seven Steps to Successful Online Help," *STC Proceedings*, 1995.

Fenchel, R. "An Integrated Approach to User Assistance," *ACM SIGDOC Bulletin*, 13:2, 1981.

Fiderio, J. "A Grand Vision: Hypertext Mimics the Brain's Ability to Access Information Quickly and Intuitively by Reference," *Byte*, October 1988, pp. 237–244.

Frisse, M. "From Text to Hypertext," *Byte,* October 1988, pp. 247–253.

Gardiner, M.M. and B. Christie, eds. *Applying Cognitive Psychology to User-Interface Design*. New York: John Wiley & Sons, 1987.

Garg, P.K. "Abstraction Mechanisms in Hypertext," *Communications of the ACM*, 31:7, 1988.

Gaylin, K. "How Are Windows Used? Some Notes on Creating an Empirically-Based Windowing Benchmark Test," *CHI 86 Proceedings*. New York: ACM, 1986.

Girill, T.R. "Display Units for Online Passage Retrieval: A Comparative Analysis," *STC Proceedings*, 1984.

Glushko, R.J. and M.H. Bianchi. "On-Line Documentation: Mechanizing Development, Delivery, and Use," *The Bell System Technical Journal*, 61:6, 1982.

Gray, S. H. *Hypertext and the Technology of Conversation: Orderly Situational Choice.* Westport, CT: Greenwood Press, 1993.

Grice, R. "Linking to Hypertext: A Critical Analysis," *STC Proceedings*, 1990.

Halasz, F.G. "Reflections on NoteCards: Seven Issues for the Next Generation of Hypermedia Systems," *Communications of the ACM,* 31:7, pp. 345–365.

Harrington, R. et al. *IBM LinkWay: Hypermedia for the PC.* New York: John Wiley & Sons, 1990.

Hasslein, V. "Marketing Survey on User Requests for Online Documentation," *STC Proceedings*, 1986.

Henderson, A. and A. Bradford. "Online Information: A Practical Approach," *STC Proceedings*, 1984.

Horton, W. "Hypertext Manifesto: Reader's Rights, Writer's Responsibility," *Technical Communication*, 36:1, 1989.

Houghton, R.C. "Online Help Systems: A Conspectus," *Communications of the ACM,* 27:2, 1984.

Hurd, J.C. "Writing Online Help," *STC Proceedings*, 1983.

IEEE. "Hypertext," (computer disk). London: IEEE, 1990.

Jenner, S.A. "Is There a Linear Approach to Hypertext?" *STC Proceedings*, 1991.

Jonassen, D. H. *Hypertext/Hypermedia.* Englewood Cliffs, NJ: Educational Technology Publications, 1989.

Jong, S. "Issues in Online Documentation," *STC Proceedings*, 1982.

_____. "The Challenge of Hypertext," *STC Proceedings*, 1988.

Katzin, E. "On-Line Documentation: Good and Not So Good," *STC Proceedings*, 1984.

Kearsley, G. *Online Help Systems: Design and Implementation.* Norwood, NJ. : Ablex Publishing, 1988.

Landow, G.P. "Relationally Encoded Links and the Rhetoric of Hypertext," *Hypertext 87 Papers*, Chapel Hill, NC: University of North Carolina, 1987.

_____. Hypertext: The Convergence of Contemporary Critical Theory and Technology. Baltimore: Johns Hopkins University Press, 1992.

Mandavilli, L.K. "Planning and Creating a Windows Online Help System," *STC Proceedings*, 1995.

Marchionini, G. and B. Schneiderman, "Finding Facts vs. Browsing Knowledge in Hypertext Systems," *IEEE Computer*, 21:1, 1988.

McAleese, R. *Hypertext: Theory and Practice.* Norwood, NJ: Ablex Publishing, 1989.

McKnight, C. et al. *Hypertext: A Psychological Perspective.* New York: E. Horwood, 1992.

McKnight, C. et al. *Hypertext in Context*. Cambridge: Cambridge University Press, 1991.

Miller, W. "The Technical Writer's Role in On-Line Documentation," *STC Proceedings*, 1986.

NATO Advanced Research Workshop on Designing Hypertext/Hypermedia for Learning. *Designing Hypermedia for Learning*, D.H. Jonassen, et al., eds. Berlin: Springer-Verlag, 1990.

Nielsen, J. *Hypertext and Hypermedia*. Boston: Academic Press Professional, 1993.

Norman, K. et al. "Cognitive Layout of Windows and Multiple Screens for User Interfaces," *International Journal of Man-Machine Studies*, 25, 1986.

Oren, T. "The Architecture of Static Hypertexts," *Hypertext 87 Papers*. Chapel Hill, NC: University of North Carolina, 1987.

Perry, T.S. "Hypermedia: Finally Here," *IEEE Spectrum*, November, 1987.

Peterson, T.J. and E.W. Rosencrants, "Creating Accessible Online Information," *STC Proceedings*, 1986.

Petrauskas, B.F. "Online Documentation: Putting Research into Practice," *STC Proceedings*, 1987.

Price, J. "Creating a Style for Online Help," *Text, ConText, and HyperText: Writing with and for the Computer*. Cambridge, MA: The MIT Press, 1988.

_____. "Structuring Help for Re-Use," *STC Proceedings*, 1995.

Quiepo, L. "User Expectations of Online Information," *IEEE Transactions on Professional Communication*, 4, 1987.

Rada, R. *Hypertext: From Text to Expertext*. London: McGraw-Hill, 1991.

Radecki, S. "Creating Hypertext Documentation: One Writer's Experience," *STC Proceedings*, 1991.

Ramey, J. "Developing a Theoretical Base for On-Line Documentation, Part I: Building the Theory," *The Technical Writing Teacher*, 13:2, 1986.

_____. "Developing a Theoretical Base for On-Line Documentation, Part II: Applying the Theory," *The Technical Writing Teacher*, 13:3, 1986.

Raskin, J. "The Hype in Hypertext: A Critique," *Hypertext 87 Papers*. Chapel Hill, NC: University of North Carolina, 1987.

Remde, J.R. et al. "SuperBook: An Automatic Tool for Information Exploration—Hypertext?" *Hypertext 87 Papers*. Chapel Hill, NC: University of North Carolina, 1987.

Ridgeway L.S. "Linking to Hypertext: Bounding Exploration Space," *STC Proceedings*, 1990.

Rockley, A. "Online Documentation: From Proposal to Finished Product," *STC Proceedings*, 1987.

Rockley, A. and G. Graham. "Hypermedia—A Web of Thought," *STC Proceedings*, 1988.

Rubens, B.K. and R. Hendricks. "The Psychological Advantage of Online Information," *STC Proceedings*, 1987.

Rubens, P. "Online Information, Traditional Page Design, and Reader Expectation," *Proceedings of the 11th Practical Conference on Communications*, 1987.

_____. "Reading and Employing Technical Information in Hypertext," *Technical Communication*, 38:1, p. 36.

Rubin, M.L. *Documentation Standards and Procedures for Online Systems*. New York: Van Nostrand Reinhold, 1979.

Schmidtke, H. "Ergonomic Design Principles of Alphanumeric Displays," *Ergonomic Aspects of Visual Display Terminals*. London: Taylor & Francis, 1980.

Schneider, M.L. "Information Hiding in Complex Displays," *Directions in Human/Computer Interaction*. Norwood, NJ: Ablex Publishing, 1982.

Schneiderman, B. and G. Kearsley. *Hypertext: An Introduction to a New Way of Organizing and Accessing Information*. Reading, MA: Addison-Wesley, 1988.

See, E. "Linking to Hypertext: A Comparative Study," *STC Proceedings*, 1990.

Seyer, P. C. *Understanding Hypertext: Concepts and Applications*. Blue Ridge Summit, PA: Windcrest, 1991.

Shirk, H. N. "Technical Writers as Computer Scientists: The Challenges of Online Documentation," *Text, ConText, and HyperText: Writing with and for the Computer*. Cambridge, MA: The MIT Press, 1988.

SIGDOC. *Going Online: The New World of Multimedia Documentation*. New York: ACM, 1992.

Slatin, J. "Toward a Rhetoric for Hypertext," *Hypermedia 88*. Houston, TX: University of Texas, 1988.

Smirnov, L.L. "Discovering the Intuitive Approach to Hypertext," *STC Proceedings*, 1991.

Smith, J.B. and S.F. Weiss. "Hypertext," *Communications of the ACM*, 31:7, 1988.

Smith, J.B. et al. "A Hypertext Writing Environment and Its Cognitive Basis," *Hypertext 87*. Chapel Hill, NC: University of North Carolina, 1987.

Soderson, C. "An Experimental Study of Structure for Online Information," *STC Proceedings*, 1987, 1990.

Stone, S. and M. Buckland, eds. *Studies in Multimedia: State-of-the-Art Solutions in Multimedia and Hypertext*. Medford, NJ: Learned Information, 1992.

Streitz, N. et al., eds. *Hypertext: Concepts, Systems and Applications: Proceedings of the First European Conference on Hypertext*. Cambridge: Cambridge University Press, 1990.

Taylor, L. "Finding the Business End of This New Wrench: Practical Guidelines for Choosing (Or Ignoring) Hypertext," *STC Proceedings*, 1990.

Towey, I.K. "'Do You Do Windows?' Designing Screens in Window-Based Applications," *STC Proceedings*, 1991.

Van Nortwick, T. "Strategy and Experiences In Accomplishing Effective Use of Hypertext," *STC Proceedings*, 1990.

Walker, J.H. "Issues and Strategies for Online Documentation," *IEEE Transactions on Professional Communication*, 4, 1987.

Wang, H. and G. Marchionini. "Improving Information Seeking Performance" in *Hypertext: Roles of Display Format and Search Strategy*. College Park, MD: University of Maryland, 1988.

Wasserman, D.C. "Critical Elements in the Design of Help and Hypertext Systems," *STC Proceedings*, 1993.

Winsberg, F.Y. "How to Design a Good Online Help Facility," *STC Proceedings*, 1986.

_____. "Online Documentation: Tutorials That Are Easy to Take," *STC Proceedings*, 1987.

Wolman, R. "A Trainer's Guide to Hypertext," *Data Training*, March 1988.

Woodhead, N. *Hypertext and Hypermedia: Theory and Applications*. Wilmslow, England: Sigma Press, 1991.

Zubark, C.L., "A 'Real World' Look at Windows Help Authoring Tools," *STC Proceedings*, 1995.

## Notes

1  For example, in right-to-left-reading cultures, books are bound on the right.

2  I am not talking about the environment-dependent execution of an infrastructure, I am talking about a universal infrastructure for online information that is environment-independent.

3  In most GUI environments, the word "screen" refers to the physical part of the monitor on which users view the information. The word "panel" refers to the online container of information.

# CHAPTER ELEVEN

# Presenting Information

*The desire to impose upon the disorder of nature some orderly pattern or arrangement makes men into poets, painters and gardeners; it also makes them prey to the illusion that a highly organized state will be civilized.*

Len Deighton

The presentation is the third layer of information subtext your users encounter. The presentation is how information looks on the page or screen. The presentation comprises the layout, which is the physical arrangement of text, graphics, and color on the page or screen and the fonts, which are the shapes and emphases of the letters you use to communicate the text.

Users call up their existing presentation schemata to interpret your information's presentation. It is easier to leverage your users' existing presentation schemata than it is to modify existing schemata or build new ones. If you have a compelling reason for users to modify existing schemata or build new ones, do so slowly, explain the benefits of the change to their problem-solving experience, and get their buy-in. Work closely with users during storyboarding to design a presentation that works for them.

There are some universal truths you can assume when designing and developing presentation:

- The most natural movement for the eye is upper left corner (primary optical area) to lower right corner (terminal anchor) as the Gutenberg diagram in Figure 11.1 shows.

  The Gutenberg diagram suggests that bottom-up and left-right reading patterns are not the most natural Western eye movements.[1]

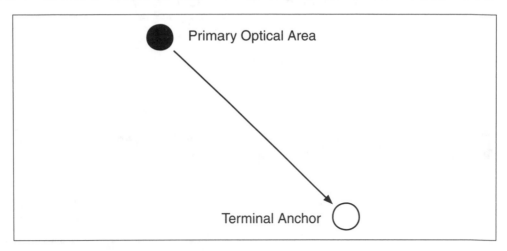

**Figure 11.1** Gutenberg diagram.

- Graphical elements (icons, white space, tables, photographs, line art, charts, drop capitals) and color attract the eye.
- White space, font, position, descending point size and sometimes font family and descending numbers delineate hierarchical heads.
- The right side of the brain processes images while the left side processes text. There is a visual cross-over in how the brain processes what the eyes see. The left side of the brain processes data from the right visual field, and the right side of the brain processes data from the left visual field. This means that the most efficient place to position graphics is in users' left visual field.
- Our perceptual processes:
  - Search for wholes and attempt to make wholes of parts
  - Group things in close proximity
  - Seek continuous patterns instead of discontinuous patterns
  - Group objects that are similar
  - Prefer symmetry over asymmetry
  - Always opt for the simplest interpretation
  - Use template matching, prototype matching, and context to recognize shapes
- Thresholds, cocktail-party effect, and sensory adaptation filter sensory data.

- Color and graphics are cultural.
- An online medium calls for a grosser level of presentation than does a hardcopy medium.

Consider this scenario:

Pat is redesigning her company's newsletter. The table of contents has always been a shadowed box in the lower right corner of the front page.

She moves the table of contents to the lower left and is surprised when complaints pour in.

Pat did two things that did not have the best interests of her users at heart: she violated her users' newsletter-presentation schema without a compelling reason, and she violated the Gutenberg diagram, which suggests that the lower right corner of the front page is the best place for the table of contents. If she had worked with users to storyboard the change, her users probably would have asked her why she was moving the table of contents. If she did not have a reason that was meaningful to her users, they would have told her, "If it ain't broke, don't fix it."

Consider this scenario:

Donna has two tables in one module of online information. One table lists acceptable values for communication timeouts, and the other table lists acceptable values for polling intervals. Donna does not understand why her users are having trouble with the data in these tables.

She does some usability testing to try to find out just what is going on and is surprised to discover that users are interchanging the data in the two tables.

Donna's information is the victim of five related phenomena:

1. Proximity

   We group like objects. Since the tables were so close together, her users perceptually grouped them.

2. Similarity

   We group objects that are similar. Since the physical appearance of the tables was identical, her users perceptually grouped them.

3. Search for wholes

We seek wholes and attempt to make wholes of parts. Since the tables were so close and so similar, her users perceptually made them one big table instead of two smaller ones.

4. Goodness of figures

We always opt for the simplest interpretation. Because of proximity, similarity, and search for wholes, the simplest interpretation for her users was that the tables were really one.

5. Representation memory

We do not store in memory re-creations of objects; we store representations. Likewise, we do not retrieve re-creations of objects; we retrieve representations. Those users who had attempted to move the data into long-term memory stored a representation of the tables and retrieved a representation of the tables. In the transmutations that occurred during storing and retrieving, her users merged the two tables into one.

If any one of these phenomena had been present, Donna's users might not have had a problem. The presence of all five phenomena, however, exponentially emphasized the importance of each. Donna can do one of three things to help her users with these tables:

1. Leverage the perceptual processes at work and make the two tables one.

2. Put each table in a separate module of information to emphasize the discrete nature of each table.

3. Make the information context sensitive so that users can access only the correct information at any given time.[2]

Layout must provide perceptual clues that enable users to process information. Users interpret layout before they begin the cognitive tasks of reading, remembering, and understanding the content of the information.

Consider this scenario:

Figure 11.2 shows a random verso-recto page set in Dave's information.

Without exception, Dave's reviewers hated this layout. They complained that it is not clear and intuitive; they have no insight into how they perceptually should group the elements on these pages.

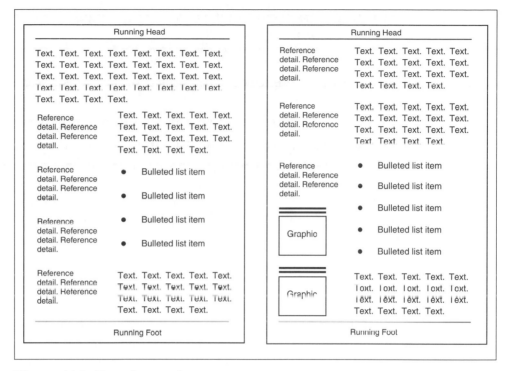

**Figure 11.2** Dave's page layout.

For example, does Dave's layout provide any clues to help users answer these questions:

- On the verso page, what do those four pieces of reference detail accompany? Do they all accompany the second text block? The bulleted list items? The last text block?

- On the recto page, is the last piece of reference detail connected to the first text block? The second text block? One of the bulleted list items? Which list item?

- On the recto page, what do the graphics accompany? One of the bulleted list items? Which one? Both of them? The last text block? Do both graphics accompany the same piece of information? Why are those graphics stacked?

This clearly is not a page layout that works for Dave's users. They cannot make perceptual sense of the way Dave has arranged the information pieces on the page.

Dave can do one or more of the following to create a clearer and more intuitive layout for his users:

- Weave the reference detail into the text blocks.
- Position the reference detail as nested paragraphs under the applicable bulleted item.
- Move the reference detail to footnotes, endnotes, or appendixes.
- Reposition the graphics so they are not stacked.
- Re-evaluate the information and his control of it. Users may have no need for so much extraneous reference detail. It may be that Dave is not in control of his information and feels insecure not including everything. This is the "kitchen sink" syndrome and is indicative of technical communicators who are "in over their head" with subject matter.
- Restoryboard the layout with his users.

Consider the following:

Brian follows his company's style guide to create a tutorial scenario explaining how to distribute an object from a network node to an end node. The guidelines call for boldface type for the following: menu names, menu options, object names, keyboard keys, user-entered data, and system responses.

Figure 11.3 shows one of Brian's examples.

When Brian sent this example out for review, his reviewers hated it. Too much boldface they said. There is so much boldface in this example that the boldface loses its perceptual meaning. Users' thresholds and sensory adaptation work to render the boldface meaningless. Users cannot scan the example for meaningful boldface clues. Brian needs to bring users and the owners of the style guide together to create meaningful applications of fonts.

Brian could also consider a more graphical illustration of the material. He could use screen captures to take users through the procedures. Users store and retrieve information more easily when it is graphical. Graphical communication would give his information a more open look and feel, and entry-level users (who are most likely to be using a tutorial) find the reinforcement between screen and page comforting.

A font is a family, point size, and emphasis. Therefore, Helvetica 12-point, Helvetica 12-point italics, and Helvetica 12-point italics underscored are three different fonts. The heuristic is to start with three basic fonts:

1. Select **Distribute Object** from the **Object** main menu.

   The **Select Network Node** submenu appears.

2. Type an **X** next to **Network Node 5**.

3. Press **Enter**.

   The **Select End Node** submenu appears.

4. Type an **X** next to **Security Object 1**.

5. Press **Enter**.

   The **Select Object** submenu appears.

6. Type an **X** next to **End Node 2**.

7. Press **Enter**.

   The following confirmation message appears:

   > **Distribute Security Object 1 from Network Node 5 to End Node 2? (Y/N)**

8. Type **Y** to distribute the object.

   (If you change your mind, you can type **N** at this point to cancel the operation.)

   The following informational message appears:

   > **Distributing Security Object 1 from Network Node 5 to End Node 2...**

   When the distribution is complete, the following informational message appears:

   > **Distribution complete**

**Figure 11.3** Brian's example.

1. First level head

   Traditionally, a first-level head is boldface, sans serif, and a larger point size than body text. For example, Helvetica 14-point boldface might be the font for a first-level head.

2. Body text

   Traditionally, body text is plain text, serif, and 10 or 12-point. For example, using a 14-point boldface Helvetica first-level head might lead you to use Times plain 12-point for your body text font.

3. Running headers and footers.

   Traditionally, running headers and footers are the same font family as first-level heads but plain text and a smaller point size than body text. For example, Helvetica plain 9-point might be a good choice for running headers and footers.

To these three basic fonts, you add as few fonts as possible. If you have a hierarchical arrangement of information, you need hierarchical heads, which would be a diminution of the first-level head. If you find your information requires more than three levels of heads, consider a reorganization of it. Each word you put in boldface, italics, another font family, or different point size adds another font. Too many fonts lead to what is known as the "ransom note effect."

When your information suffers from the ransom note effect, the subtext you are trying to communicate with the font change is lost on users. Their thresholds, cocktail-party effect, and sensory adaptation have filtered out any meaning the fonts may have had. In some advertising, marketing, and newsletters, several fun fonts may be appropriate, but in technical communication, stick with the classic serif (Times, Times New Roman, Palatino) and the classic sans serif (Helvetica, Arial, Avant Garde, Geneva).

Users form pattern and prototype-matching schemata based on the fonts you use in your presentation. If they are used to first-level heads always being Helvetica boldface 14-point, then each time they encounter this font, they expect it to be a first-level head. Likewise, if they scan your page and see Helvetica boldface 14-point and Helvetica boldface 12-point heads, they probably interpret it using a presentation schema that assumes a hierarchical structure in which the 12-point head is a subhead to the 14-point head.

In hardcopy information, you control every detail of layout and font. This is not the case in online information.

Consider this scenario:

Ashley has designed a unit of online information. She has spent a great deal of time on the layout. She worked in close partnership with her users to arrive at a layout that was meaningful.

The product and information go to field test. Ashley makes a site visit to see how users are doing with her online information. She is aghast to find that they have resized the information panels and destroyed her layout.

In an online environment where users can size and resize information panels, you cannot rely on detailed layout. You have to lay out your information at a much grosser level in online information development than you do in hardcopy information development. In a unit of hardcopy information, you can dictate every last detail of layout, but in the world of online information, users can size an information panel to fill their 20-inch screen or size it down to a 2-inch by 2-inch square.

The basic placement of heads, text, and graphics do not change, but panels that had been a single panel can become six scrollable panels. A single row of controls can become a triple row of controls. Four paragraphs can become either four sentences when users expand the information panel, or four paragraphs that extend over eight scrollable panels when they reduce the information panels.

Just as detailed layouts are often lost in online information, so are hierarchical structures. It is easier on you and your users to present your information in heterarchies rather than in hierarchies in online information. When users scan a hardcopy page, there are ample visual clues as to the information hierarchy: different fonts, white space, and position. In online information, users expect more random-access stand-alone units of information. They do not want to scroll through many panels looking for topics and subtopics. Online information has a web-like layout of heterarchical related topics instead of a linear layout of hierarchical topics.

In the online world, users may also control fonts and default colors. You may have designed your online information in Helvetica and Palatino, but if users have not installed these fonts on their system, their system substitutes whatever fonts are available. This is another good reason to stick with the standard classic fonts. Use the default development colors as well as standard classic fonts. In your development environment, hyperlinks may appear in green, but in the users' production environment, they may appear in red. In online information, do not bother changing the default colors. Do not spend your time and effort trying to get a nice cyan body text with navy heads and green hyperlinks. It might all be lost when it gets to the users' environment.

Resist the temptation to add color to online information. By default, online information usually has enough color. If you weaken the perceptual meaningfulness of color by overdoing it, you lose the subtext you were trying to communicate to your users.

Some guidelines to help you with hardcopy and online information presentation are:

- Involve users as presentation-design partners.

  Involve users in storyboarding so they can tell you what they need and expect in the way of presentation.

  Do some competitive benchmarking of information whose presentation users tell you they like. Learn from the competition's successes. Benchmark information whose presentation users dislike as well, so you can avoid the competition's failures.

  Usability test presentations. Design test suites that measure the speed, ease, and accuracy of users' performing tasks with various presentations to determine the best presentation.

- Choose consistent presentations among like units of information and complementary layouts among media subtypes.

  While a reference manual should not have the same layout as a users' guide, your organization can adopt consistent layouts for reference manuals and consistent layouts for users' guides that are complementary. This exploits users' existing presentation schemata and helps them develop new presentation schemata.

- Use white space proactively.

  White space is a graphic that you should use proactively to indicate organization, separate modules of information, convey relationships, emphasize pieces of information, direct users' focus, and afford an open look and feel to your information. Aim for 20 to 40 percent white space in hardcopy information and 40 to 60 percent white space in online information.

- Place graphics so they fall on the left visual field.

  Exploit left brain-right brain processing. Place graphics so that they fall on the left visual field, where data is processed by the right half of the brain.

- Exploit users' natural perceptual processes of proximity, similarity, closure, gestalts, symmetry, and goodness of figures.

  Take advantage of these processes that users automatically employ. Users assume that graphic elements near each other or near textual elements accompany one another. Users build schemata from similarity and symmetry in presentations and always opt for the simplest interpretation of a presentation. Users do not like parts; they seek wholes, and if your presentation does not afford wholeness or closure, users invent it.

- Adhere to the Gutenberg diagram.

  Leverage users' natural eye flow from upper left corner to lower right corner. Avoid making users' eyes travel bottom up or right left.

- Make hierarchies and heterarchies obvious.

  In hardcopy information, exploit users' existing schemata for hierarchical and heterarchical presentation. In online information, leverage users' existing schemata or help them build new schemata for heterarchical presentation.

- Make the relationships among information elements intuitive.

  Users should be able to interpret the presentation of information intuitively before they cognitively process the content of the information.

Some guidelines that apply only to online information presentation are:

- Design online presentations at a grosser level than hardcopy presentations.

  You do not have control over the finer points of online presentation, so do not invest your effort and time in it. Design the basic placement of heads, text, and graphics, but resign yourself to the fact that users size online information panels to their liking.

- Design to the smallest screen your users are likely to have.

  If you determine that 85 percent of your user community has 14-inch monitors, design your presentation for a 14-inch monitor and let the other 15 percent of your users size their information panels accordingly. Even when designing to the smallest screen your users are likely to have, there is no guarantee users will not size the panels.

- Design strong, relational heterarchies, as hierarchies are often lost online.

  Do not depend on hierarchical presentations to carry subtext in online information. The web-like, random-access, stand-alone na-

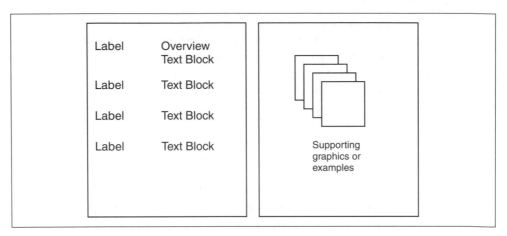

**Figure 11.4** Structured writing.

ture of online information modules destroys the ability of hierarchies to carry communication in and of themselves. In online information development, design to strong heterarchical presentations.

There are several presentation-intensive hardcopy writing systems that force particular presentations:

- Structured writing

  Structured writing is a two-column, double-page format that presents information topics as maps (sections or chapters) of information. Each map has an overview, several blocks (paragraphs), and a supporting graphic or example. Each block has a label (side head). Horizontal lines separate the overview from the blocks, and the blocks from each other. Use of labels and stringent chunking afford easy skimming, scanning, and keyword (label) searches. R. Horn's Information Mapping is a common example of structured writing.

  Figure 11.4 shows a structured writing presentation.

- Playscript

  Playscript is a two-column, single-page format that presents information as actions (usually in the imperative) that actors perform. White space separates the individual actions. Playscript is good for process and procedural information and enhances skimming and scanning.

  Figure 11.5 shows two variations of Playscript presentation.

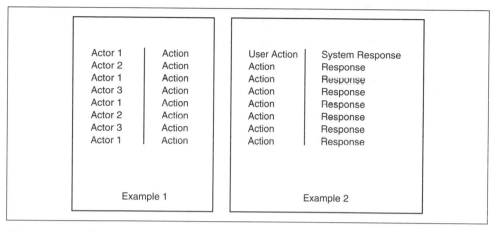

**Figure 11.5** Playscript.

- STOP

  STOP stands for Sequential Thematic Organization of Proposals and is a single-column, double-page format that presents information as headline, thesis statement, text block, and supporting graphics or examples.

  Figure 11.6 shows a STOP presentation.

- FOMM

  FOMM stands for Functionally Oriented Maintenance Manuals and is a single-column, single-page format that presents hardware main-

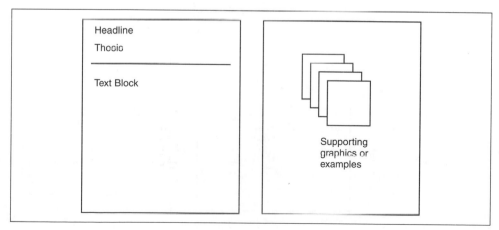

**Figure 11.6** STOP.

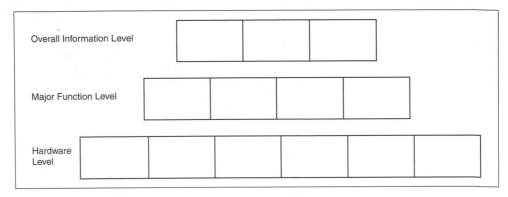

**Figure 11.7** FOMM.

tenance information in a top-down graphical format. The format has three layers: overall information, functional information, and hardware component information. FOMM emphasizes the use of tables, charts, and schematics, and minimizes the use of text.

Figure 11.7 shows a FOMM presentation.

- Logic boxes

Logic boxes are a single-column, dual-page format that present procedural information as objective, notes, steps, and supporting graphic or example. Logic boxes employ a telegraphic, minimalist style that eschews introductions and transitions.

Figure 11.8 shows a logic-box presentation.

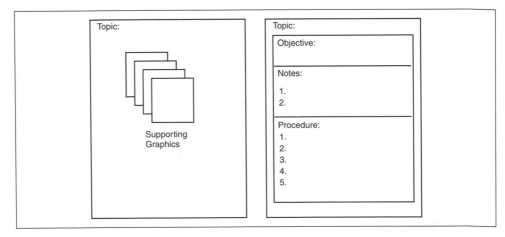

**Figure 11.8** Logic box.

# Summary

The presentation is the third layer of information subtext your users encounter. The presentation is how information looks on the page or screen. The presentation comprises the layout, which is the physical arrangement of text, graphics, and color on the page or screen and the fonts, which are the shapes and emphases of the letters you use to communicate the text.

There are some universal truths you can assume when designing and developing presentation:

- The most natural movement for the eye is upper left corner to lower right corner.
- Graphical elements and color attract the eye.
- White space, font, position, descending point size and sometimes font family and descending numbers delineate hierarchical heads.
- The right side of the brain processes images while the left side processes text.
- Our perceptual processes seek wholes, continuity, symmetry, and simplicity.
- Thresholds, cocktail-party effect, and sensory adaptation filter sensory data.
- Color and graphics are cultural.
- An online medium calls for a grosser level of presentation that does a hardcopy medium.

Layout must provide perceptual clues that enable users to process information. Users interpret layout before they begin the cognitive tasks of reading, remembering, and understanding the content of the information.

When users scan a hardcopy page, there are ample visual clues as to the information hierarchy: different fonts, white space, and position. In online information, users expect more random-access stand-alone units of information. They do not want to scroll through many panels looking for topics and subtopics. Online information has a web-like layout of heterarchical related topics instead of a linear layout of hierarchical topics.

There are several presentation-intensive hardcopy writing systems that force particular presentations: structured writing, Playscript, STOP, FOMM, and logic boxes.

## Further Reading

Anderson, R.C. "Schema-Directed Process in Language Comprehension," *Cognitive Psychology and Instruction*. A. Lesgod, et. al., eds. New York: Plenum Press, 1978.

Barton, B.F. and M.S. Barton, "Simplicity in Visual Representation: A Semiotic Approach," *Journal of Business and Technical Writing*, 1, 1987, pp. 5–26.

Beiderman, I. "Recognition by Components: A Theory of Human Image Understanding," *Psychological Review*, 94.

Bernard, R.M., C.H. Petersen, and M. Ally. "Can Images Provide Contextual Support for Prose?" *Journal of Educational Communication and Technology*, 1981, 29:2.

Bernhardt, Stephen. "Seeing the Text," *College Composition and Communication* 37 (1) February 1986.

Boyer, N. and J.R. Salazar, "Principles of Interaction: A Guide to Good Screen Design," *STC Proceedings*, 1990.

Brockmann, R.J. *Writing Better Computer User Documentation: From Paper to Hypertext*. New York: John Wiley & Sons, 1990.

Craig, J. *Designing with Type*. New York: Watson-Guptill, 1971.

Creed, L. "The Tip of the Visual Design Iceberg: A Short Lesson," *STC Proceedings*, 1991.

Curtiss, D. *Introduction to Visual Literacy: A Guide to the Visual Arts and Communication*. Englewood Cliffs, NJ: Prentice-Hall, 1987.

Deitrick, D.K. "Using Logic Boxes to Simplify Documentation," *STC Proceedings*, 1990.

Duin, A.H. "Minimal Manuals vs. Elaboration In Documentation: Centering On The Learner," *STC Proceedings*, 1990.

Elser, A.G. "Using Graphics to Help Users Build Mental Models," *STC Proceedings*, 1995.

Faruque, O. *Graphic Communication As a Design Tool*. New York: Van Nostrand Reinhold, 1984.

Hartley, J. *Designing Instructional Materials*. 2nd edition. New York: Nichols, 1985.

Horn, R. "Structured Writing and Text Design," *The Technology of Text: Principles for Structuring, Designing, and Displaying Text*. D. Jonasses, ed. Englewood Cliffs, NJ: Educational Press, 1982.

_____. *Strategies for Developing High-Performance Documentation*. Waltham, MA: Info Mapping, 1992.

Hurlburt, A. *Publication Design*. New York: Van Nostrand Reinhold, 1971.

Kern, R. "Modeling Users and Their Use of Technical Manuals," *Designing Usable Texts*. T.M. Duffy and R. Waller, eds. Orlando, FL: Academic Press, 1985.

Killingworth, M.J. and M. Gilbertson. "How Can Text and Graphics Be Integrated Effectively," *Problem Solving in Technical Writing*. L. Beene and P. White, eds. New York: Oxford University Press, 1988.

Kostlenick, C. "Visual Rhetoric: A Reader-Oriented Approach to Graphics and Designs," *The Technical Writing Teacher*, 1.

Lewis, Elaine. "Design Principles for Pictorial Information," *Effective Documentation: What We Have Learned from Research*. S. Doheny-Farina, ed. Cambridge, MA: MIT Press, 1988.

Little, R. and M. Smith. "Improving FOMM Troubleshooting," *Technical Communication*, 1983.

Macindoe, C. Scott. "An Assessment of Functionally Oriented Maintenance Manuals (FOMMs) *Technical Communication*, 32:3, 1983.

Mandel, S. *Effective Presentation Skills*. Los Altos, CA: Crisp Publications, 1987.

McLeish, D. "The Visual Spectrum: Balancing Text and Graphics in Computer Manuals," *STC Proceedings*, 1991.

Pinelli, T.E. et al. "A Survey of Typography, Graphic Design, and Physical Media in Technical Reports," *Technical Communication*, 2, 1985.

Redish, J. "Integrating Art and Text," *STC Proceedings*, 1997.

Southard, S.G. "Practical Considerations in Formatting Manuals," *Technical Communication*, 3, 1985.

Stankowski, A. *Visible Presentation of Invisible Processes*. Teufen, Switzerland: Arthur Niggli Ltd., 1967.

Szlichcinski, K.P. "The Syntax of Pictorial Instructions," *Processing of Visible Language*. P.A. Kolers, et al, eds. New York: Plenum, 1980.

Tedford, W.H. et al. "The Size-Color Illusion," *Journal of General Psychology*, 91:1, 1977.

Tufte, E.R. *The Visual Display of Quantitative Information*. Cheshire, CT: Graphics Press, 1983.

Turnbull, A.T. and R. Baird. *The Graphics of Communication*. 3rd edition. New York: Holt, Rinehart, and Winston, 1975.

Walklin, C. *Designing with Letters*. New York: Drake Publishers, 1974.

Whittick, A. Symbols: *Signs and Their Meaning and Uses in Design*. 2nd edition. London: L. Hill, 1971.

Wilde, R. *Problems, Solutions: Visual Thinking for Graphic Communicators*. New York: Van Nostrand Reinhold, 1986.

Wright, P. "The Quality Control of Document Design," *Information Design Journal*, 1.

## Notes

1  R. Krull and P. Rubens indicate that the Gutenberg diagram may apply only to hardcopy information. They suggest that the color of online information causes users to jump from color to color as if they were viewing a painting instead of a unit of information. In fact, they call the mode of reading online information "paint mode."

2  When deciding which information to make context sensitive, you must also decide whether users need to access that information only through context sensitivity. If it is information users may need in both context sensitive and noncontext sensitive settings, consider single-sourcing that information and mapping it to both context sensitive information and index topics.

# CHAPTER TWELVE

# Designing and Developing Content

*A method of solution is perfect if we can foresee from the start, and even prove, that following that method we shall attain our aim.*

Gottfried W. von Leibnitz

The content of your information is the text; it is what you are communicating; it is the substance of the solution you are brokering; it is the goal of your users. They have worked their way through the subtext layers of medium, navigation, and presentation to arrive at the text, which they apply to solving a problem in their world.

The three critical things you must have when you begin your content work are the fruits of the partnership you have sown with your users:

1. Your understanding of the physical and psychological processes, needs, and expectations that compose your users' world

2. Your users' profile

3. Your information's subtext profile

You should come to the content stage of information development with a clear understanding of your users' general sensory and perceptual processes, needs, and expectations:

- Sensory-perception continuum processing
- Schemata use, creation, and modification

- Thresholds, cocktail-party effect, and sensory adaption
- Pattern and prototype matching
- Habit use, creation, and modification
- Learning theory and styles
- Motivational stages and needs
- Memory stages, types, and processing
- Reading types, accesses, and goals
- Action structures
- Problem-solving processes and obstacles

You add a users' profile that identifies their:

- Perceptual sets
- Place on user curves
- Learning styles
- Feedback needs
- Habits, habit families, and habit strengths
- Reading strategies
- Existing schemata that you can leverage
- Existing schemata that you have to help them modify
- New schemata that you have to help them build
- Problem-solving obstacles
- Relationship to the problem domain

You add an information subtext profile for each unit of information that specifies:

- Media type and subtype
- Navigational infrastructure
- Presentation standards
- Storyboard that reflects the media type and subtype, navigational infrastructure, and presentation standards

Now you begin your information's text profile that:

- Defines the problem
- Responds to the problem

When helping users identify and respond to the problem, think of your information as an inverted tree: roots in the air, trunk connecting roots and branches, and branches on the ground. The roots are the foundation; they nurture the rest of the tree. This is the concept and background information users need to understand the problem. The trunk is the main response to the problem. It is the response you are teaching users. It may not be the only response. The branches are the auxiliary information such as alternate responses, exceptions, notes, emphases, and supporting information. Sometimes small branches spring out of the trunk, such as notes or cross-references, but if too many branches grow out of the trunk, the trunk weakens and splits and cannot support the entire unit.

## Defining the Problem

Before you can define the problem for your users, you must thoroughly understand the problem and its solutions. This is where your knowledge of the problem domain is critical. You must thoroughly understand your subject matter or you cannot hope to define the problem and offer solutions. It is not enough to accept and edit input from subject matter experts. You must understand that input as it relates to the problems your users want to solve. This really is the heart of technical communication.

Users depend on you to define the problem in such a way that they can relate to it. Users do not approach information from a functional perspective; they approach it from a problem-solving perspective.

Consider this scenario:

Adele is sitting on the front porch watching her two children play with their new puppy. Her children are young: five and seven years old. Her job is secure, but she is worrying about her career path. She is an assistant store manager for a major supermarket chain. She has every expectation that she will manage her own store some day.

While she can provide well enough for her and her children now, she is concerned about the future. She wants her children to go to college, and she knows that in ten years, college costs will be astronomical.

A friend gave her some brochures on mutual funds. She is thinking she ought to look into investing in some mutual funds.

What is the problem Adele wants to solve? When she picks up the brochure on mutual funds, is the problem to be solved that she wants to invest in mutual funds? No. Adele does not get up one morning and say, "Today I invest in mutual funds." She gets up every morning, however, and says, "How can I make sure there is enough money for my children to go to college?" The problem Adele wants to solve is how to ensure she has enough money in ten years to send her children to college.

So, Adele reads the brochure on mutual funds. She learns what load and no-load mutual funds are, what an indexed mutual fund is, even how mutual funds perform in relation to certificates of deposit and annuities. What she does not learn is how to ensure she has enough money in ten years to send her children to college, which is the problem she wants to solve.

Users often pick up a unit of information thinking it contains the answer to their problem. They trust that you know what their problem is. The technical communicator who created the mutual funds brochure did a good job of teaching the basics of mutual funds. The technical communicator, however, did not anticipate that users picking up the brochure would not know how to define the problem they want to solve. If the technical communicator had put mutual funds in context as only one financial instrument, included a checklist to help users determine if mutual funds are the right investment for them, and pointed users to other information sources, Adele would have found that perhaps mutual funds are part of what her investment portfolio should be, and she would have had a path to follow to find the complete solution to her problem.

Consider this scenario:

> Roger's boss has purchased new software and wants Roger to use it to project their customers' buying trends over the next 18 months.

> Roger fiddles around with the software, pulling down menus, calling up the charts and graphs dialog box, and skimming through some of the online help.

> He has no idea where to begin. So...he calls up the online information and begins reading in earnest.

> It tells him all the features and functions, gives him hints and tips on making dazzling exploding pie charts, and explains how to merge database information into a report and print the report. It does not, however, give him any idea of how to fit all the pieces together to solve his problem: creating a report that projects customer-buying trends over the next 18 months.

No doubt all of the information Roger needs is in the online information. The technical communicator wrote concise, accurate procedures, investigated time-saving hints and tips, and anticipated every type of trend users would want to project. Why, then, four hours later, is Roger still sweating and swearing at his desk trying to figure out how to perform a task his manager thought would take no more than an hour?

As with most users, Roger wants to solve a problem that is an end-to-end task comprising many functions, features, and subtasks. He does not want to import database information or input trend-analysis variables or create a chart or print a report. He wants to do all of it in one task. He wants to look up some information on projecting future trends and find a big picture of everything he needs, how to put it all together, and a problem-solving scenario that imitates his real-world problem-solving tasks.

In this scenario, Roger is obviously a beginner-level user of the new software. As such, he needs the online information to help him:

* Store specific knowledge about using the software

    Beginner-level users store domain-specific knowledge in small, fragmented, disparate units. They do not understand the big picture or how the information fits together.

    Roger needs help creating a using-this-software schema that shows him how to store specific information about using this software in large, solution-oriented, interconnected units. He needs to learn how to easily retrieve the information and link it to other large units of knowledge he already possesses.

    The technical communicator did an admirable job creating the subtext of medium, navigational infrastructure, and presentation. In developing content, however, the technical communicator revealed a status of beginner-level user. The information reflects small, fragmented, disparate units of information, does not provide a big picture of how the information fits together, and does not present a framework of solution-oriented, interconnected units of information that helps Roger build a schema and successfully use the software.

    While we expect beginner-level users in our user communities, our users do not expect beginner-level status in their technical communicators.

* Apply specific knowledge about using the software

    Beginner-level users apply specific knowledge in a series of halting, disjointed, manual steps. Roger needs information that leverages schemata he already has. As a technical communicator, you must help him modify existing schemata or build new ones, and move him to the point of automaticity using the new software.

- Identify problems he wants to solve with the software

As a beginner-level user, Roger can observe and evaluate the new software only at a surface level; his observations are disjointed, out-of-context, and appearance-oriented. He does not have an integrated functional schema of the software and cannot relate the new software to any other software he has used.

He cannot posit problems in terms of the new software. He knows the problem he needs to solve, but he cannot frame it in reference to the new software. He needs help creating an integrated schema that he can relate to what he already knows and what he will learn in the future.

- Generate and test hypotheses that teach him how to solve problems using the software

Since he is a beginner-level user, Roger cannot detect clues in the software that would lead him to solving his problem with the software. He cannot generate hypotheses to test what the software can do to help him solve problems.

If the technical communicator had created the information using a user profile, the information would reflect examples, extended examples, and problem-solving scenarios that Roger could relate to his everyday work world.

These examples, extended examples, and problem-solving scenarios would give Roger the big picture, take him from using the software in halting manual steps to using it almost automatically, help him build an integrated schema of the software that he can relate to his present and future body of knowledge, and show him how to generate and test hypotheses so he can use the software to solve other problems in his daily work world.

Neither Adele nor Roger has a context for the problem or the factual, semantic, schematic, or strategic problem-domain knowledge they need to solve their problem. The information they have brought into their world does not provide them with a solution to the big picture.

Consider the following scenario:

Mearl is a network database administrator for the Western region of a large manufacturing firm. His job is to ensure that customer, order, and inventory databases are available on the network 24 hours a day, seven days a week. The central repository for the database information is called the hub system.

Communications errors with the hub system have started to impact productivity, so Mearl is going to move the data from the hub system to a back-up system and establish the back-up system as the new hub system. This is the problem Mearl wants to solve. While he has used this particular network software for two years, he has never moved the hub data and established a new hub.

He turns to the system administrator's manual and finds a chapter on migrating the hub. When he reads the information on this chapter, he finds that it is information on migrating the hub system to a new release of software, not migrating the data and the status of the hub system itself.

He looks under "hub" in the index. Among the entries, he finds "registering the hub." He turns to that information and finds how to register the hub system, which is what he did when he set up the network with this software. He cannot find information on moving the hub data and establishing a new hub.

Mearl then looks up "moving", "data," and "database" in the index, but does not find the information he needs. Meanwhile, every minute he spends trying to find the information is another minute his company is losing productivity.

He turns to the troubleshooting section of the manual. There he finds a section of what to do when there is trouble communicating with the hub. Mearl finally calls the customer support number and finds out that he has to do three things: 1) back up the hub database, 2) load the backed up database on the new hub system, 3) distribute a new hub pointer to all network nodes.

The procedures for doing these three things are in the documentation, but Mearl did not know that his problem comprised these three components. Mearl is much like Roger in that he knows his problem, but after two years of working with the software, he still did not have an integrated schema that enabled him to break down his problem into component tasks.

Users often either do not know what problem they want to solve or do not know the component tasks of the problem they want to solve. They depend on you to know what the problem is and how it breaks down.

They also depend on you to give them the big picture and help them create an integrated schema so they can solve problems as they arise.

You must provide the factual, semantic, schematic, and strategic problem-domain knowledge users need in order to understand the big picture and create an integrated schema. See Chapter 5, Problem Solving, for more information on factual, semantic, schematic, and strategic problem-solving knowledge.

As much as you help users determine what the problem is, you must also help them determine what the problem is not. Much like the paper-clip in the box scenario of Chapter 5, users sometimes take the long way around a problem because they do not know the short cut.

Some guidelines to help you aid your users in identifying the problem are:

- Put the problem in context.
- Ensure that users have the correct level of problem-domain knowledge.
- Help users form the big picture and create integrated schema.
- Be clear on what the problem is not as well as on what it is.
- Present the shortest, most direct route to identifying the problem.
- Do not dilute the main thrust of identifying the problem with extraneous information.

## Responding to the Problem

Correctly framing the problem is half the content. The other half is helping users respond to the problem. You must present problem solving in a way that takes advantage of users' existing schemata, memory processes, learning styles, reasoning approaches, place on user curves, feedback and motivational needs, and ability to create action structures. You must anticipate and overcome users' obstacles to problem solving. Anytime you can leverage existing schemata, you make your and your users' jobs easier. For example, if users already know how to use Microsoft Word for Macintosh, you can leverage that knowledge to help them build an integrated problem-solving schema for WordPerfect for Macintosh.

Examples, extended examples, and problem-solving scenarios presented in categorical, linear, or conditional syllogistic logic are excellent ways of helping your users modify and create schemata to respond to problems. Start with concepts they already know; stress the similarities before leading them to deduce the exceptions. This creates a psychological comfort zone for your users. Terminology maps and topical road maps that compare and contrast concepts also help users modify and create schemata. For example, Microsoft Word for Macintosh and WordPerfect for Macintosh have a great many mutual functions, controls, and terms. If you were leveraging knowledge of one to help users learn the other, you would begin by comparing these similarities, ensuring that users are comfortable with them and enabling users to demonstrate their mastery of them. Only then should you move on to the differences.

You must anticipate and overcome your users' obstacles to problem solving. Consider this scenario:

> Barbara works in an office that is automating its manual accounts receivable procedures. Barbara has handled the accounts receivable for 11 years, and she has a complex system of handwritten notes and stickies that helps her track all of the information she needs about each account.

> Since the automated system does not enable either handwritten notes or stickies, Barbara cannot see how the system will be a success. Naturally, when her boss hands her the user's guide and tells her to learn the new method, Barbara's perceptual set and functional fixedness inhibit her ability to learn. She falls prey to learned and taught helplessness, sees her usefulness to the company falling by the wayside, and vents her frustration and anger on the new automated process.

To Barbara, a computer is not a tool for doing her work. Her T-tables, adding machine, pencil, and stickies are tools that she is comfortable with and that have served her well in the past. When overcoming users' obstacles to problem solving, the technical communicator sometimes has to don the hat of salesperson. Not that the information should be marketing information or sales fluff, but it must acknowledge users' obstacles and invite them to change perceptual sets and functional fixedness by showing them the benefits of new ways of looking at what they do. Refer to Chapter 5, Problem Solving, for information on obstacles to problem solving.

As you develop your content, remember that short-term memory is our working memory. Everything we do, we do as a result of short-term memory processing. Chunking, serial-position effect, and image reinforcement help users successfully process information in short-term memory.

Consider Frank's plight:

Frank wants to remove the folding closet doors from the closet in his den. He gets out his handy-dandy home repair manual and looks up "doors" in the index. He finds "removing" as an entry and turns to that information.

An 18-step procedure that is completely textual greets him. He begins reading through the procedure. One of the steps mentions a Phillips head screwdriver; six steps later, another step mentions a special tool for removing molding; still later, another step mentions finishing nails to replace the facing after removing the molding.

Frank reads through the procedure, gathers the tools, and begins removing his closet doors. He finds that it takes him almost an hour and a half for a job that should have taken half an hour at the most.

The technical communicator did a fine job indexing and making the information available. Frank was able to remove his closet doors, so the information was technically accurate. Frank was able to articulate the problem he wanted to solve and was able to find information that told him how to solve it. His task would have been easier, however, if the technical communicator had:

- Put a short list of necessary tools before the procedure
- Included an estimate of how long the procedure would take
- Chunked the information by collapsing procedural steps under process steps
- Re-enforced the textual procedure with graphics

Refer to Chapter 4, Memory, for information on the stages and processes of memory.

If your users want to move up the user curves, you must help them traverse the curves, providing adequate feedback at each stage to motivate them to continue.

Consider this scenario:

Margo is learning a new application that automatically adds and cancels credit life insurance for revolving personal loans at the bank where she works. Until now, the bank has been processing insurance manually, so Margo has no experience using a computer to perform this task. She is an entry-sensorimotor-trust-level user, but needs and wants to move up the user curves quickly to the power-abstract thinking-confidence level.

The hardcopy tutorial for this application revolves around extended scenarios that build on each other, gaining in complexity. At the end of the tutorial, the user should be able to perform all critical tasks that result in adding and canceling credit life insurance for revolving personal loans.

The first tutorial scenario is accessing the Customer Search screen and returning to the Main menu. The second scenario is accessing the Customer Information screen from the Customer Search screen. The third scenario is accessing the Purchase Insurance screen from the Customer Information screen.

At the end of the third scenario, Margo has spent 45 minutes and still cannot perform a task. She is disgusted with the tutorial, and her frustration with the new application mounts.

The technical communicator's instincts about using a tutorial approach with building-block scenarios was on target. This is an excellent approach for users who are low on the user curves but want to move up those curves. However, the technical communicator did not enable Margo to move up the curve or to have a feeling of accomplishment. The information stymies Margo and enslaves her low on the user curves. The information is too granular. After three scenarios, Margo wants to be able to perform a task, not just move from screen to screen.

The technical communicator could have met Margo's needs and expectations better by:

- Presenting the problem-solving information by component tasks rather than component screens

- Incorporating several component tasks into one scenario

- Quickly moving users to successful completion of a representative task

- Providing feedback at the task level rather than at the navigation level

While you may need to break down the tasks into their most elemental phases to understand them and design effective content, users do not learn tasks at an atomic level. They learn them at a problem-solving level. Being able to get to three screens does not solve any of Margo's problems. Performing tasks on those screens and receiving feedback does. Refer to Chapter 3, Learning, for information on user curves and feedback needs.

Part of moving up user curves is moving tasks from being effortful to being automatic. An excellent way of doing this is building associations into users' integrated schemata.

Consider this scenario:

Dave is writing a policy and procedures manual for an insurance firm. One of the procedures addresses how to open the office, which includes how to prepare the office's mid-size computer for the day's business.

A critical point is that the person opening the office must advance the computer's system date to the calendar date of the current business day. Dave chooses to make advancing the system date a separate procedure and not include it in the procedure on opening the office. He feels the information is so important that it warrants its own procedure.

During editorial review, Dave's editor questions the reasoning behind making advancing the system date a procedure and asks Dave to incorporate it into the procedure on opening the office.

Often technical communicators think that the way to stress the importance of information is to call attention to it. This can be disruptive to users' attempts to build schemata. Integrating information and helping users form associations among pieces of information is more effective. This is the point Dave's editor was making. Certainly advancing the system date is important. Making it an integral part of the procedure on opening the office solidifies that importance in users' minds, because they make an association between opening the office and advancing the system date. This association helps them build an integrated schemata of opening the office, which always includes advancing the system date.

Users solve problems by creating and executing action structures. They use your information to do this. To help users successfully create and execute action structures, you must help them evaluate their environment (identify the problem), create a goal (conceptually move from identification to response), and execute a series of actions that accomplishes that goal (respond to the problem).

Consider the following:

Eulinda is preparing a proposal in response to a request for proposal (RFP) that her company received. The RFP clearly identifies the problem and the deadline for resolving the problem. Eulinda's proposal must build the conceptual bridge from problem identification to response, articulate the goal, define a series of actions that achieves the goal, and identify criteria by which the soliciting firm can evaluate how well Eulinda's company has obtained the goal.

Eulinda's clear, well-written, thoughtful proposal addresses all of these but the last. Her proposal ends with a discussion of how her company can achieve the goal. She feels that she has done a good job on the proposal and is confident her company will be among the finalists for the contract. She is dismayed to learn two weeks later that her company is out of the running.

An action structure is circular. Evaluation leads to goal, which leads to actions, which lead back to evaluation. Eulinda's users had no way of getting back to evaluation. They could not determine whether the action structure would be successful, since she did not provide a means of evaluating the success of the series of actions she designed to meet the goal.

Some guidelines to help you aid your users in responding to the problem are:

- Leverage existing schemata, memory processes, learning styles, place on user curves, feedback and motivational needs, and ability to create action structures.

- Anticipate and overcome users' obstacles to problem solving and do not let them fall into learned and taught helplessness.

- Use examples, extended examples, and problem-solving scenarios to leverage existing knowledge and help users build integrated schemata.

- Present problem-solving and feedback at the task level, remembering that a user task may comprise several component tasks.

- Help users form associations among pieces of information to enable them to build integrated schemata.

- Ensure that your information supports the three phases of a basic action structure as well as the circular nature of action structures.

Refer to Chapter 7, Actions, for information on action structures.

## Summary

The content of your information is the text. You must have three things before beginning your content: understanding of the physical and psychological processes, needs, and expectations that compose your users' world; your users' profile; and your information's subtext profile.

The two main components of content are identifying the problem users want to solve and helping them respond to the problem. Before you can define the problem for your users, you must thoroughly understand the problem and its solutions. Users depend on you to define the problem in such a way that they can relate to it. Users do not approach information from a functional perspective; they approach it from a problem-solving perspective. You must present problem solving in a way that takes advantage of users existing schemata, memory processes, learning styles, reasoning approaches, place on user curves, feedback and motivational needs, and ability to create action structures. You must anticipate and overcome users' obstacles to problem solving.

## Further Reading

Bringhurst, R. "Concrete Methods that Promote Active Learning in Software Manuals," *STC Proceedings*, 1993.

Carroll, J.M. *The Nurnberg Funnel: Designing Minimalist Instruction for Practical Computer Skill*. Cambridge, MA: MIT Press, 1990.

Casey, C. and L. Lindahl. "Richard Saul Wurman: Helping Us Understand Information," *STC Proceedings*, 1995.

Dart, G.P., Jr. "Practical Human Factors for Document Design," *STC Proceedings*, 1993.

Gordon, S. and V. Lewis. "Enhancing Hypertext Documents to Support Learning from Text," *Technical Communication*, 39.

Grech, C. "Computer Documentation Doesn't Pass Muster," *PC/Computing*. April 1992.

Isaksen, S.G. et al. *Creative Approaches to Problem Solving*. Dubuque, IA: Kendall/Hunt Publishing, Co., 1994.

Livingstone, D. "Improving Documentation with Learning Techniques," *STC Proceedings*, 1993.

McClelland, P.J. and A. Bourdel. "Write Once, Use Many: Why and How We Make Product Information Modular," *STC Proceedings*, 1993.

Mirel, B. et al. "Designing Manuals for Active Learning Styles," *Technical Communication*, 38:1.

Rathbone, R.R. *Communicating Technical Information: A Guide to Current Uses and Abuses in Scientific and Engineering Writing*. Reading, MA: Addison-Wesley Publishing Company, 1966.

Wright, P. and F. Reid. "Written Information: Some Alternatives to Prose for Expressing the Outcomes of Complex Contingencies," *Journal of Applied Psychology*, 57:2, 1973, pp.160–166.

# Writing for
# Other Cultures

Technical communicators face special challenges when writing information for cultures other than their own. When writing for an audience that is a subset of your culture, you can be sure that your users understand the references, metaphors, icons, and colors that you use. When you write for an audience that is not part of your own culture, however, you can be sure of none of this.

While the processes of sensation and perception, learning, memory, problem solving, and acting are universal, the concepts, schemata, references, graphics, subtext, and eye movement across a page or screen are not. When writing for other cultures, you must write in a way that ensures that your target cultures can access your information.

When writing for other cultures, you are writing information that either a translation vendor is going to translate into one or more foreign languages or someone whose first language is not English is going to read. If you are sending the information to translation, in addition to multicultural considerations, you have to consider the needs and limitations of the translation process and how to interact with a translation vendor.

There are basically three types of translation:

1. Manual

   A person or group of persons translates each word of your source information into the target language or languages.

2. Machine

   A computer reads your source information and translates it into the target language or languages.

3. Machine-assisted

   A translation operator programs glossaries, boilerplate, and algorithms into a computer, which translates your source information into the target language or languages. If there is something in the source that the computer cannot translate, it flags it for the operator to translate.

There are advantages and disadvantages to all three types of translation. Table A.1 summarizes the advantages and disadvantages of each type.

Whatever type of translation you choose, you should always negotiate post-translation proofing and testing of the information as part of the per-word translation cost. You should also consider whether your translation vendor supports localization, translating the source in the country of the target culture. Localization is more of an issue in some cultures than in others. It is extremely important in Asian and Middle Eastern cultures, for example, because the cultural protocols of what appears on page or screen are more stringent than in Western cultures.

You must also consider how you transmit files to a translation vendor, how the translation vendor returns files to you, and how you and the vendor communicate problems during the translation process.

Regardless of the target language, you must build in translation expansion space. For example, "Keep cartridge sealed until ready to use" is seven words and 40 letters and spaces in English but 10 words and 70 letters and spaces in French ("Gardez la cartouche dans son emballage jusqu'au moment de l'utilisation"). Start by adding 15 percent right off the top, then use Table A.2 to determine how much more translation expansion space you should build into your English information.

For example, if you have a unit of information with 2000 words and 13,000 letters and spaces, you should build in 45 percent expansion space (15 percent + 30 percent). This unit of information, then, expands by 45 percent when translated, which is something you need to know when estimating pages and panels, figuring production time, and determining how much binding to order.

**Table A.1** Advantages and Disadvantages of Various Types of Translation

| *Type* | *Advantages* | *Disadvantages* |
|---|---|---|
| Manual | Most accurate of the three types | Most expensive of the three types |
| | You can be more involved with manual translation than you can with the other types | Not cost-effective for large amounts of information |
| | Most cost-effective for small amounts of information such as reference cards, medical inserts, flyers, brochures, and pamphlets | Takes more time than the other two types |
| | Is the only means to translate graphics; even machine-assisted translation depends on a translation operator to construct and translate graphics | |
| Machine | Least expensive of the types | Prone to literal, often poorly translated information |
| | Can translate a great amount of source information in a short amount of time | You are not involved in the translation process |
| | | Cannot translate graphics |
| Machine assisted | Combines the speed of machine translation with the accuracy of human involvement | Cannot translate graphics |
| | You provide the glossaries and boilerplate that the computer uses to translate the material | More expensive than machine translation |
| | Less expensive than manual translation | |
| | Cost-effective for large amounts of information | |

**Table A.2** Expansion Space

| Number of Characters | Add Expansion Space |
| --- | --- |
| 1-10 | 100-200 percent |
| 11-20 | 81-100 percent |
| 21-30 | 61-80 percent |
| 31-50 | 41-60 percent |
| 51-70 | 31-40 percent |
| 71+ | 30 percent |

There are ten general areas of concern when writing for translation:

1. Grammatical constructions
2. Special characters
3. Cultural references
4. Humor
5. "Isms"
6. Vocabulary
7. Usage
8. Graphics and icons
9. Color
10. Special files

## Grammatical Constructions

Not every culture supports all grammatical constructions. Among those you should avoid when writing for translation are:

- Possessives

  Non-English-speaking cultures do not indicate possession with 's. They use a genitive construction. Instead of saying, "The book's index" say, "The index of the book."

- Contractions

  Non-English-speaking cultures do not use contractions. For example, instead of using "isn't," "can't," or "won't," use "is not," "cannot," and "will not."

- Passive voice

  Even in English, passive voice is not a good habit for technical communicators. It indicates nonuser-centered information for the most part.[1] Even English readers who are prelingually deaf or dyslexic have trouble deciphering the passive voice, especially the agentless passive. Readers for whom English is a second language have a very difficult time deciphering the passive voice.

  Non-English-speaking cultures do not use the passive construction. French, for example, creates either a reflexive construction (French speaks itself here) or uses the third person neutral (One speaks French here).

- Imperative

  Some non-U.S. cultures take offense at the imperative (command) form of verbs. You can use a "softer" form of the imperative to convey the same information. For example, instead of saying, "Insert the diskette into drive A" you can say, "Make sure the diskette is in drive A." Both are imperatives, but the second appears less abrasive.

  You can also try to avoid the imperative altogether with something like, "The diskette should be in drive A." You can also use a graphic to illustrate a command. However, it is sometimes hard to write procedural information and avoid the imperative.

- Noun clusters

  Many languages do not use noun clusters, so translating them is a nightmare that results in long, unusable sentences. Even in English, this example is hard to understand: "Find the glare screen bracket peg adjuster screw."

  The rule of thumb is use no more than three nouns in a noun cluster. I would suggest even fewer if possible.

- Positional words

  Positional words are words that change the meaning of the sentence depending on their position. For example, when native English speakers hear, "I only have eyes for you" they know that the meaning is "I have eyes only for you."

  Native speakers of any language make acoustical adjustments on the fly as they listen to speech. One of these acoustical adjustments is assigning the true meaning of positional words such as, "only," "merely," "just," "mainly," and "simply."

When you write for translation, you have to be careful when using positional words and be sure you position them correctly in your sentence.

- Compound, complex, and compound-complex sentences

  Simple sentences reflect a 1:1 ratio between sentence and number of ideas. It is far easier to translate one idea per sentence than it is to muddle through a jumble of ideas that you have strung together with punctuation and conjunctions. Simple sentences are shorter as well, and as the next bullet indicates, sentences for translation should have no more than 16 words.

- Sentences longer than 16 words

  The rule of thumb is that sentences for translation should never exceed 16 words; average length should be 10 words.

- Comma-separated series

  A list with incorrect punctuation is a translation disaster. It is easier on both the translator and the reader if you format your information in lists rather than series. It also helps you achieve chunking and white space.

- Abbreviations, initialisms, and acronyms

  Some languages such as Arabic and Hebrew do not have abbreviations. Some languages such as Mandarin and Kanji use the Roman letters for abbreviations, initialisms, and acronyms then explain them with pictographic characters in parentheses.

  The fewer abbreviations, initialisms, and acronyms you have in information for translation, the easier it is on the translation vendor and the end user. It is also less expensive, because translation costs are per-word costs. If you must use abbreviations, initialisms, and acronyms, you have to give the translation vendor a special file (special files are covered later in this chapter).

- "That" and "which" used interchangeably to introduce restrictive and nonrestrictive clauses

  Native English speakers acoustically correct the incorrect use of "that" and "which" to introduce restrictive and nonrestrictive clauses, respectively. When you write for translation, it is important to use the correct relative pronoun.

There is a great deal of difference between "These are the translation rules, which I follow" (I follow all of the translation rules) and "These are the translation rules that I follow" (I follow a subset of the rules; I choose not to follow all of the rules).

- And/or constructions

  Non-English languages do not use the and/or construction, so spell it out in your source. Say, "use commands and macros" instead of, "Use commands and/or macors."

- Plurals formed by adding (s)

  Non-English-speaking cultures do not form plurals by adding "s" or "es," so the (s) to denote plural does not apply in those cultures. Say, "Users can customize their icons" instead of, "Users can customize their icon(s)."

- Date format

  In the United States, 5/9/95 means May 9, 1995, but in other cultures it means September 5, 1995. When writing for translation, always spell out the date to avoid confusion.

## Special Characters

Not all language keyboards support all characters, and not all cultures use all special characters to mean the same thing. Special characters you should avoid in information for translation are:

- # to indicate "pound"
- $ to indicate currency
- · to indicate multiplication
- " to indicate inches and "ditto" and ' to indicate feet
- — (em dash) to indicate parenthetical information
- ? to indicate help

## Cultural References

Every culture has its own references that do not translate across cultures. Avoid these types of cultural references in information for translation.

- Geographical nicknames

  A Russian user might not understand a reference to the Big Apple, the Big Easy, or the Mile High state.

- Literature

  An Asian user might not understand a reference to "Frankly my dear, I don't give a damn," Mr. Toad's wild ride, or the scarlet letter A.

- Holidays

  An Ethiopian user might not understand a reference to Mother's Day, Thanksgiving, or Spring Break.

- Legends

  A Peruvian user might not understand a reference to Paul Bunyan, Washington and the cherry tree, or the mighty Casey.

- Puns

  A user in Spain might not appreciate N. E. Thyme, A. N. Other, or Dr. Stasick.

- Mores

  A user in Greece might not understand a reference to the protocols of "sir" and "ma'am" in the South, not making eye contact with a highway patrol officer, or always tipping the Keno operator.

- Celebrities

  A user in China might not understand a reference to the Divine Miss M, Air Jordan, or the Sultan of Swing.

- Jargon and lingo

  A user in Wales might not understand a reference to URL, red alert, or crash cart.

- Slang

  A user in Sri Lanka might not understand a reference to deuce and a quarter, gum shoe, or "best thing since sliced bread."

- Names

  In the United States, John Doe, John Q. Public, and Mary Smith are stereotypical names that we use to indicate Anyman or Anywoman, but other cultures do not use them. If you must use names in information for translation, use these names for first names:

- Ann
- Betty
- Tom
- Joe

and these names for last names:

- White
- Green
- Jones
- Smith

When translation vendors come across these names in source information, they select equally common, stereotypical names in the target cultures.

## Humor

Humor is cultural and does not translate well. What is funny in Zaire may not be funny in Canada. More than any other type of communication, humor depends on people's shared experiences, and people from disparate cultures do not have the wealth of shared experiences they need to share humor.

Sometimes, however, you want to write something with a humorous slant. In these instances, it is necessary to have the information written in the target culture. For example, you might have a brochure introducing a new product and you want to take a lighthearted approach to convincing people to buy this product. The Greek brochure would not read like the Kanji brochure, which would not read like the Russian brochure.

Sales and marketing information rely heavily not only on humor but also on cultural references. It is better to have a native of the target culture create this information in the target language.

## "Isms"

The most important "isms" to avoid in information for translation are:

- Sexism
- Racism
- Nationalism

What is an offensive "ism" to one culture, however, may not be to another. For example, in a graphic showing a group of business people, Western cultures would be offended if both men and women were not portrayed. In Middle Eastern cultures, a woman in a business position or a position of authority is offensive. You must understand the "isms" of your target cultures.

To be on the safe side, graphically portray androgynous stickperson-like figures if a graphic serves Western, Asian, and Middle Eastern cultures. If multimedia is part of your product, do not use a woman's voice-over for Middle Eastern cultures. Write as much as possible in the third person plural to avoid having to refer to "him" or "her," or recast your information in the second person.

Be sensitive to nationalistic prejudices. Do not use a nationalist reference or graphic that would incite a particular culture. Be careful about what your graphics' subtext is saying when you mix genders, races, and nationalities.

"Isms" are a particularly sensitive issue; research your target cultures enough to know what offends.

## Vocabulary

There are some words that are especially troublesome in translation:

- Billion

  The word "billion" means 1,000,000,000 in the United States, but 1,000,000,000,000 in the United Kingdom. When referring to a billion of something, spell out the word "billion."

- Foreign and Domestic

  These words tend to flip-flop when readers outside the country of origin read them. For example, a British technical communicator might use the word "domestic" to refer to the United Kingdom, but when readers in India read "domestic," they think it refers to India.

  Likewise, that British technical communicator might use "foreign" to mean non-United Kingdom countries, while the readers in India assume it means non-India countries.

  Spell out the names of countries you are referring to or say something like, "in countries other than the United Kingdom."

- Invalid

  Even in English-speaking cultures, the word "invalid" has a dual meaning: not valid and a person who is infirm. In some cultures, "invalid" means broken or out of order. To avoid confusion, say "not valid" or rewrite the sentence to eliminate the term. For example, instead of saying, "The system does not allow invalid file names" say, "The system does not allow duplicate file names or file names containing embedded blanks."

- Translation

  In the United States, we often use the word "translation" to refer to data. Other cultures do not, however. They use the word "conversion."

- Male and female

  In some cultures, the terms "male" and "female" apply only to nonhuman animals and it is an insult to use them in reference to humans. The terms "man" and "woman" are universally accepted.

## Usage

When writing for translation, precision and clarity are of utmost importance. Native English speakers usually understand usage that may be grammatically incorrect; however, you cannot rely on translation vendors or non-native speakers of English to understand the intent of your grammar. You have to be especially careful about using:

- Can and may

  Many English speakers in the United States have given up the distinction between can and may, but in other cultures the distinction is important. "Can" denotes ability, while "may" denotes permission or probability.

- Since meaning because

  The word "since" has two meanings: ever since and because. To avoid confusion with the word "because," use "since" to mean only "ever since."

- When meaning if

  English speakers in the United States often mistakenly use "when" and "if" interchangeably. "When" indicates an event that is inevitable, and "if" indicates an event that has a dependency on another event.

For example, "When the system administrator assigns a user profile" does not mean the same thing as, "If the system administrator assigns a user profile."

- Alternate and alternative

English speakers in the United States often incorrectly use these two words synonymously, although they are not synonyms. "Alternate" means every other one, skipping the ones in between; "alternative" means another choice.

- Affect and effect

These two words give many English speakers trouble. "Affect" is a verb meaning "to influence," while "effect" is a noun that means "result" or a verb that means "to bring about."

- Agree to and agree with

In English, the nuances of these verbs rest on the prepositions "to" and "with," so that English speakers often confuse them. "Agree to" means "to consent," while "agree with" means "to be in harmony with."

- Anticipate and expect

English speakers in the United States often mistakenly use "anticipate" and "expect" interchangeably. "Anticipate" indicates that you have taken steps in preparation for an event, while "expect" indicates that you consider an event likely to occur.

For example, "Anticipating a strike by union workers, we have trained management to perform line functions" is correct, while, "Expecting a strike by union workers, we have trained management to perform line functions" is incorrect. Likewise, "We anticipate a strike" is incorrect, while, "We expect a strike" is correct.

- Assure, ensure, and insure

These words give many English speakers trouble. "Assure" means "to promise" in reference to people. "Ensure" and "insure" are verbs meaning "to make certain," though the preference is to reserve "insure" for information dealing with insurance.

Use these verbs with care, because they imply guaranty and have legal implications.

- Augment and supplement

  Some English speakers confuse the meanings of these two words as verbs. As a verb, "supplement" means "to make complete," while "augment" means "to increase." "Supplement" is also a noun, which means "something added."

- Complement and compliment

  Because these two words are homonyms, their use as nouns, verbs, and adjectives is often confusing for English speakers.

  As nouns, "complement" means "that which makes something complete," and "compliment" means "flattery."

  As verbs, "complement" means "to make complete," and "compliment" means "to flatter."

  As adjectives, "complementary" means "related to making complete," and "complimentary" means "related to flattery" or "something that is free."

- Compose and comprise

  While these words are antonyms, many English speakers use them synonymously. "Compose" means "to make up or be included in," while "comprise" means "to include." Remember the mnemonic "The parts compose the whole, and the whole comprises the parts."

  Often English speakers use the incorrect phrase "is comprised of" to mean "comprise."

- Continuous and continual

  These two words give a great many English speakers trouble. "Continuous" means "without stopping," and "continually" means "intermittently."

  It is a good idea to rewrite information so as to avoid including these often misused words. For example, instead of saying, "Continually check the valve pressure and make the necessary adjustments" say, "Check the valve pressure at regular intervals and make the necessary adjustments." "Continuously check the valve pressure" would mean that the person should check the valve pressure over and over, never stopping.

- Discrete and discreet

  These are two more homonyms that give English speakers trouble. "Discrete" means "being separate," while "discreet" means "showing prudent judgment."

- Disinterested and uninterested

  A great many English speakers do not know how to use these adjectives correctly. "Disinterested" means "without prejudice," while "uninterested" means "without interest."

  For example, a "disinterested observer" is not the same thing as an "uninterested observer." You probably would seek out a disinterested observer to settle a dispute, whereas you probably would not want an uninterested observer to settle anything.

- Due to and because of

  English speakers often incorrectly use these two phrases interchangeably. "Due to" is an adjective phrase meaning "attributable to" and usually follows a form of the verb "to be." "Because of" is a prepositional phrase that means "as a result of."

  For example, "The cracks in her walls were due to the Northridge earthquake" is correct, but, "The cracks in her walls were because of the Northridge earthquake" is incorrect. Likewise, "She had cracks in her walls because of the Northridge earthquake" is correct, whereas, "She had cracks in her walls due to the Northridge earthquake" is incorrect.

- Oral and verbal

  These two words are very confusing for some English speakers. "Oral" means "spoken," while "verbal" means "in words" and can refer to words either spoken or written.

  For example, "An oral agreement" means an agreement that was only spoken, not written, while "a verbal agreement" could mean either an agreement that was spoken or one that was written.

  To avoid confusion, use "oral" to mean "spoken" and "written" to mean "written." Avoid the use of "verbal."

## Graphics and Icons

Graphics and icons are cultural; when you write for translation, you must use "safe" graphics and icons, that is, those that communicate across cultures and do not offend any cultures. The rule of thumb is not to use any body parts or animals in icons and graphics. Use androgynous stick-like figures so as not to offend cultures that do not tolerate graphical representations of women. Table A.3 lists some graphical elements and icons and their cultural associations. For a complete discussion of icons and iconic communication, see the resources in the Further Reading section at the end of this appendix.

Some icons have poignant associations such as the yellow stars Hitler made Jews wear, the pink triangles he made homosexual men wear, and the black triangles he made lesbians wear. Jesse Jackson and his Rainbow Coalition use a multicolored flag as their icon, and homosexuals use a similar multicolored flag as their icon. Some cultures look upon cats, dogs, and rabbits as food while others look upon them as domesticated companions. Some cultures consider beef a fine meal, while Hindus hold cows sacred.

This section has addressed just a few of the many icons and graphical elements that appear in technical information. When writing for other cultures, do your homework. Choose your icons carefully. Do not let otherwise excellent information suffer from a cultural misconception.

**Table A.3** Cultural Associations of Icons

| Symbol | Culture | Association |
| --- | --- | --- |
| **anchor** | | |
| | Christian | orderliness, virtue, patriotism, subordination |
| | universal | hope, steadfastness, stability, tranquillity |
| **ant** | | |
| | Chinese | orderliness, virtue, patriotism, subordination |
| | Greek | harvest |
| | Hindu | transitoriness |
| | universal | industriousness |
| **ape** | | |
| | Celtic | magic, otherworld, fertility, marriage |
| | Chinese | mischief, conceit, mimicry |
| | Christian | malice, cunning, lust, sin |
| | Hindu | benevolence, gentleness |
| **apple** | | |
| | Celtic | magic, otherworld, fertility, marriage |
| | Chinese | peace, concord |

*(continues)*

**Table A.3** Cultural Associations of Icons (*Continued*)

| Symbol | Culture | Association |
|---|---|---|
| | Christian | ambivalence, temptation, sin |
| | Greek | health, immortality |
| | universal | fertility, joyousness, knowledge, wisdom, divination, luxury, deceit, death |
| **arrow** | | |
| | Amerindian | sun's rays |
| | Christian | martyrdom, suffering |
| | Greek | sun's rays, darts of love, union, light, pain, disease |
| | Hindu | earth, storms, fertility, healing rain |
| | Islamic | wrath and punishment |
| | universal | phallus, masculinity, lightning, virility, power |
| **ax** | | |
| | African | magic |
| | Buddhist | severance of life and death |
| | Celtic | divine being, chief, warrior |
| | Chinese | justice, judgment, authority, punishment |
| | Christian | martyrdom, destruction |
| | Egyptian | sun |
| | Hindu | fire |
| | Scandinavian | divinity, chief, warrior |
| | universal | power, thunder, fecundity, sacrifice, help |
| **bear** | | |
| | Amerindian | supernatural power, strength, fortitude |
| | Celtic | sun |
| | Chinese | bravery, strength |
| | Christian | devil, cruelty, greed |
| | Japanese | benevolence, wisdom, strength |
| | universal | new life |
| **bee** | | |
| | Celtic | wisdom |
| | Chinese | industry, thrift |

| Christian | diligence, purity, chastity, courage, economy, prudence, cooperation, sweetness |
| Egyptian | birth, death, resurrection, industry, chastity, harmony, royalty |
| Greek | industry, prosperity, immortality, purity |
| Islamic | faith, intelligence, wisdom, harmlessness |
| Roman | misfortune (swarm), justice, sobriety, monarchy |
| universal | immortality, rebirth, industry, order, purity |

**bell**

| Buddhist | wisdom |
| Chinese | respect, veneration, obedience, harmony |
| Hebrew | vestments, four elements, thunder, lightning |
| Hindu | rank, dignity |
| Teutonic | nobility |

**bird**

| Buddhist | auspiciousness |
| Chinese | longevity, good fortune |
| Christian | winged souls |
| Egyptian | soul |
| Hindu | intelligence |
| Islamic | faith |
| Japanese | creativity |
| Scandinavian | freedom |
| Taoist | sun, cosmic powers |
| universal | transcendence, thought, imagination |

**book**

| Buddhist | wisdom, language, expression |
| Chinese | scholarship |
| Islamic | creativity |
| universal | learning, wisdom |

**bull**

| Buddhist | morality, ego, god of the dead |
| Celtic | divine power and strength |
| Christian | brute force |
| Hebrew | might of Jahveh |

*(continues)*

**Table A.3** Cultural Associations of Icons (*Continued*)

| Symbol | Culture | Association |
|--------|---------|-------------|
| | Iranian | soul of the world, germ of all creation |
| **butterfly** | | |
| | Celtic | soul, fire |
| | Chinese | immortality, leisure, joy |
| | Greek | immortality |
| | Japanese | feminine vanity |
| | Maori | soul |
| | universal | soul, immortality, rebirth, resurrection |
| **candle** | | |
| | Christian | divine light |
| | Hebrew | divine presence |
| | universal | light, illumination, uncertainty |
| **cat** | | |
| | Amerindian | stealth |
| | Celtic | chthonic powers |
| | Chinese | night, powers of evil, transformation |
| | Christian | Satan, darkness, lust, laziness |
| | Egyptian | growth of seed in womb |
| | Græco-Roman | liberty |
| | Japanese | transformation, repose |
| | witchcraft | familiar and disguise of witches |
| **circle** | | |
| | Amerindian | universe, cosmos |
| | Buddhist | existence |
| | Chinese | heavens, perfection |
| | Christian | church |
| | Egyptian | sun |
| | Greek | universe, time, fate |
| | Hindu | existence |
| | Islamic | heaven, divine light |
| | Taoist | supreme power |

| | | |
|---|---|---|
| | universal | totality, wholeness, simultaneity, perfection, self, infinity, eternity |

**cock**

| | | |
|---|---|---|
| | Buddhist | carnal passion and pride |
| | Chinese | courage, valor, benevolence, faithfulness |
| | Christian | vigilance, weakness, repentance |
| | Egyptian | vigilance, foresight |
| | Hebrew | fertility |
| | Iranian | royalty |
| | Scandinavian | underworld |
| | universal | courage, vigilance, dawn |

**compass**

| | | |
|---|---|---|
| | Chinese | right conduct |
| | universal | justice, source of life |

**conch**

| | | |
|---|---|---|
| | Buddhist | oratory, learning |
| | Chinese | royalty, prosperous voyage |
| | Islamic | ear that hears divine words |
| | Mayan | waters |

**cornucopia**

| | | |
|---|---|---|
| | universal | abundance, bounty, fertility |

**cube**

| | | |
|---|---|---|
| | Chinese | earth deity |
| | Hebrew | Holy of Holies |
| | Islamic | stability |
| | Mayan | earth |
| | universal | truth, perfection, completion |

**dagger**

| | | |
|---|---|---|
| | universal | phallus, masculinity, war |

**dog**

| | | |
|---|---|---|
| | African | fire-bringer |
| | Amerindian | rain-bringer, fire-maker, messenger |

*(continues)*

**Table A.3**  Cultural Associations of Icons (*Continued*)

| Symbol | Culture | Association |
|--------|---------|-------------|
| | Buddhist | guardian |
| | Celtic | healing, heroes, war gods |
| | Chinese | fidelity, devotion, prosperity |
| | Christian | fidelity, watchfulness |
| | Islamic | impurity |
| | Japanese | protection |
| **door** | | |
| | universal | hope, opportunity, initiation |
| **duck** | | |
| | Amerindian | mediator |
| | Chinese | conjugal happiness and fidelity, felicity, and beauty |
| | Japanese | conjugal happiness and fidelity, felicity, and beauty |
| | Hebrew | immortality |
| **eagle** | | |
| | Amerindian | revelation, mediator, day |
| | Australian aboriginal | deity |
| | Aztec | celestial power |
| | Buddhist | vehicle of Buddha |
| | Celtic | healing waters |
| | Chinese | sun, authority, warriors, courage, tenacity, keen vision, fearlessness |
| | Christian | spirit, ascension, aspiration, spiritual endeavor |
| | Greek | spiritual power, royalty, victory, favor |
| | Hebrew | renewal |
| | Scandinavian | wisdom |
| | Sumero-Semitic | noon sun |
| **ear** | | |
| | universal | spiral, birth |
| **earth** | | |
| | Amerindian | cosmic center |
| | Celtic | corruptible body |

|  | Chinese | feminine, yin principle |
|---|---|---|
|  | universal | universal genetrix |

**finger, first and fourth raised**

|  | universal | protection against evil, insult if pointing at a person |
|---|---|---|

**finger, on mouth**

|  | universal | silence |
|---|---|---|

**finger, pointing**

|  | universal | magic, insult |
|---|---|---|

**finger, three raised**

|  | Christian | blessing |
|---|---|---|

**finger, two raised**

|  | Greek | blessing, help, strength |
|---|---|---|
|  | universal | teaching, judgment |

**fish**

|  | Buddhist | freedom from restraint, emancipation from desires and attachments |
|---|---|---|
|  | Celtic | foreknowledge of the gods |
|  | Chinese | abundance, wealth, regeneration, harmony |
|  | Christian | baptism, immortality, resurrection |
|  | Egyptian | phallus, creativity, fertility |
|  | Greek | love, fecundity, power of waters |
|  | Hebrew | food of the blessed |
|  | Hindu | wealth, divinity, power of waters |
|  | Japanese | love |
|  | Roman | funerary, power of waters |
|  | Scandinavian | love, fertility |
|  | universal | phallus, fecundity, creation, powers of water |

**flame**

|  | Amerindian | dwelling place of the Great Spirit |
|---|---|---|
|  | Aztec | ritual death |
|  | Buddhist | wisdom |
|  | Chinese | divinity, danger, anger, ferocity, speed |

*(continues)*

**Table A.3** Cultural Associations of Icons (*Continued*)

| Symbol | Culture | Association |
|--------|---------|-------------|
| | Christian | religious fervor, divine revelation |
| | Egyptian | inspiration |
| | Græco-Roman | hearth, inspiration |
| | Hebrew | voice of God, divine revelation |
| | Hindu | transcendental light, knowledge, wisdom, destruction |
| | Iranian | place of divinity, soul of man |
| | Islamic | light, heat, divinity, hell |
| | universal | transformation purification, renewal, impregnation, power, protection, visibility, passion, immolation, fusion, passage from one state to another |
| **fleur-de-lis** | | |
| | universal | light, life, trinity, royalty |
| **globe** | | |
| | Christian | dominion by faith |
| | Græco-Roman | fortune, fate |
| | universal | world, self-containment, power, imperial dignity |
| **hammer** | | |
| | Chinese | sovereign power |
| | Christian | passion of Christ |
| | Græco-Roman | vengeance |
| | Hindu | thunder |
| | Japanese | wealth, good fortune |
| | universal | masculinity, forces of nature, justice, avenging |
| **hand** | | |
| | Celtic | rays of sun |
| | Christian | power and might of God |
| **hand, both clasped** | | |
| | Chinese | friendliness, allegiance |

**hand, both raised**

    universal                        supplication, weakness, ignorance, dependence, surrender

**hand, both together**

    Buddhist                       meditation, receptivity

    Hindu                           meditation, receptivity

**hand, both together in front of heart**

    Buddhist                       wisdom, method

    Hindu                           wisdom

**hand, clenched**

    universal                        threat, aggression

**hand, concealed**

    Chinese                       respect, deference

**hand, covering eyes**

    universal                        shame, horror

**hand, folded**

    universal                        repose, humility

**hand, holding bag**

    Christian                      Judas Iscariot, betrayal

**hand, left**

    Chinese                       yin, femininity

    universal                        receptivity, surrender

**hand, on breast**

    universal                        supplication

**hand, open**

    Islamic                         benediction, adoration, hospitality

**hand, pointing at foot**

    Hindu                           deliverance

*(continues)*

**Table A.3**  Cultural Associations of Icons (*Continued*)

| Symbol | Culture | Association |
|---|---|---|
| **hand, raised** | | |
| | Buddhist | protection |
| | Hindu | peace, protection |
| | universal | adoration, worship, prayer, salutation, amazement, horror |
| **hand, raised palm outwards** | | |
| | Christian | benediction |
| **hand, raised to head** | | |
| | universal | thought, care |
| **hand, right** | | |
| | Buddhist | power over earth |
| | Chinese | yang, masculinity |
| | universal | power |
| **hand, right palm upwards** | | |
| | Buddhist | giving |
| | Hindu | giving |
| **hand, right raised** | | |
| | Buddhist | dauntlessness |
| | Hindu | dauntlessness |
| **hand, three fingers raised** | | |
| | Christian | trinity |
| **hand, two clasping one another** | | |
| | universal | union, friendship, allegiance |
| **hand, two crossed at wrists** | | |
| | universal | binding |

**hand, with three fingers or mutilated**

| | |
|---|---|
| universal | phases of the moon |

**hare**

| | |
|---|---|
| African | moon |
| Amerindian | father, guardian, creator, transformer |
| Celtic | hunting |
| Chinese | moon, longevity |
| Christian | fecundity, lust |
| universal | rebirth, rejuvenation, resurrection, intuition |

**heart**

| | |
|---|---|
| Aztec | center of man, religion, love |
| Buddhist | essential nature of Buddha, purity, indestructibility |
| Celtic | generosity, compassion |
| universal | center of being, compassion, understanding, love |

**key**

| | |
|---|---|
| Christian | keys to heaven |
| Hebrew | raising of the dead, birth, fertilizing rain |
| Japanese | love, wealth, happiness |

**knife**

| | |
|---|---|
| Buddhist | vengeance |
| Christian | martyrdom |

**lion**

| | |
|---|---|
| Buddhist | defender of law, bravery, spiritual zeal |
| Chinese | valor, strength, energy |
| Christian | power, might |
| Egyptian | protection |
| Hebrew | might, cruelty |
| Iranian | royalty, light |
| Japanese | king of beasts |
| Taoist | withdrawal, emptiness of the mind |

**monkey**

| | |
|---|---|
| Buddhist | greed |
| Chinese | ugliness, trickery |

*(continues)*

**Table A.3**  Cultural Associations of Icons (*Continued*)

| Symbol | Culture | Association |
|---|---|---|
|  | Christian | vanity, luxury, the devil |
|  | Hindu | divine power |
| **network** |  |  |
|  | universal | complex relationship beyond time-space sequence |
| **owl** |  |  |
|  | Amerindian | wisdom |
|  | Chinese | evil, crime, death |
|  | Christian | darkness, solitude, mourning, bad news |
|  | Egyptian | death, night, coldness |
|  | Hebrew | blindness |
|  | Hindu | god of the dead |
|  | Japanese | death |
|  | Mexican | night, death |
| **palm tree** |  |  |
|  | Arabian | tree of life |
|  | Chinese | retirement, dignity, fecundity |
|  | Christian | righteousness |
|  | Hebrew | righteous man |
| **pen** |  |  |
|  | Christian | learning |
|  | Egyptian | awakening of the soul |
|  | Islamic | intellect |
| **rainbow** |  |  |
|  | African | guardian of treasures |
|  | Amerindian | ladder of access to other world |
|  | Buddhist | highest state before nirvana |
|  | Chinese | union of heaven and earth |
|  | Christian | pardon, reconciliation |
|  | Islamic | four elements |

|   |   |
|---|---|
| Scandinavian | bridge, the way |
| universal | transfiguration, heavenly glory |

**serpent**

|   |   |
|---|---|
| African | royalty, immortality |
| Amerindian | lunar and magic power, eternity, harbinger of death |
| Buddhist | anger |
| Celtic | healing |
| Chinese | destruction, deceit, cunning |
| Christian | Satan, temptation, craftiness |
| Egyptian | wisdom, power, knowledge |
| Greek | resurrection, healing, wisdom |
| Hebrew | evil, temptation, sin |
| Hindu | cosmic power, chaos, fire |
| Islamic | life |
| Japanese | god of thunder and storms |
| Scandinavian | malevolent forces of the universe |

**skull**

|   |   |
|---|---|
| Buddhist | renunciation of life |
| Christian | vanity of worldly things |
| Hindu | god of the dead |
| universal | death |

**sun**

|   |   |
|---|---|
| African | feminine power, supreme deity |
| Amerindian | universal spirit |
| Buddhist | light |
| Celtic | feminine power |
| Chinese | male principle |
| Christian | ruler, light, love |
| Hebrew | divine will, guidance |
| Hindu | entrance to knowledge, immortality |
| Islamic | all-seeing, all-knowing |
| Japanese | emblem of Japan |
| Scandinavian | all-seeing |
| Taoist | celestial power |
| universal | cosmic power |

*(continues)*

**Table A.3** Cultural Associations of Icons (*Continued*)

| Symbol | Culture | Association |
|--------|---------|-------------|
| **tortoise** | | |
| | Amerindian | source of cosmic tree |
| | Chinese | strength, endurance, longevity |
| | Christian | modesty |
| | Hindu | first living creature |
| | Japanese | good luck, support |
| | Mexican | terrible aspect of the Great Mother |

# Color

As Chapter 6, Accessing Information, indicates, color is cultural. The only universal colors are natural mappings such as red apples and green leaves. Table A.4 lists some colors and their cultural associations.[2]

**Table A.4** Cultural Associations of Color

| Color | Culture | Association |
|-------|---------|-------------|
| **black** | | |
| | Amerindian | mourning |
| | Buddhist | bondage |
| | Chinese | yin, winter, water |
| | Christian | death, despair, sorrow, mourning, evil |
| | Egyptian | rebirth, resurrection |
| | Hebrew | understanding |
| | Hindu | downward movement |
| | Western | death, evil |
| **blue** | | |
| | Buddhist | coolness, wisdom |
| | Cajun Voodoo | peace |

|  |  |
|---|---|
| Chinese | heaven, spring, wood |
| Christian | truth, eternity, faith |
| Hebrew | mercy |
| Japanese | villainy |
| Middle Eastern | virtue, faith, truth |
| Western | male, calm, authority |

**gold**

|  |  |
|---|---|
| Celtic | fire |
| Hindu | light, life, truth |

**gray**

|  |  |
|---|---|
| Christian | death |
| Hebrew | wisdom |
| universal | mourning, depression, penitence |

**green**

|  |  |
|---|---|
| Amerindian | peace |
| Buddhist | life (pale green—death) |
| Cajun Voodoo | business |
| Christian | immortality, hope |
| Hebrew | victory |
| Hindu | death |
| Islamic | holiness |
| Japanese | future, youth, energy |
| Middle Eastern | fertility, strength |
| Western | safe, sour |

**lavender**

|  |  |
|---|---|
| Cajun Voodoo | conqueror |
| Western | homosexuality, gay pride |

**orange**

|  |  |
|---|---|
| Cajun Voodoo | control |
| Chinese | love, happiness |
| Japanese | love, happiness |
| Hebrew | splendor |

**pink**

|  |  |
|---|---|
| Cajun Voodoo | love |
| Western | femaleness, helplessness |

*(continues)*

**Table A.4** Cultural Associations of Color (*Continued*)

| Color | Culture | Association |
|-------|---------|-------------|
| **purple** | | |
| | Christian | truth, humility, penitence |
| | universal | royalty, power, pride |
| **red** | | |
| | Amerindian | joy |
| | Cajun Voodoo | power |
| | Celtic | death, disaster |
| | Chinese | joy, happiness, luck |
| | Christian | love, power, dignity, martyrdom |
| | Hebrew | severity |
| | Hindu | activity, creativity |
| | Japanese | anger, danger |
| | Western | danger |
| **white** | | |
| | Amerindian | birth, life |
| | Buddhist | redemption |
| | Cajun Voodoo | protection |
| | Chinese | death, mourning |
| | Christian | purity, joy, innocence, virginity |
| | Egyptian | mourning |
| | Hebrew | joy |
| | Hindu | self-illumination, light |
| | Japanese | death, mourning |
| | Western | purity, virtue |
| **yellow** | | |
| | Amerindian | death |
| | Cajun Voodoo | steady work |
| | Chinese | honor, royalty |
| | Hebrew | beauty |
| | Japanese | grace, nobility |
| | Middle Eastern | happiness, prosperity |
| | Western | caution, cowardice |

## Special Files

When you send your information to translation, there are some special files that must accompany it so that the vendor can give you the most accurate translation:

- Glossary

  You need to give the translation vendor a glossary of terms that might help with translating the source. Generally, the translation glossary has all of the information that the end-user glossary has and then some. For example, you may want to go into more technical detail in the translation glossary than you would in the end-user glossary

- Test data files

  Test data files are applicable to examples and screen captures. Test data files contain the data you used to seed the application for examples and screen captures.

  For example, you are documenting a spreadsheet application and you want to set up an extended example and show screen captures supporting that example. In this example, you have two users: Mary Green and Tom White. You also have two files: Payroll 1 and Sales 1. The test data file would contain the data you used to set up these fictitious users and seed these example files so that the translation vendor can set up corresponding users and files in the translated information.

- Images files

  Images files work along with test data files to help the translation vendor capture screens. Screen captures are not line art files that you can give to the translation vendor for translating. They are usually bitmaps or PostScript files that cannot be edited. Translation vendors have to set up each screen just as you did, then capture it.

  The images file is a step-by-step accounting of how you got to each screen and what you did on each screen to set it up for capturing. Images files differ from test data files in that they do not contain the seed data for the screen capture, but instead, the procedure you used to get to each screen.

  For example, an images file might contain:

- Screen Capture # 95-HF-001

    1. Open application by double clicking the product icon.
    2. Select Open from the File menu.
    3. Select Sales 1 from the file list.
    4. Capture screen.

- Screen Capture # 95-HF-002

    1. Select Chart from the Graph menu.
    2. Select Bar from the Graph dialog box.
    3. Capture screen.

- Abbreviations, initialisms, and acronyms

    You must give the translation vendor an alphabetized list of all the abbreviations, initialisms, and acronyms you used in the source along with what they stand for.

- Notes to translator

    Notes to translator is a file that contains anything you think the translation vendor should know. This might include product terms that you do not want to externalize to the end user but that might facilitate translation, any special notes about graphics, any embedded comments you have included in files, and any special circumstances surrounding the files that the vendor is translating.

- Test suites

    Part of the translation service should include verifying the translation. To do this, translation vendors need test suites from you. The test suites should indicate what to exercise in the product and what result to expect.

## Further Reading

Axtel, R.E. *Do's and Taboos Around the World*. New York: John Wiley & Sons, 1990.

Bennett, W.S. "Machine Translation and Multilingual Technical Communication," *STC Proceedings*, 1995.

Cooper, J.C. *An Illustrated Encyclopaedia of Traditional Symbols*. London: Thames and Hudson, 1990.

Dreyfuss, H. *Symbol Sourcebook: An Authoritative Guide to International Graphic Symbols*. New York: Van Nostrand Reinhold, 1984.

Elliot, K.H. "A Layered Approach to Translating Online Documentation," *STC Proceedings*, 1993.

Fernandes, T. *Global Interface Design : A Guide to Designing International User Interfaces.* Boston: AP Professional, 1995.

Frutiger, A. *Signs and Symbols: Their Design and Meaning.* New York: Van Nostrand Reinhold, 1989.

Helfman, E. S. *Signs and Symbols Around the World.* New York: Lothrop, Lee & Shepard Company, 1967.

Hoft, N. L. *International Technical Communication: How to Export Information About High Technology.* New York: John Wiley & Sons, 1995.

_____. *The Icon Book: Visual Symbols for Computer Systems and Documentation.* New York: John Wiley & Sons, 1994.

Horton, W. "Overcoming Chromophobia: A Guide to the Confident and Appropriate Use of Color," *IEEE Transactions on Professional Communication*, 34:3.

Jones, S. et al. *Developing International User Information.* Bedford, MA: Digital Press, 1992.

Kumhyr, D.B, et al. "Internationalization and Translatability," *STC Proceedings*, 1995

Lorence, P. "Designing Multilingual Documents: Some Principles, Observations, and Guidelines," *STC Proceedings*, 1995.

Miles, M. R. *Image as Insight: Visual Understanding in Western Christianity and Secular Culture.* Boston: Beacon Press, 1985.

Nielsen, J., ed. *Designing User Interfaces for International Use.* Amsterdam: Elsevier, 1990.

Ogawa, M. "Translating Software Manuals from English to Japanese," *STC Proceedings*, 1995.

Robinson, L. J. *A Dictionary of Graphical Symbols.* London: Avis, 1972.

Russel, A. and M. Thomson. "Planning for Translation: What We've Learned the Hard Way," *STC Proceedings*, 1993.

Smart, K. and R. Bringhurst. "International Considerations in Creating Computer Documentation," *STC Proceedings*, 1993.

Thompson, P. and P. Davenport. *The Dictionary of Graphic Images.* New York: St. Martin's Press, 1981.

Whittick, A. *Symbols, Signs and Their Meaning.* Newton, MA: C. T. Branford Company, 1960.

## Notes

1   There are a few times when passive voice is acceptable, but these are rare. Strong, clear writing is active-voice writing.

2   Some of the color associations come from W. Horton (1991) and J. C. Cooper (1990).

# Human Factors Resources

There are a great many resources available to technical communicators interested in human factors. At the time this book was printed, this partial list of resources was current.

- Societies

  Association for Computing Machinery (ACM)
  Special Interest Group on Computer-Human Interaction (SIGCHI)
  P.O. Box 12115
  Church Street Station
  New York, NY 10249

  Human Factors and Ergonomics Society
  P.O. Box 1369
  Santa Monica, CA 90406-1369

  IEEE Systems, Man, and Cybernetics Society at:
  http://www.isye.gatech.edu/ieee-smc/

  Usability Professionals Association
  10875 Plano Road
  Suite 115
  Dallas, TX 75238

- Internet newsgroups (use your newsreader to subscribe to the following)

  bit.listserv.techwr-l
  comp.dsp
  comp.edu

comp.fonts
comp.graphics
comp.human-factors
    see the FAQ for this newsgroup at:
    http://www.dgp.toronto.edu/people/ematias/faq/contents.html
comp.text
comp.text.desktop
comp.theory
ieee.general
misc.books.technical
sci.psychology
sci.psychology.research
soc.culture.<culture name>
    There are several pages' worth of soc.culture groups. Some examples are:
- soc.culture.bolivia
- soc.culture.korean
- soc.culture.nordic
- soc.culture.swiss
- soc.culture.usa

- World Wide Web (point your web browser to these URLs)

ACM SIGCHI at:
    http://www.acm.org/sigchi/
ACM SIGCHI 95 Conference Proceedings at:
    http://www.acm.org/sigchi/chi95/Electronic/chi95cd.htm
ACM SIGDOC at:
    http://www.acm.org/sigdoc/
ACM SIGLINK at:
    http://www.acm.org/siglink/
ACM Transactions on Information Systems at:
    http://www.acm.org/pubs/tois/
British Human-Computer Interaction (HCI) Group at:
    http://www.york.ac.uk/~sjbs1/british-hci-www/british-hci-grp.html
*Computer-Mediated Communication Magazine* at:
    http://sunsite.unc.edu/cmc/mag/current/toc.html
Computer-Mediated Communication Studies Center at:
    http://sunsite.unc.edu/cmc/center.html

Engineering and Computer Technology at:
    http://www.einet.net/galaxy/Engineering-and-Technology/Computer-Technology.html
Ergo Web at:
    http://ergoweb.mech.utah.edu/
Ergonomics and Human Factors Society at:
    http://vered.rose.utoronto.ca/HFESVE_dir/HFES.html
Ergonomics and training meta site at:
    http://www.usernomics.com
Ergonomics in Teleoperation and Control Laboratory at:
    http://vered.rose.utoronto.ca/
HCI Index of Related Sources at:
    http://is.twi.tudelft.nl/hci/sources.html
HCI Laboratory at the University of Maryland at College Park at:
    http://www.cs.umd.edu:80/projects/hcil/index.html
HCI project index at:
    http://is.twi.tudelft.nl/hci/
HCI Resources at:
    http://www.ida.liu.se/labs/aslab/groups/um/hci/
Human Engineering Methods Research Laboratory at:
    http://phaedra.larc.nasa.gov/HEM-Top.html
Human Factors and Human Ecology at:
    http://galaxy.einet.net/galaxy/Engineering-and-Technology/Human-Factors-and-Human-Ecology.html
Human Factors Division Home Page at:
    http://www.dciem.dnd.ca/DCIEM/HF/home.html
International Journal of Man-Machine Studies at:
    http://hyperg.tu-graz.ac.at:80/6706AB6D/CHCIbib.ijmms
Lulea Sweden University Human Factors Program at:
    http://www.ludd.luth.se/~anthony/ergo/ergo.html
UIWORLD at:
    http://www.io.tudelft.nl/uiworld/intro.html
United Technologies Research Center HCI lab at:
    http://danville.res.utc.com/WORLD/vr_hci.html
USC Human Factors Program at:
    http://www.usc.edu/dept/issm/hf.html
Virginia Tech Human Factors Engineering Center at:
    http://hci.ise.vt.edu:80/hfcc/
WWW Virtual Library, HCI at:
    http://www.cs.bgsu.edu/HCI/

WWW Virtual Library, Industrial Engineering at:
  http://isye.gatech.edu/www-ie/

- Miscellaneous

  Ohio State University's bibliography of HCI texts at:
    ftp:archive.cis.ohio-state.edu

  *SIGLINK Newsletter: Quarterly Newsletter of the Special Interest Group on Hypertext,*
  Association for Computing Machinery (ACM)
  1515 Broadway
  New York, NY 10036

  Usability test LISTSERV—to subscribe, send a SUBSCRIBE UTEST command to:
    LISTPROC@HUBCAP.CLEMSON.EDU

  WWW virtual library HCI links—for information, send e-mail to:
    instone@s.bgsu.edu

- Cyberspace Search Engines

  You can use any of the following search engines to search on topics such as ergonomics, human factors, cognitive psychology, usability testing, icons, symbols, color, typography, reading, and anything else you can think of:
  EiNet Galaxy at:
    http://www.einet.net/galaxy
  Lycos at:
    www.lycos.com
  Searchable gopher index at:
    gopher://iq-occ.iquest.net
  Webcrawler at:
    www.webcrawler.com
  World Wide Web Worm (WWWW) at:
    http://www.cs.colorado.edu/home/mcbryan/WWWW.html
  Yahoo at:
    www.yahoo.com
  Z39.50 gateways (including Library of Congress) at:
    http://lcweb.loc.gov/z3950/

# Glossary

**absolute threshold**   The absolute threshold is the smallest amount of sensation we can detect 50 percent of the time. Absolute thresholds depend on both the sensation we are experiencing and our psychological state at the time we are experiencing the sensation.

**access, reading**   Reading access is one of the three components of a reading strategy. There are two kinds of reading access: sequential and random. Accessing information sequentially is finding information based on what precedes and follows it. Accessing information randomly is finding information regardless of what precedes or follows it.

**acoustic encoding**   Acoustic encoding is translating sensory data into neuronal impulses the brain can understand using the sound of words. It is more durable than visual encoding, but less durable than semantic encoding.

**acquiring**   Acquiring is the first step in the conceptualizing process. It is the mechanism we use to formulate concepts.

**action structure**   An action structure is one of three components in an action. It is the physiological and psychological processes of performing an action. A basic action structure comprises three parts: evaluation, goal, and execution. An enhanced action structure comprises six parts: receiving sensory input, interpreting sensory input, integrating perceptions, forming the intention to act, designing a series of actions, and executing the series of actions.

**affordances**   An object's affordances are its actual and perceived properties that determine what we can do with the object and that invite us to interact with the object.

**agent**   An agent is one of three components in an action. The agent is the person performing the action structure.

**algorithms**   Algorithms are one of the five problem-solving strategies. They are step-by-step procedures we use to solve problems.

**associative memory**   Associative memory is one of the five types of declarative memory. Associative memory is memory for the tags we associate with data when we store it in long-term memory.

**attentive processes**   Attentive processes are processes that involve cognitive functions such as learning, memory, and understanding. Contrast with preattentive processes.

**auditory feedback**   Auditory feedback is one of three categories of feedback. Auditory feedback is feedback we can hear such as the click of the keyboard keys as we type.

**availability heuristics**   Availability heuristics enable us to base our judgments on concepts readily available in long-term memory. If a concept comes readily to mind, we assume that it is commonplace.

**behaviorist learning theory**   Behaviorist learning theory suggests that it is better to focus not on mental acts that we cannot observe, but rather on objective, quantifiable behavior, the connection between actions, and the role of reward in behavior. Contrast with cognitive learning theory.

**brainstorming**   Brainstorming is a group problem-solving session where group members make suggestions and a scribe writes down all the suggestions. There are no value judgments in brainstorming; anything goes.

**categorical syllogism**   Categorical syllogisms compare categories of concepts to another concept. For example:
>    All dogs are mammals
>    Hesiod is a dog
>    Hesiod is a mammal

**CBT**   *Computer-Based Training* is self-paced and sometimes interactive training for users who are learning new software or hardware.

**classical conditioning**   Classical conditioning is one of the seven types of procedural memory. It is memory for a response that is a result of a paired stimulus and reinforcer and that continues even when the reinforcer is not present. The most famous example of classical conditioning is Pavlov's dogs in which the ringing of a bell (stimulus) precedes food (reinforcer) and eventually creates salivation (response) even when the food is not present.

**closure**   Closure is one of the six laws of grouping. It is our tendency to complete figures that have gaps.

**cocktail-party effect**   The cocktail-party effect is our ability to focus on what is important in our environment while filtering out what is not important.

**cognitive learning theory**   Cognitive learning theory suggests that it is better to focus on mental acts that we cannot observe such as conceiving, believing, and expecting than on strictly objective, quantifiable behavior. Contrast with behaviorist learning theory.

**cognitive skill learning**   Cognitive skill learning is one of the seven types of procedural memory. Cognitive skill learning is memory for higher cognitive functions such as understanding, interpretation, and expectation.

**color vision**   Color vision is a normal eye's ability to see seven million different shades of color. Contrast with color-vision deficiency.

**color-vision deficiency**   Color-vision deficiency is an abnormal eye's inability to see seven million shades of color. There are four types of color-vision deficiency: protanopism, deuteranopism, tritanopism, and monochromatism.

**combining**   Combining is the third step in the conceptualizing process. It is the mechanism we use to create schemata from concepts.

**common fate**   Common fate is one of the six laws of grouping. It is our tendency to see objects moving in the same direction (toward a common fate) as a whole rather than as disparate objects.

**communication**   Communication is the mechanism we use to transfer knowledge between the world and our heads. It comprises knowledge, giver, receiver, and feedback.

**concepts**   Concepts are the building blocks of thought. They are psychological representations of groups of objects or ideas that share relationships among common, typical characteristics.

**conceptualizing**   Conceptualizing is one of the four components of problem solving. It is forming psychological representations of objects or ideas that share relationships among common, typical characteristics. Conceptualizing is a four-step process: acquiring, distinguishing, combining, and using.

**conditional syllogisms**   Conditional syllogisms set up an "If A, then B" conditional relationship between concepts. For example:

> If you hear music, the radio is on
> You hear music
> The radio is on

**cones**   Cones are chromatic light receptors in the retina of the eye that enable us to see color. Contrast with rods.

**confirmation bias**   Confirmation bias is one of the four obstacles to problem-solving. It is our tendency to search for solutions that confirm our ideas.

**constraints**   An object's constraints are its actual properties that limit what we can do with the object.

**context-dependent memory cue**   A context-dependent memory cue is putting yourself in the same context you were in when you encoded the data while you are trying to retrieve the data. Recall of information is better if we are in the same context we were in while encoding the information.

**continuity**   Continuity is one of the six laws of grouping. It is our tendency to perceive smooth, continuous patterns rather than discontinuous ones.

**critical reading**   Critical reading is one of five reading goals. Critical reading is reading for evaluation. It may be either a declarative or procedural reading type and is a sequential reading access.

**declarative memory**   Declarative memory is memory for events, facts, and images. Declarative memory is a function of both short-term and long-term memory and comprises five types of memory: episodic, associative, semantic, lexical, and image.

**deductive reasoning**   Deductive reasoning is the logical process of inferring the particular from the general. Contrast with inductive reasoning.

**deuteranopism**   Deuteranopism is one of the four types of color-vision deficiency. It is an inability to distinguish red and green, due to a lack of green cones. Contrast with protanopism.

**distinctive features**   Distinctive features is one of the three shape-recognition strategies. We distinguish letters by their distinct patterns of features, then we match patterns by analyzing the distinct features of letters we are comparing.

**distinguishing**   Distinguishing is the second step in the conceptualizing process. It is the mechanism we use to differentiate concepts we have acquired.

**encoding**   Encoding is one of the four steps in the memory process. Encoding is translating sensory data into neuronal impulses the brain can understand. There are three types of encoding: visual, acoustic, and semantic.

**engram**   An engram is Karl Lashley's term for a neuronal change in the brain that indicates memory.

**episodic memory**   Episodic memory is one of the five types of declarative memory. Episodic memory is memory for events. There is a special type of episodic memory called flashbulb memory. Flashbulb memory is clear, detailed, poignant, and often stressful. A common example of a flashbulb memory is the memory of learning that President Kennedy had been shot.

**equipotentiality**   Equipotentiality is Karl Lashley's term for holographic memory. See holographic theory of memory.

**faulty encoding theory of forgetting**   The faulty encoding theory of forgetting states that we forget data because we did not thoroughly process the information in short-term memory.

**feedback**   Feedback is any indication of what we have done with an object. Positive feedback indicates that we have successfully used an object. Negative feedback indicates that we have not successfully used an object. In communication, feedback is any indication that the receiver has gotten knowledge from the giver. There are three categories of feedback: auditory, visual, and tactile.

**figure-ground relationship**   Figure-ground relationship is our ability to recognize objects as being separate from other stimuli and as having a distinct, meaningful form. Every object has at least two parts: the object itself that we recognize as a distinct whole, called the figure, and the object's surroundings, called the ground.

**fixation point**   A fixation point is the resting place between saccades as our eyes move along a line of text. The words between fixation points are called fixations. Fixations are usually two to three words in length.

**forgetting**   Forgetting is the inability to retrieve data from long-term memory into short-term memory. There are seven theories of forgetting: lost engrams, modified schemata, repression, interference, weakened associations, faulty encoding, and motivated forgetting.

**fovea**   The fovea is a slight indentation in the retina. Rods and cones are densest at the fovea; therefore, foveal vision is the sharpest and clearest vision we have. Our eyes constantly move to focus images on the fovea.

**functional fixedness**   Functional fixedness is one of the four obstacles to problem solving. It is our inability to see the functionality of objects as flexible.

**goal**   A goal is the result of an action structure. It is what we want to do as a result of evaluating our environment.

**goal, reading**   A reading goal is one of the three components of a reading strategy. There are five reading goals: skimming, scanning, searching, reading for reception, and reading for critical evaluation.

**goodness of figures**   Goodness of figures is a perceptual tool we use to interpret visual data. It states that we opt for the simplest interpretation of visual information. Also called the law of Pragnantz.

**GUI**   GUI stands for graphical user interface. A GUI is an iconic interface that you manipulate with a mouse. Also called a point-and-shoot interface.

**gulf of evaluation**   An object's gulf of evaluation is one of two gulfs we use to determine the object's usefulness. It is the amount of effort we expend trying to figure out how to use the object. The wider the gulf of evaluation, the less useful the object.

**gulf of execution**   An object's gulf of execution is one of two gulfs we use to determine the object's usefulness. It is the difference between how we intend to use an object and what the object allows us to do with it. The wider the gulf of execution, the less useful the object.

**habit**   A habit is a learned connection between a stimulus such as a stop sign and a response such as stopping. See habit strength, habit family, and habit family hierarchy.

**habit family**   A habit family is a set of related habits. See habit, habit family hierarchy, and habit strength.

**habit family hierarchy**   Within each habit family is a habit family hierarchy, which is a pecking order for habits. The most effective habits are the highest in the habit-family hierarchy and are the ones we tend to use first in a new situation. See habit, habit family, and habit strength.

**habit strength**   The strength of the connection between a stimulus and a response is called the habit strength. See habit, habit family, and habit family hierarchy.

**habituation**   Habituation is one of the seven types of procedural memory. Habituation is memory for sensory adaptation.

**Hering's opponent color theory**   Hering's opponent color theory is the second half of our visual color processing. It states that the central nervous system analyzes the trichromatic color messages of the eye's cones in terms of three opponent color pairs: red/green, blue/yellow, and black/white. The trichromatic color theory is the first half of visual color processing.

**heterarchy**   A heterarchy is a horizontal arrangement of equal units. Contrast with hierarchy.

**heuristics**   Heuristics are one of the five problem-solving strategies. They are rules of thumb we acquire through experience and use to solve problems. There are two special types of heuristics: availability and representative.

**hierarchy**   A hierarchy is a vertical arrangement of super- and subunits. Contrast with heterarchy.

**holographic theory of memory**   The holographic theory of memory states that memory is a nonlocal phenomenon that is distributed equally throughout the brain.

**hypothesis testing**   Hypothesis testing is one of the five problem-solving strategies. It is generating and testing appropriate hypotheses to solve a problem.

**image memory**   Image memory is memory for pictures and mental images we construct from pictures, events, and picture-evoking words.

**inductive reasoning**   Inductive reasoning is the logical process of inferring the general from the particular. Contrast with deductive reasoning.

**insight**   Insight is a Gestaltist concept that is a sudden flash of inspiration that provides the solution to a problem.

**interference theory of forgetting**   The interference theory of forgetting states that previously stored data gets in the way of our ability to access newly stored data and vice-versa.

**just noticeable difference (JND) threshold**   The JND threshold is the smallest amount of sensation we can detect between any two stimuli 50 percent of the time. JND thresholds are proportional; we notice a 10 percent change in 50 pounds more than we notice a 10 percent change in two ounces.

**laws of grouping**   Laws of grouping is a perceptual tool we use to interpret objects. Laws of grouping are a Gestalt approach to perceptual organization which emphasize well-organized, meaningful wholes instead of isolated parts. There are six laws of grouping: proximity, similarity, continuity, symmetry, closure, and common fate.

**learned helplessness**   Learned helplessness occurs when we repeatedly fail at using an object successfully. We learn that we are "helpless" when it comes to using the object. Compare with taught helplessness.

**learning**   Learning is a relatively permanent change in behavior based on experience. Learning theory falls into two broad categories: cognitive and behaviorist.

**lens**   The lens is the transparent part of the eye behind the pupil. The lens focuses light on the retina.

**lexical memory**   Lexical memory is memory for the graphological and phonological features of words. We store the meaning of words in semantic memory.

**linear syllogisms**   Linear syllogisms compare relationships among concepts in a sequential fashion. For example:

> John has more apples than Mary.
> Mary has more apples than Sue.
> John has more apples than Sue.

**localized theory of memory**   The localized theory of memory states that memory is a function of local synaptic change. Contrast with holographic theory of memory.

**long-term memory**   Long-term memory is the third and last stage of memory. It is where we permanently store data. Once we move data into long-term memory, we never lose it, although we may not be able to retrieve it. There are two types of long-term memory: declarative and procedural.

**lost engrams theory of forgetting**   The lost engrams theory of forgetting states that we forget data because we have physiologically lost an engram. This theory is applicable only to the localized theory of memory.

**magical number seven**   George Miller coined the term "magical number seven plus or minus two" to refer to the five to nine chunks of meaningful information we can hold in short-term memory.

**mappings**   An object's mappings are its properties that suggest natural relationships between the object and how we can use the object successfully.

**media subtype**   A media subtype is a finer categorization of information within a media type. A help system is a media subtype of an online information media type.

**media type**   A media type is a gross categorization of the information such as hardcopy or online.

**medium**   The medium is the second layer of subtext users encounter in your information.

**memory**   Memory is any indication that learning persists. We infer memory from behavior. Biologically, memory is a morphological neuronal change in the brain. This change is called an engram.

**memory cues**   Memory cues are mechanisms we use to retrieve data from long-term storage into short-term storage. There are four types of memory cues: environment, mood, sensory tickler, and mnemonic device.

**mind mapping**   Mind mapping is a group problem-solving session that builds on brainstorming. During mind mapping, group members group ideas and eliminate redundancies. See brainstorming.

**mnemonic device memory cue**   A mnemonic device memory cue is a way to draw disparate pieces of information together around a single, centralized, memorable anchor. Every Good Boy Does Fine is a mnemonic device to remember the EGBDF treble clef line notes.

**modified schemata theory of forgetting**   The modified schemata theory of forgetting states that we forget data because we modify schemata both as we encode them and as we retrieve them; therefore, it is possible to modify schemata so much that we can no longer access the original data but only the modified schemata.

**monochromatism**   Monochromatism is one of the four types of color-vision deficiency. It is the inability to see color due to a lack of cones. Monochromats see only shades of gray.

**motivated forgetting theory of forgetting**   The motivated forgetting theory of forgetting states that we forget data because we intentionally lock away memories that are painful or embarrassing. Contrast with the repression theory of forgetting.

**motivation**   Motivation is the why of learning.

**motor skill learning**   Motor skill learning is one of the seven types of procedural memory. Motor skill memory is memory for performing motor skills such as walking, typing, and tap dancing.

**multiple stores theory of short-term memory**   The multiple stores theory of short-term memory states that we have multiple short-term memories. Each short-term memory processes different types of information such as verbal, textual, and graphic.

**navigational infrastructure**   Your information's navigational infrastructure is the second layer of subtext users encounter. The navigational infrastructure is the skeleton on which you hang your information. It is the way users move around in your information.

**negative instance**   A negative instance is the occurrence of a concept that disconfirms our general truth about that concept.

**negative transfer**   Negative transfer is one of the four obstacles to problem solving. It is the process by which past experiences in problem solving inhibit or prevent our ability to solve current problems. Contrast with positive transfer.

**neuron**   A neuron is a nerve.

**neurotransmitters**   Neurotransmitters are chemical messengers in the brain that carry communication between neurons by jumping the synaptic gap at the synapse of neurons.

**noise**   Noise is anything that interferes with communication.

**obstacles to problem solving**   Obstacles to problem solving are one of the four components of problem solving. They are psychological blocks or mindsets that prevent our solving problems. There are four obstacles to problem solving: problem-solving set, confirmation bias, functional fixedness, and negative transfer.

**opportunistic actions**   Opportunistic actions are actions that take advantage of circumstance rather than planning and analysis.

**optic nerve**   The optic nerve is a bundle of neurons that carries neuronal signals from the eye to the brain.

**paperwalk**   A paperwalk is taking users through an information's storyboard, draft, or prototype on paper.

**perception**   Perception is the cognitive process of interpreting data we take in through our senses.

**perceptual illusions**   Perceptual illusions are visual perceptions that appear true but are false. There are six perceptual illusions: Pöggendorff effect, Ponzo illusion, relative size, Müller-Lyer illusion, subjective contours, and Necker cube.

**perceptual learning**   Perceptual learning is one of the seven types of procedural memory. Perceptual memory is memory for perceiving data differently with exposure and practice.

**perceptual set**   A perceptual set is an experience-based predisposition to interpret data in a given manner.

**positive instance**   A positive instance is the occurrence of a concept that confirms our general truth about that concept.

**positive transfer**   Positive transfer is the process by which positive past experiences in problem solving aid or promote our ability to solve current problems. Contrast with negative transfer.

**preattentive processes**   Preattentive processes are automatic processes that do not involve higher, cognitive functions. Preattentive processes are primarily a function of sensory input. Contrast with attentive processes.

**presentation**   The presentation is the third layer of information subtext your users encounter. The presentation is how information looks on the page or screen. The presentation comprises the layout, which is the physical arrangement of text, graphics, and color on the page or screen and the fonts, which are the shapes and emphases of the letters you use to communicate the text.

**priming**   Priming is one of the seven types of procedural memory. Priming is the use of cues to activate memory. An example of priming is that the word "yellow" activates the memory of both "lemon" and "cowardice."

**problem domain**   A problem domain is the particular area of expertise in which you are trying to solve a problem. For example, physics is the problem domain if you are trying to solve a physics problem.

**problem solving**   Problem solving is responding to a situation for which there is no well-established response. There are four components of problem solving: conceptualizing, reasoning, problem-solving strategies, and obstacles to problem solving.

**problem-solving set**   A problem-solving set is one of the four obstacles to problem solving. It is our tendency to see things through the lens of experience and our inability to see problem elements in a novel way.

**problem-solving strategies**   Problem-solving strategies are one of the four components of problem solving. They are psychological processes we use to solve problems. There are five problem-solving strategies: trial and error, hypothesis testing, algorithms, heuristics, and insight.

**procedural memory**   Procedural memory is memory for motor skills, cognitive skills, and reflexes. Procedural memory is a function only of long-term memory and comprises seven types of memory: motor skill learning, cognitive skill learning, perceptual learning, classical conditioning, priming, habituation, and sensitization.

**protanopism**   Protanopism is one of the four types of color-vision deficiency. It is the inability to distinguish red and green, due to a lack of red cones.

**prototype matching**   Prototype matching is one of the three shape-recognition strategies. We store generalized shape patterns (prototypes) in long-term memory, and we compare those patterns to objects to see if there is a match that helps us interpret the visual data. Because the prototypes are generalized, we are able to recognize unlimited variations on an object's shape. Contrast with template matching.

**proximity**   Proximity is one of the six laws of grouping. It is our tendency to group things that are near each other.

**reactionary actions**   Reactionary actions are actions that we take in response to an external force.

**reading**   Reading is a two-part process: the first part is the physiological process of taking in visual data; the second part is the psychological process of understanding that data. The modern English word "reading" comes from the old Anglo-Saxon word "rædan," which means "to advise oneself."

**reading strategy**   A reading strategy is a mechanism we use to assimilate information from text. Reading strategies have three components: type, access, and goal.

**reasoning**   Reasoning is one of the four components of problem solving. It is applying logic to data in order to find truth in that data. There are two types of reasoning: inductive and deductive.

**recalling**   Recalling is one of the three types of retrieval. Recalling is bringing something into conscious awareness.

**receptive reading**   Receptive reading is one of the five reading goals. Receptive reading is reading for thorough comprehension. It may be either a declarative or procedural reading type and either a sequential or random reading access.

**recognizing**   Recognizing is one of the three types of retrieval. Recognizing is being aware that you have experienced something before.

**recursion**   Recursion is the phenomenon of having to reread a passage to get the entire meaning.

**redundancy**   Redundancy is the presence of more lexical data than we need to cognitively process information during reading. Redundancy helps us read more quickly, easily, and efficiently.

**relearning**   Relearning is one of the three types of retrieval. Relearning is learning something again and takes less time than learning something for the first time.

**representative heuristics**   Representative heuristics enable us to make snap judgments of concepts based on how well those concepts represent the stereotype of that concept.

**repression theory of forgetting**   The repression theory of forgetting states that we forget data because we have unconsciously locked away painful memories. *See also*, motivated forgetting theory of forgetting.

**retina**   The retina is the light-sensitive inner surface of the eye on which the lens focuses light from visual stimuli. The retina contains rods for black and white vision, cones for color vision, and neurons for initiating the processing of visual data.

**retrieval**   Retrieval is one of the four steps in the memory process. Retrieval is getting data out of long-term memory back into short-term memory where we act on that data.

**rods**   Rods are achromatic light receptors in the retina that enable us to see black and white. Contrast with cones.

**saccades**   Saccades are the little jumps that our eyes make as they move along a line of text.

**saccadic eye movement**   Saccadic eye movement is the way our eyes jump from fixation point to fixation point along a line of text.

**scanning**   Scanning is one of five reading goals. Scanning is reading for general gist. It is a declarative reading type and may be either a sequential or random reading access.

**schema**   A schema is a collection of concepts we use to form a mental framework or model to understand and interact with the world.

**sclera**   The sclera is the white part of the eye.

**searching**   Searching is one of the five reading goals. Searching is reading with attention to the meaning of specific information. It is a declarative reading type and may be either a sequential or random reading access.

**semantic encoding**   Semantic encoding is translating sensory data into neuronal impulses the brain can understand using the meaning of words. It is the most durable kind of encoding.

**semantic memory**   Semantic memory is memory for the meaning of facts, concepts, and vocabulary.

**sensation**   Sensation is the physiological process of taking in data through our senses.

**sensitization**   Sensitization is one of the seven types of procedural memory. Sensitization is being highly sensitized to specific events or situations.

**sensory adaptation**   Sensory adaptation occurs when our senses get used to a stimulus and do not respond to it. Similar to habituation.

**sensory registers**   Sensory registers are the first of three stages of memory. There is a sensory register for each sense. They take in sensory data and extend sensation traces so that data can move into short-term memory.

**sensory tickler memory cue**   Sensory tickler memory cues are sensations that unlock memories we are usually unaware of.

**shape-recognition strategies**   Shape-recognition strategies are a perceptual tool we use to interpret visual data. They help us determine whether we recognize visual information. There are three shape-recognition strategies: prototype matching, template matching, and distinctive features.

**short-term memory**   Short-term memory is the second of three memory stages. Short-term memory is our limited-capacity working memory. We rehearse, encode, and retrieve data in short-term memory. Short-term memory makes thinking and use of language possible.

**similarity**   Similarity is one of the six laws of grouping. It is our tendency to group together things that are similar.

**skimming**   Skimming is one of the five reading goals. Skimming is reading to find specific information quickly. It is a declarative reading type and may be either a sequential or random reading access.

**slot theory**   The slot theory of short-term memory states that we have five to nine slots in short-term memory and that each slot can hold one chunk of meaningful data.

**state-dependent memory cue**   A state-dependent memory cue is putting yourself in the same state you were in when you encoded the data while you are trying to retrieve the data. We can retrieve some data only if we enter the same psychological state we were in when we encoded the data.

**storyboarding**   Storyboarding is taking a mind map and making a visual blueprint of information. Storyboards address both text and subtext.

**subtext**   Subtext is how you communicate text. The medium, navigation, and presentation compose an information unit's subtext. The subtext is the how of what you are communicating. Contrast with text.

**syllogism**   A syllogism is a logical argument that contains three prepositions: the first two are general truths, and the third is the particular conclusion derived from those general truths. Syllogisms form the framework for deductive reasoning. There are three types of syllogisms: categorical, linear, and conditional.

**symmetry**   Symmetry is one of the six laws of grouping. It is our tendency to perceive a coherent, symmetrical figure if symmetrical figures bound an area.

**synapse**   A synapse is the junction between two neurons.

**synaptic gap**   A synaptic gap is the microscopic gap between neurons at a synapse. Synaptic gaps facilitate memory.

**system image**   The system image of an object is the part of the object that we see and with which we interact.

**tactile feedback**   Tactile feedback is one of the three categories of feedback. It is feedback we can feel, such as the coldness of an ice cube.

**taught helplessness**   Taught helplessness occurs when the poor instruction we receive in using one part of an object "teaches" us that we cannot use any part of the object. Compare with learned helplessness.

**telegraphic writing**   Telegraphic writing is a writing style that dispenses with articles, pronouns, conjunctions, and transitional expressions.

**template matching**   Template matching is one of the three shape-recognition strategies. We store detailed shape patterns (templates) in long-term memory, and we compare those patterns to objects to see if there is a match that helps us interpret the visual data. Since the patterns are detailed, we have to store a pattern for each variation of an object, which requires enormous memory-storage capacity. Contrast with prototype matching.

**text**   Text is the content of your information. It is what you are communicating. Contrast with subtext.

**thresholds**   A threshold is the lowest intensity at which we can sense data. There are two sensory thresholds: absolute and just noticeable difference (JND).

**tip-of-the-nose phenomenon**   Tip-of-the-nose phenomenon is recognizing a scent but being unable to recall its name.

**tip-of-the-tongue phenomenon**   Tip-of-the-tongue phenomenon is a term that R. Brown and D. McNeill coined for that maddening stage of retrieval between recall and recognition. You know everything about the data you are trying to recall except the data itself.

**trial and error**   Trial and error is one of the five problem-solving strategies. It is trying one possible solution after another until the problem is solved.

**trichromatic color theory**   The trichromatic color theory is one half of visual color processing. It states that every light stimulus excites various combinations of red, green, and blue cones in the eye. Also called the Young-Helmholtz trichromatic color theory. Hering's opponent color theory is the second half of visual color processing.

**tritanopism**   Tritanopism is one of the four types of color-vision deficiency. It is the inability to distinguish blue and yellow due to a lack of blue-light-absorbing pigment. It is often the result of retinal disease.

**type, reading**   A reading type is one of the three components of a reading strategy. There are two reading types: reading to learn (declarative) and reading to do (procedural).

**using**   Using is the last step in the conceptualizing process. It is the mechanism we use to employ schemata we have created from concepts.

**visibility**    An object's degree of visibility is the degree to which crucial parts are obvious and convey the object's affordances, constraints, and mappings.

**visual capture**    Visual capture refers to the fact that vision is preeminent among our senses.

**visual encoding**    Visual encoding is translating sensory data into neuronal impulses the brain can understand using the image of words. It is the least durable kind of encoding.

**visual feedback**    Visual feedback is one of the three categories of feedback. Visual feedback is feedback we can see such as the mark pencil lead makes on paper.

**weakened association theory of forgetting**    The weakened association theory of forgetting states that we forget data because we may confuse the infinite number of tags under which we store data.

**word-letter phenomenon**    The word-letter phenomenon is our ability to recognize letters more easily if they are parts of meaningful words rather than if they are single letters.

**word-superiority effect**    The word-superiority effect is our ability to recognize individual letters and whole words more easily if they are in a meaningful context.

**Young-Helmholtz**    See trichromatic color theory.

# Index